D0054325

CRAZY FOR GOD

Other Books by Frank Schaeffer

FICTION

(The Calvin Becker Trilogy)

PORTOFINO

ZERMATT

SAVING GRANDMA

BABY JACK

NONFICTION

KEEPING FAITH—A Father-Son Story about Love and the United States Marine Corps (Coauthored with Sgt. John Schaeffer USMC)

FAITH OF OUR SONS—A Father's Wartime Diary

VOICES FROM THE FRONT—Letters Home from America's Military Family

AWOL—The Unexcused Absence of America's Upper Classes from Military Service—And How It Hurts Our Country (Coauthored with Kathy Roth-Douquet)

CRAZY FOR GOD

How I Grew Up as One of the Elect, Helped Found the Religious Right, and Lived to Take All (or Almost All) of It Back

FRANK SCHAEFFER

CARROLL & GRAF PUBLISHERS
NEW YORK

CRAZY FOR GOD

How I Grew Up as One of the Elect, Helped Found the Religious Right, and Lived to Take All (or Almost All) of It Back

Carroll & Graf Publishers
An Imprint of Avalon Publishing Group, Inc.
11 Cambridge Center
Cambridge, MA 02142

First Carroll & Graf edition 2007

Cataloging-in-Publication Data is available from the Library of Congress.

ISBN-10: 0-7867-1891-9
ISBN-13: 978-0-7867-1891-7

9 8 7 6 5 4 3 2 1

Printed in the United States of America

for my daughter Jessica

CONTENTS

PROLOGUE

You can be the world's biggest hypocrite and still feel good about yourself. You can believe and wish you didn't. You can lose your faith and still pretend, because there are bills to be paid, because you are booked up for a year, because this is what you do.

One morning in the early 1980s, I looked out over several acres of pale blue polyester and some twelve thousand Southern Baptist ministers. My evangelist father—Francis Schaeffer—was being treated for lymphoma at the Mayo Clinic, and in his place I'd been asked to deliver several keynote addresses on the evangelical/fundamentalist circuit. I was following in the proudly nepotistic American Protestant tradition, wherein the Holy Spirit always seems to lead the offspring and spouses of evangelical superstars to "follow the call."

A few weeks earlier, after being introduced by Pat Robertson, I had delivered a rousing take-back-America speech to thousands of cheering religious broadcasters. And not long afterward, I would appear at a huge pro-life rally in Denver. Cal Thomas—once the vice president of Jerry Falwell's Moral Majority, later a Fox News commentator—would introduce me as "the best speaker in America." The "anointing," someone said, was "clearly on this young man!" They were saying that I was a better speaker than my famous father.

At that moment, the Schaeffers were evangelical royalty. When I was growing up in L'Abri, my parents' religious community in Switzerland, it was not unusual to find myself seated across the dining room table from Billy Graham's daughter or President Ford's son, even Timothy Leary. The English actress Glynis Johns used to come for Sunday high tea. I figured it was normal. They were just a few of the thousands who made it through our doors. Only later did I realize that L'Abri attracted a weirdly eclectic group of people who otherwise would not have been caught dead in the same room. My childhood was, to say the least, unusual.

When Gerald Ford died in January 2007, I recalled that on the day he had assumed the presidency, his daughter-in-law Gayle was babysitting my daughter Jessica as her job in the work-study program at L'Abri, where Mike Ford, the president's son, was a student.

Mom and Dad met with presidents Ford, Reagan, and Bush Sr. and stayed in the White House several times. In the 1990s when my mother Edith—then in her eighties—heard that George W. Bush might run for the presidency, she exclaimed, "What? But Barbara asked me to pray especially for young George. She didn't think he had what it took to do anything."

Given the fact of my family connections to the Republican Party, it was somewhat ironic that when James Webb was elected to the Senate from Virginia by a razor-thin margin in 2006, giving the Democrats their first new majority in years, I was credited with helping Webb. Or, to put it another way, judging by the hate e-mail I got from my father's fundamentalist followers and other assorted Republicans and conservatives, I deserved some of the blame.

I had long since left the evangelical subculture when I wrote an op-ed for the *Dallas Morning News* that was picked up by several hundred blogs and posted on the front page of James Webb's campaign Web site. I had defended Webb against a series of scabrous attacks wherein his novels were smeared and he was even labeled a "pedophile" because he had described a sexual tribal ritual. I noted that Webb is a serious novelist whose work has been widely praised by many, including Tom Wolfe, who called Webb's books "the greatest of the Vietnam novels."

I also took the Republicans to task for doing to Webb what they had done to another war hero, Senator John McCain, back in the 2000 Republican primaries. I went so far as to say that, in disgust, my wife Genie and I were switching from being registered Republicans to independents.

A few days after this op-ed was published, I wrote another piece, this time for the *Huffington Post,* about the reaction to my departure from the Republican Party. This was picked up by dozens of Democrat-friendly blogs. As the congratulatory e-mails poured in, I was reminded of the welcome given new believers when they convert from some particularly hideous life of sin. Then the *Drudge Report* and dozens of other right-wing and/or evangelical outlets alerted their faithful to my treason.

Furious e-mails flooded in. They fell into two categories: The evangelical "Church Ladies" said they hadn't read Webb's novels but were shocked by his immorality nonetheless and went to three- and four-page single-spaced quivering lengths to justify the Republicans' tactics; the second group were simply profanity-spewing thugs. The Church Lady e-mails contrasted markedly with the insults. It was as if I'd stumbled into a Sunday school picnic at a Tourette syndrome convention.

"As a Christian the best question you could ask is what would Jesus do? He wouldn't give Webb's books a pass just because he's a veteran. . . ."

"Mr. Schaeffer: Don't let the door hit your ass on the way out you FUCK!"

"Mr. Webb has no excuse for using profanity. . . ."

"Good fucking riddance—you fucking cry baby!"

"I have never read any of Mr. Webb's novels. However, the excerpts [in the *Drudge Report*] are very disturbing. . . . As for the Bible, yes it has all the things you mentioned: rape, murder, adultery, masturbation, etc. However, the Lord did not give us graphic details. . . . And I hope as Christians we can remember that and be a voice crying out against ALL the ugly things. . . ."

"We don't need your lame ass motherfucking comments or your support. . . ."

When combined, the hundreds of e-mails seemed to boil down to: "Do what we say Jesus says—and if you don't, we'll kick your head in!" The reaction confirmed why any sane person would run, and keep on running from the right-wing/evangelical/Republican morass as far as their legs would carry them, something I'd been doing for more than twenty years. But I had brought this upon myself. The truth is that, with my father, I had once contributed mightily to the creation of the right-wing/evangelical/Republican subculture that was attacking me.

My life has been one of all-consuming faith—not *my* faith, but the faith of others that I seem to have caught like a disease and been almost obliterated by. What does God want? I am still trying to find out. And having once been a "professional Christian," my vision is muddied by the baggage I carry. Every action, every thought, every moment I stumble into is judged by an inner voice. Everything seems to have a moral component: eating—because there are hungry people; sex—don't even start. What I write, don't write, who I talk to, don't talk to, and how I raised my children, their characters, accomplishments, failures, whether they "love the Lord" or not, everything points to my relationship with God, real or imagined.

The habit of fundamentalist faith persists in my gut, even long after I rejected it. I'm meeting my agent Jennifer on the Upper West Side. She thinks I'm sane. I pretend I am. But somewhere in the back of my mind is a vague unease. She isn't saved. She's some sort of lapsed something. Should I be doing anything about that? Will God bless my next book deal if I deny him before men, or in this case before my agent? When Jen asks me to tell her about my new book, shouldn't I ask her if she wouldn't like to accept Jesus first?

It turns out that it was easier to move beyond my parents' beliefs intellectually than to abandon my gut responses. So who instilled those responses? In other words, who were we? It depends on what moment you choose to become a fly on the Schaeffer wall. People are not as one-dimensional as the stories about them. There is no way to write the absolute truth about any family, much less my family.

The only answer to "Who are you?" is "When?"

Author's Note: I'm sure I have placed some events in the wrong years or have written that something happened in one place when it happened in another. This is a *memoir,* not a biography. (I have also changed some people's names to protect the more-or-less innocent.) To footnote this story or to have done research into dates and places and to correct the chronology would have been to indulge the conceit that my book is an objective history. It is not. What I've written comes from a memory deformed by time, prejudice, flawed recall, and emotion.

PART I

Childhood

1

Being raised inside a miracle tends to make you feel singled out. I wanted to fit into the world. I still do. And yet the darkly weird moments of my childhood did not cancel out the light.

When I walked down the back road from our chalet to the village of Huémoz it was impossible to get anywhere without stopping to look at the view. I don't think I once left Chalet Les Mélèzes, charged up the back steps, then ran down the back road without at least one view-absorbing pause. Sometimes I'd stop and stare at the mountains so long, I'd forget what I'd been planning to do. The view of the Alps always seemed like a special reward to our family for doing God's will. "If we had stayed in America, we'd never have a view like this," Mom would say.

Fifty years later, when I fly back to Switzerland I sit on the left-hand side of the connecting flight from Zurich to Geneva. That way I can see our valley, pick out my mountains.

Before I moved to America, there was never any doubt about which way I was facing; down to the Rhône Valley with its patchwork of fields, orchards, roads, and villages miles below, up to the flower-studded hayfields and steep forest-clad hills behind our village, or across the valley to the peaks towering over everything. We were *Les Américains* on the edge of a tiny village, fundamentalist Christians running a mission called L'Abri, surrounded by Swiss peasants who hated the fact we'd invaded their farming community. Our theology taught us that we were mere sojourners in an alien land, temporary subjects of earth, citizens only of heaven. We were separated from the world, even from all those other born-again American Christians back home who, to outsiders, must have looked very much like us. But to we Schaeffers, most Protestants were the "other." Perhaps they were part of ministries that asked for money rather than really trusting the Lord to meet their needs. Perhaps they had compromised on some point of theology. We did the Lord's work in the Lord's way.

Living with a mother and father who defended their theological ideas all day, in a household where lunch and dinner were often two or three hours long as the discussions continued—"discussions" is not really the right word, since what happened was that a guest would ask a question and then Dad, Fidel Castro-like, would hold forth for several hours—I grew up with a gift for verbal communication. By the time I was nine or ten, I could mimic my parents and compose an articulate answer to almost any theological question. And I had a flair for vocabulary that maybe only a dyslexic raised with no TV, and who had a mother who read out loud, could acquire. Adults who talked to me told my parents that I was the most well-spoken child they had ever met. What they didn't know was that my verbal abilities were like a circus trick. Professional proselytizers were raising me: sweet, sincere—but preoccupied—proselytizers.

On any given day from the time I was about seven on, you could have asked my parents where I was and they would have had no idea. They literally lost track of me, more or less forgot I existed, except at one specific time of the day. At bedtime, Mom read me nineteenth- and early twentieth-century novels by people like Louisa May Alcott and Jean Stratton Porter. Mom also read Dickens, C. S. Lewis, Sherlock Holmes stories, and everything by P. G. Wodehouse and all of Mark Twain (with the exception of his ramblings about why he was an atheist and his speculation about how many tens of thousands of years an angel's orgasm lasts). And Mom read every book of the Bible to me so many times that I still know more about ancient Israel than modern America.

2

Dad was born in 1912 to "working-class ignorant pagan parents in Philadelphia" (according to Mom). Mom was born in China in 1914 to "dear and sensitive highly educated missionary parents." (Mom again.) Mom lived in China at a China Inland Mission compound until she was five, as a privileged colonial in a walled compound with a Chinese nanny and other servants whose job it was to care for and amuse the little foreign girl. Then her parents sailed back to America, where her father taught Greek and Hebrew.

When Mom's parents had come back to America in 1919, it was meant to just be for a one-year furlough. But my Mom's mother had a heart condition that prevented her from returning to China. Mom's parents lamented this and argued with the China Inland Mission board, who made that decision.

When Mom got to America, she says that she felt like a displaced person, certainly not Chinese but not American either. My mother's memories of her early childhood are remarkably vivid, even at ninety-two when she has forgotten so much else. Mom remembers arguing with children who knew she had lived in China, and who would taunt her with the ditty "Chinky-chinky Chinaman sitting on a fence, trying to make a dollar out of fifteen cents!" Mom would counter: "And he could, too!"

Mom pined for the life in the Chinese compound, at least as she thought she remembered it. Perhaps that longing shaped her fierce desire to found her own mission to recreate something her family had lost—that golden childhood time just beyond reach. In Mother's nostalgic memories, life in China became a sacred time for her. Mom recalled life in a compound filled with friendly Chinese converts, the "needy" Chinese who came to her parents. Her memories were so vivid that at age eighty-three, Mom even wrote a lovely children's book about her life in the compound, *Mei Fuh—Memories from China.*

Mom's older sisters Janet and Elsa had been dumped in mission boarding schools and hardly saw their parents until they moved back to America as young teens. A few years after returning home, Aunt Janet joined the Communist Party. Later, Aunt Elsa married a mental patient who tried to murder her. Janet left the Communists and hooked up with the Closed Plymouth Brethren, a sect so "separated" from the world that she stopped sleeping with her husband. And as the sect got crazier, she went right along with them, stopped "fellowshipping" with her two sons, wouldn't eat in the same room, and finally moved out, because she couldn't even be under the same roof as her family of "unbelievers." Meanwhile, Aunt Elsa's husband Ralph mistook her for a vulture and shot at her. (He missed.)

Jessie, my mother's mother, had been married and widowed. Mom told me that her mother said her first marriage was the only time she was in love, that she was fond of my mother's father, my grandfather George Seville, but nothing more. I think my mother's tremendous passion for life, for anything she did, came from a rebellion against her genteel parents' lukewarm relationship. Perhaps Mom was determined to be hot where her parents were cool.

Compared to Aunt Janet, my mother was sane. Compared to Aunt Elsa, she was lucky.

When she was a teen Mom used to sneak out to dance. Mom's professor father and blueblood mother were genteel to a fault and easily fooled by their daughter, whom they spoiled. Her dad made a point of always serving her as if she was an honored guest. Pictures of Mom when she was little show her exquisitely dressed and always posing, dramatically and with a secure sense of her own extrovert charm.

My mother was raised as a devout fundamentalist Christian. But her parents' version of fundamentalism was an educated and cultured fundamentalism. They read the Bible and believed it was literally true in every detail. But they also spoke several languages, and Bible reading was accompanied by plenty of P. G. Wodehouse, chunks of recited Shakespeare, funny limericks, amusing puns, and a deep interest in classical music and art.

Mom was a "Mediterranean" beauty with dark eyes, a softly rounded nose, high cheekbones, and long waist-length black hair that she wore up in a bun. She was not tall, but her figure was perfect. She may have been partly Jewish.

There was a family theory about her maiden name Seville. Mom's father's people came to America from England in the early nineteenth century. (Her mother's people came over on the second voyage of the Mayflower.) It was thought that George Seville's family may have been Jewish. There was a Seville family connection to Scotland. When the Spanish Roman Catholics were persecuting Jews, they made them take last names, and the Jews took the names of their cities. Then Spaniards were wrecked on the Scottish coast after the defeat of the Armada. And so—as our family theory went—maybe one of Mom's ancestors was one of those Spanish/Scottish

Jews. That would have suited Mom perfectly. She loved all things Jewish and in the 1970s wrote a book—*Christianity Is Jewish.*

Once, when my mother was in her late sixties, I saw a man come up to her on an airplane and ask her if she was Audrey Hepburn. My mother didn't really look like Ms. Hepburn, but she was so beautiful, and exuded such energy, that people assumed she had to be somebody.

Mom was very aware that she was special. She would, from time to time, talk about what *could* have been, what she *could* have done if she had had less-strict parents, what she *might* have been if she hadn't married Dad. What *if* she had finished college instead of dropping out to marry my father to work and put him through seminary? What *if* she had married money? "There were *lots* of wealthy and cultured young men, and not so young too, who wanted to have me."

Mom lived her life in tension between her unrealized ambition to be recognized for something important, refined, and cultured and her belief that God had called her to do Christian work that required her to sacrifice herself, not least her image of who she really felt she was when the cultural elites she admired, or at least envied, mocked fundamentalism.

Mom sometimes stamped her foot (literally) if H. L. Mencken's name was mentioned. And she would say of his antifundamentalist satires: "But *we're* not like that! He would *never* have written those horrible things if he had ever met *me!*"

My mother loved culture. I don't know if this was because she loved books, art, and music for their own sake, or if this was part of her desire to not be mistaken for "just some fundamentalist" or "one of those American Christians," as she sometimes called other believers.

When we went on our vacations to Italy, Mom brought books and read out loud to us on the beach, in our rooms, even at dinner. Bertie Wooster, Huck Finn, Shylock, Aslan, Peter, Susan, and Lucy, not to mention Odysseus, Prince Caspian, or the Little Prince, got tangled up in many a Mediterranean sunset, accompanied us up to Mom and Dad's bedroom, then lurked in the shadows as we sprawled on my parents' bed for "just one more chapter, *please,* Mom!" before sleep.

My mother was a great and expressive actress and read better out loud than anyone I've heard since. Every book she read lived. And Mom never said so specifically, but it was clear that reading was a necessity, not a luxury.

When Mom and Dad traveled to England, Mom would visit Blackwell's Children's Book Shop and come home laden with Penguin and Puffin paperbacks. And since those included everything written by such luminary children's authors as E. Nesbitt, who set her stories in Victorian England, I grew up knowing more about the monarchy, the difference between a scullery and parlor maid, hackney cabs, and how to make and serve tea properly than about American daily life, unless you count life on the prairie with Ma and Pa or life on the Mississippi as observed from a raft.

Mom *loved* books. And my mother never read down to her children. She always was reading books "meant for slightly older children." By the time I was nine or ten, Mom was reading me classics, from *Wuthering Heights* to *Pride and Prejudice.*

Once I started to read for myself, I discovered that Mom had given me a flying start. The world was literally an open book. As I turned the pages, I met many familiar friends.

Mom was a music lover, too. And she could not enjoy anything unless she shared it. If my parents were going to a concert, we children were taken along. Each year, Mom bought tickets to three or four concerts at the Montreux classical music festival. She also took our family to several ballets over the years, to several operas and many chamber orchestra concerts, and to all sorts of recitals. And she did this even back when we had very little money, when we were sometimes eating meatless meals for months if giving to the mission was down. We had no car and often couldn't afford a taxi ride to the station after a concert. But my mother got us there somehow anyway.

My first encounter with opera was watching *Don Juan*, which my parents took me to at the Paris Opera House when I was seven and traveling with them on one of their speaking trips. We were in the cheap seats, what seemed like miles from the stage. But Dad handed me his binoculars and, though I fell asleep, I woke up in time to see Don Juan sinking into the flames of hell, singing his way into oblivion. I was hooked.

There was a tension between what Mom believed and her wider interests in art, music, and culture. Mom could not ignore the sorts of people who were most certainly *not* fundamentalist: the artists, composers, and choreographers she so admired, or the sorts of secular people she might bump into at concerts and in museums. So I think my mother spent a lifetime trying to change the image of Bible-believing Christians. She decided she would be so wonderful in every way that her example would undo all the damage done to the image of what it was to be a Bible-believing Christian set by those other, all-too-ordinary Christians.

Mom wanted her children to know that she could have done lots more glamorous things than "just be a missionary." And Mom never wanted to look like what she was: a pastor's wife.

She dressed with taste and style for every occasion. And Mom was never more animated than when she was talking about the cultured, wealthy, or important people she met. She would not just mention their names but would go into detailed stories of their lives, as if she was reading (or writing) a novel about them. I think Mom wanted to *be* one of them.

My mother's favorite people were those who were famous for some cultural achievement. She met the great violinist Yehudi Menuhin on the beach in Italy once and was more or less in a swoon for weeks while telling us in detail what he had said, what she had said. . . . And more than half a century later, when B. B. King gave her a backstage pass for a concert at the Montreux Jazz Festival, Mom—at age ninety—wore that laminated security pass around her neck for the better part of a year, as if it was priceless jewelry.

My mother saw her mission as nothing less than repairing the image of fundamentalism. Sometimes this image-repair just involved serving exquisite high teas or reading good books. At other times it got complicated. For instance, in 1986, to launch her book *The Gift of Music,* Mom raised fifty thousand dollars—"To reach out to the kind of New Yorkers that no other Christians ever reach"—and rented Avery Fisher Hall at Lincoln Center, hired the Guarneri Quartet, and invited her friends from all over the country to join her for a concert followed by a reception.

When Mom met people, then told her children about her encounters, the story line was always the same: They were lost, and Mom saved them. Or at least she had changed them. Mom's favorite phrase was "Before he met me, he said he never knew there were Christians who were so. . ."—fill in the blank—cultured, knowledgeable about art, music, food, clothes, compassionate, and refined.

My mother took Dad to his first art museum, the Philadelphia Museum of Art. "Now Fran talks all about art, but when I met him he knew nothing, my dear, nothing!" Mom helped Dad "deepen his faith" after he became a Christian. Mom showed Dad how to have an always-use-real-silver-and-good-china-and-put-candles-on-the-table-at-dinner, cultured family, since his parents had been "so working class."

My mother became the basis of "Elsa," the mother in my first novel, *Portofino,* and the rest of the *Calvin Becker Trilogy (Zermatt* and *Saving Grandma).* And I still see the world through her eyes. She was there at every stage, including mopping up my vomit—without recrimination—when I took some bad peyote buds after smoking pot when I was fifteen.

Whatever I believe, or say I believe now, the shape of my life is defined by my mother's prayers—whether these have actually been answered or whether the force of her personality was enough to make it so. In that quietest inner place, my mother is still young, beautiful, and present, leaning forward listening with rapt attention at a concert, or with a book on her lap, eyes sparkling and opening up the universe of *Treasure Island,* or as poor Oliver picks his way though the harsh Victorian urban underworld.

3

If Dad had been an actor, he might have been cast to play James Cagney's little brother, maybe in some 1930s movie set down by the docks. But by the time I was a teenager, a lifetime of intellectual work had given Dad a craggy, bags-under-the-eyes Einstein look and softened his face.

My father was my mother's opposite. Born and raised in Germantown, Philadelphia, he grew up hard, in hard times. Dad was short and stocky. He had thick leg muscles and heavy forearms with strong wide-palmed hands. His legs just kept getting thicker as he hiked all over the Alps. His Moods—they deserve a capital letter—dictated everything about our daily lives. Dad suffered from bouts of fury punctuated by depression. All Mom needed to say was "Fran is in a Mood," and we crept around trying to stay out of sight till Mom gave the all-clear.

Dad's brooding face reflected his early life as a working-class son of poor parents. He had a little scar on his cheek where he'd been stabbed in a street fight when he was delivering ice off a horse-drawn cart. When I was ten or eleven, Dad taught me to fight. He was very matter-of-fact and said: "You need to know how to defend yourself." Dad's idea of fighting was this: just get in close, break something, and run.

While Mom was being served breakfast in bed by her Chinese

servants, then later by her genteel parents, who cut her toast into buttered "ladyfingers" and boiled her "a perfect three-and-a-half-minute soft-boiled egg each morning," Dad was eating corned beef hash warmed over, being beaten with a strap by his mother, and selling ice from the time he was ten or eleven off a wagon.

Dad's father ran away from his home when he was twelve years old. My grandfather served in the Navy in the Spanish-American War, when, as he told Dad, "The ships were made of wood but the men made of iron." And while raising Dad, his father worked as a "stationary engineer" in a large office building maintaining the heating and electrical plant. He got this job even though he only had a third-grade education. Dad told me about getting into the huge boilers and chipping out the lime deposits with his father.

My father heard his first classical music when the Boy Scouts took his troop to a concert. He loved it, and from then on Dad would argue with his mother to let him listen to broadcasts of symphonies when she wanted to hear popular music, played on the old crystal set Dad's father built.

Dad got "saved" in 1929 in a tent revival; he was seventeen. This was after reading the Bible. Sometimes Dad said he got saved "just reading the Bible." Other times he said it was in that tent revival. Other times he would explain to the students that it was while he was studying Greek philosophy and at the same time giving the Bible a "last chance" by reading it, and that it occurred to him that the Bible answered the philosophical questions raised by the Greeks.

About two years after Dad got saved, he met Mom when he stood up in a church meeting to challenge a "liberal" pastor who was questioning the literal truth of scripture. Judging by my mom's account, Dad's real salvation was when he met her. Dad's reward for accepting Christ was to get a saint for a wife, a sexy saint.

Dad's newly converted zealot heart twined with Mom's zealot heart, though Dad was but a mere "newborn babe in Christ." And Dad became a pastor, called by God, or pushed by Mom, or both.

By the time I came along, Mom and Dad were thriving and making a living on propagating their ideas and defending them. And the verbal images they spun out of thin air had to be strong. They were describing a world you can't see, the invisible link between mortality and immortality. They were bringing alive the biblical epoch to twentieth-century young people, competing with modernity by talking up a storm, convincing smart people that the spiritual world is more real and essential than the evidence of one's eyes. And they were good at it.

Dad had one big idea: God has revealed himself to us through the Bible. And he spent a lifetime trying to fit everything into that one idea, and explain away anything that didn't fit. Dad's apologetic method—combining scripture, theology, and culture—became his trademark, a kind of rationalist approach to the mysteries of faith, as instantly recognizable to his millions of evangelical followers as a Rothko is to anyone who has seen more than one canvas painted after he hit his blocks-of-color stride. ("Apologetics" being defined as the method and means and content of one's argument for the faith, a way of reasoning, one's method of evangelization.)

Dad was also a dedicated hiker and camper, a starter of campfires "even with wet wood," and a man who could fix and build things. Dad always kept his father's tools handy. His father's hammer, plane, and chisel were like sacred objects in our home, along with his father's old Lionel train set.

Dad passed on one saying of his father's to me. It related to how to survive working high in the rigging of a wind-tossed sailing ship. *"Keep one hand for yourself, boy!"* Dad would often exclaim, applying his father's wisdom to all sorts of situations in life, from how to argue, to hiking and tree-climbing safety rules.

Dad had a reverence for the way his father had done so much with so little. Everything my grandfather learned was something he taught himself—the engineering knowledge needed to run a building's heat and electrical generating plant; how to wire his house, which he did with Dad helping; how to build his first radio. You never called the repairman in the household Dad grew up in; you did it yourself.

My father kept his old Boy Scout manual, his father's tools, and his father's Navy shaving mug next to his bed on a little shelf behind a curtain. It was like a little shrine. As a child, I often looked at my father's precious mementos, but I never took them out of Mom and Dad's bedroom. Dad also kept his own metalwork "exam pieces" from high school shop class behind that curtain. They included a stained-glass monogram of the letter "S" and several pieces of beautifully crafted wrought iron. "*I* made those," Dad would say.

When Mom would talk about how wonderful her father was and how he could speak and teach Mandarin, Greek, Hebrew, and Latin, Dad never said much. But later he might quietly mention to me that his dad could fix anything. And sometimes there would be tears in his eyes when he would talk about how his "Pop" wired that old house while laboring to read the electrical manual he was learning from.

"Pop never had the opportunities I had," Dad would say, "but you would have liked him, boy."

When Dad turned in his first philosophy paper at Hampden-Sydney College, his professor invited him over to his house a few days later. Dad found him sitting in a rocking chair next to an old pot-bellied stove and smoking a pipe. For a while the man said nothing, just smoked and watched Dad and smiled inscrutably. Then at last the professor spoke.

"Schaeffer," he said, "I have a problem with you. I don't know how to resolve it. This is the best philosophy paper from a first-year student that has ever been turned in since I've been teaching. It is also the worst spelling I've ever seen. What should I do with you?"

"I have a suggestion," said Dad; "I suggest you always grade my papers on the ideas and pay no attention to my spelling. I've never been able to spell. And I can't fix that."

There was a long pause. Dad said he was nervous but tried not to move, or even take his eyes off that old professor's face.

"You know what, Schaeffer, I think I'll do just that," said the professor at last.

This was a big break for my father. He spoke of the incident with such emotion that his voice would shake. It was an unusual thing for a professor to do, back in the days when spelling and grammar, even handwriting, still figured heavily into a college grade.

Dad was very aware of each step in his journey to a "bigger world," as he called it. There were the Boy Scouts and that symphony, and then there was one high school teacher who Dad recalled with tears. She had "opened all the doors" for him by encouraging him to start to read books for pleasure. She "opened my eyes," Dad would say. And years later, my father tracked her down and wrote to her, and remarkably she was still alive, and in 1968 (or thereabouts) Dad sent her a signed copy of his first book, *Escape From Reason*, and a letter telling her that she was why he had "done anything" with his life.

4

Dad was pastor of several small churches in the Northeast and in St. Louis. Then he became a missionary in 1947. Sponsored by his mission board, Dad located in Switzerland because from there he could get anywhere in Europe to do his mission work with young people in war-torn cities. The next year, Mom and my three sisters joined Dad.

The Swiss had sat out the Second World War as neutrals, trading security for the lives of the Jews they turned back to the Nazis, banking for all sides, selling weapons to everyone, and waiting for other countries to send their young men to die to make them safe from the Nazi empire. So in 1947 the Swiss infrastructure was intact. And Dad would travel almost every week to the cities all over Europe where he was helping to start youth ministries. And on those trips his quest for self-betterment continued, and he would visit the art museums, buy guidebooks, and study what he was seeing.

At first my family lived in Lausanne and then moved to the small alpine village of Champéry, where I was born in 1952. Then we got kicked out of Champéry when I was three. My parents were expelled from the Roman Catholic canton (state) of Valais because they led a local man to Christ. In other words, Mom and Dad talked him into becoming a born-again Calvinist fundamentalist Protestant like us.

The local priest was not amused. And the bishop of Sion (the capital of Valais, just a few miles from the border of "very Roman Catholic Italy") was not amused. Swiss democracy notwithstanding, he arranged to have my parents' residency permits canceled to get the "religious influence"—the official reason given for our family's expulsion—away from his flock. That was when we moved to Huémoz, where I grew up.

Huémoz is in the Protestant canton of Vaud and is a lot more open to the sky than Champéry. The mountains look friendlier, easy to see whole, not looming close as they do over Champéry. Our old village was "a lot darker," Mom would say, "and I don't mean just because there was so little sunlight compared to Huémoz. It was darker in *every way!*"

I heard the word "dark" a lot while growing up, and most of the time it was other people's spiritual darkness that was being spoken of. There was a lot of that around. People, places, history, villages, cantons, whole continents were filled with spiritual dark or spiritual light, depending on what they believed about what we believed. If they agreed completely with us, then they got the rarest of accolades: truly kindred spirits.

Everything we did was to be a witness. (To "witness" was to "share Christ"; in other words, talk about your faith in hopes that you would convince the person listening to convert. To witness also meant to live in such a way that people would "see Christ" in you and want to convert because your life was so admirable.)

People's eternal destinies hinged on a word or tiny event, maybe on no more than an unfriendly look. Even an improperly served high tea on Sunday afternoon could send someone to hell. What if the sandwiches were prepared wrong and they went away with the impression that we were like all those so-called ministries where they didn't even know how to butter thinly sliced bread out to the edges? What if the person visiting was given a plastic spoon and we were mistaken for uncouth Pentecostals? We had to be people that others wanted to join, attractive ambassadors for Christ in word and deed.

"My dear mother," Mom said, "used to say that every meal should be served as if the Queen of England might drop by."

"Really, Mom?"

"Why, yes, darling. In Mother's day, of course, that was Queen Victoria. But Queen Elizabeth is just a person, too, and she needs Christ as much as any of those terribly confused Anglicans do. And her family skis in Klosters and there are some English people we met on the last English trip who know one of her ladies-in-waiting, so you never know. I've been praying for her."

We often reviewed our family's history to discern God's hand on our lives, something like the people of Israel looking back in thanksgiving to discern God's hand on them as they were brought out of Egypt. Just before our exodus from Champéry, I got polio. Mom always said "That year was the greatest testing we ever went through. Looking back, it's not surprising Satan attacked us."

"Why?" I asked. "Because of what happened next," Mom would say.

"What was that?" I'd ask, knowing what the answer was, but compelled to ask by an unspoken rule that this sort of spiritual heart-to-heart was edifying.

"L'Abri was about to start, and Satan knew that and was doing everything he could to stop us from founding The Work."

"Does Satan know the future?"

"Yes, dear, he does."

"But I thought only God knows everything."

"That's right, but foreknowledge isn't the same thing as foreordaining."

"Oh?"

"God chose you to be born, to accept The Finished Work Of His Son On The Cross, to be one of his Elect. Satan can't do anything like that."

"I guess not."

"Satan knew that if we started L'Abri, the Lord was about to use us very powerfully."

"And he knew about all the people who'd get saved?" I asked.

"That's right, dear."

"But if it's predestined, why did Satan bother to try and stop us?"

"Because, dear, he's always trying to fight God."

"But God always wins?"

"Yes, and that is why Satan fell, he thought he could win."

"So he was stupid?"

"No, dear, Satan is a wily adversary. Don't ever underestimate him."

"And that's why I got polio?"

"Yes, dear. Your leg is part of the battle-in-the-heavenlies. You are like a soldier who got wounded. It was during The Year Of Testing, but, by God's Grace, we all came through, and your father did not lose his faith, though he certainly fell into the temptation of doubt. Poor Fran," Mom said with the deep sigh that always accompanied her many versions of "poor Fran."

If Dad didn't get a joke, it was "poor Fran." When he couldn't figure out what fork to use in a restaurant, it was "poor Fran." Mom rarely said those words to Dad's face. But we children could read her thoughts. A certain eye roll, a certain sigh, and I could hear "poor Fran" even if her mouth wasn't moving.

5

Fundamentalists never can just disagree. The person they fall out with is not only on the wrong side of an issue; they are on the wrong side of God. In the 1940s, my parents had a big fight with a fundamentalist leader I never met, Carl McIntyre. Years later, the mention of his name was enough to put Dad in a Mood. They fell out in a way that got personal, and McIntyre lied about my father, or so Mom said. What the lies were, I never knew. My sister Susan says that McIntyre accused Dad of being a communist and that this was "All part of the McCarthy-era witch hunts." Anyway, the upshot was that Dad left the mission that sent him to Europe in 1947. Then my parents founded the ministry of L'Abri in 1955.

A church split builds self-righteousness into the fabric of every new splinter group, whose only reason for existence is that they decide they are more moral and pure than their brethren. This explains my childhood, and perhaps a lot about America, too.

The United States is a country with the national character of a newly formed church splinter group. This is not surprising. Our country *started* as a church splinter group. The Puritans left England because they believed they were more enlightened than members of the Church of England, and they were eager to form a perfect earthly community following a pure theology. They also had every intention of some day returning to England, once they had proved that something close to heaven on earth could work, and reforming their "heretical" fellow citizens.

America still sees itself as essential and as destiny's instrument. And each splinter group within our culture—left, right, conservative, liberal, religious, secular—sees itself as morally, even "theologically," superior to its rivals. It is not just about politics. It is about being *better* than one's evil opponent. We don't just disagree, we demonize the "other." And we don't compromise.

We Schaeffers never compromised. At times it seemed that only God knew how important we were, how right, how pure. But isolation and rejection by "The World" only confirmed our self-importance. The sense of being like the tribes of Israel wandering the desert, with enemies on all sides, was the underlying reality of my childhood. I think it was shared by my three sisters—Priscilla, Susan, and Debby—too, though because I was so much younger I really didn't get to know them until we all grew up. Before that, it was like having three extra mothers.

My oldest sister Priscilla was kind, but my early memories of her are vague. She married when I was five and moved to St. Louis with her husband John Sandri. Later she and John came back and joined L'Abri. Susan, my next oldest sister, was dramatic, loud, and desperately trying to get me educated, something my parents had somehow absentmindedly forgotten to do. Susan went to study in Oxford and married Ranald Macaulay when I was nine. They moved in next door and also joined L'Abri. Debby, my youngest sister, was intensely sweet. She married when I was twelve, moved away for a few years, then moved back with her husband Udo Middelmann and joined L'Abri.

We children fell somewhere between my pietistic, gorgeous mother and my dour, ordinary-looking father. We veered from extreme dramatic piety (Susan) to doubt (me), from energetic proselytism (Debby) to spiritual wrestling (Priscilla), from solid and self-assured (Susan) to gorgeous and nervous (Priscilla), from short and passionate (me) to even shorter and virtually quivering with a sincere desire to save humankind (Debby). However, we all shared a sense of being separated from the world.

We were busy judging everyone's spiritual state. We had a lot to do. Only God might be able to see their hearts and innermost thoughts, but we had a pretty good idea of how it was going to go for plenty of folks on the Judgment Day. Not so well.

Susan took grim satisfaction at the looming damnation of just about everyone but us. Debby wept and redoubled her efforts. Priscilla got nervous and threw up. I hid.

If my sisters ever had doubts about their faith, I never knew, at least when I was very young. And of course Mom had no doubts. Only Dad had doubts. We knew about those because Mom told us.

Mom never said what they were about, just that "Fran questioned everything that year," and "Your father's faith is not as strong as mine," long pause, a slight shake of the head, "Poor Fran." Sigh.

All Dad ever said about his doubts was "I wrestled before the Lord while walking back and forth in the hayloft of Chalet Bijou in Champéry, for many days and nights on end. I was ready to give it all up. I questioned everything!"

Maybe my bad leg was God's punishment of Dad. Mom

never said this, but somehow I got that idea. This made sense to me when I was a young child. It is an idea that still makes sense to some evangelical readers who stumble on my novels like *Zermatt* or my "anti-Christian" op-eds. From time-to-time they write to me that they expect me to drop dead, literally, as soon as God catches up on his work.

One thing they hate about *Zermatt* is that the missionary father loses his faith. They don't like the sex either, but it is the threat of losing one's faith that seems to infuriate them. If life can't be tied up in a neat package, if you let those doubts begin to gnaw at your guts, where will it end?

It is no coincidence that about 99 percent of evangelical books are written to help people order their lives according to an invisible world when everything in the visible world is challenging faith. The title of almost every evangelical book could be "How to Keep Your Faith in Spite of . . ." fill in the blank, college, art, science, philosophy, sex, temptation, literature, media, TV, movies, your homosexual tendencies, your heterosexual tendencies . . . in other words, every breath you take.

Each night, Mom read me Bible stories. Lots of the ones I liked best—the juicy killing, adultery, death, and revenge ones—were filled with people suddenly getting leprosy, being plagued by worms that ate them from the inside out, and other usually fatal problems under the general heading of being "struck down by God" and/or "chastised." This happened for reasons related to not believing *right,* especially not having enough faith, or the right kind of faith, or maybe they had lots of faith but it was in bad theology, or led to worshipping various false gods, or they married people who worshipped false gods, or sinned by worshipping our God, the One True

Reformed Calvinist God, but did it wrong the way Cain did when he came to God with unclean hands bearing vegetables and fruit when a lamb was required. Or maybe they forgot to do what God said to do and didn't kill every man, woman, and child of some wicked peoples he had expressly told them to exterminate, including the cattle and household pets.

God would sometimes punish the sinner by striking down an innocent bystander—though since all people are fallen under Adam's curse, no one is really innocent—for instance, King David, whose lust-child was killed by God as a way to send David a stern warning. David mourned for a while, and then he took a bath and wrote a psalm about it. So maybe I was lucky because Dad questioned God and I only lost the use of one leg. Anyway, the paralysis felled me when I was two, either as a warning to Dad, a preemptive punishment, or a test of my parent's faith.

I was incredibly fortunate that the Swiss doctor Mom took me to in Monthey—the town at the base of the mountain below Champéry—didn't kill me. This "polio specialist" talked Mom into allowing him to replace some of my spinal fluid with a "special serum" he made from tapping the spinal fluid of chimpanzees. The doctor had the chimps locked in a lab in the local hospital and was working on an idea that injecting their spinal fluid into a human spine could arrest, or reverse, paralysis.

Dad's respect for my mother's expertise on all things to do with "raising the children" was complete. Dad left all medical decisions "up to Edith" as well as letting her decide anything to do with our education, prayer life, and introduction to the facts of life. When it came to treatment for my polio, the rule of "Edith will decide" was followed.

Mom knew this doctor was crazy, and she prayed for guidance.

Apparently she got told by God to proceed, and I was wheeled off by the nuns who were nurses in this "very Roman Catholic hospital." Mom said she waited on her knees, crying, in the ward.

They administered one treatment and brought me back to Mom. The next day, I was to have a second treatment, but at the last moment the doctor told my mother that he didn't think it was necessary. Later, Mom told me that it was "such a wonderful answer to prayer that God moved his heart and that doctor spared you."

I always wondered why she had to pray that the doctor would change his mind and "spare" me. Couldn't she just have said no, with or without God? Twenty-five years later when I told this story to Dr. Koop, a family friend who was about to be appointed by President Reagan as Surgeon General, he said that you couldn't design a better method to murder a small child.

Throughout my childhood, Mom often repeated the story and said it was the hardest decision of her life, but "Who knows, perhaps that old doctor's ideas really did save your other leg because you walked again and they all said you wouldn't."

"I have monkey blood in me?" I asked, feeling strangely delighted.

"Not monkey *blood,* darling: chimpanzee spinal fluid. Thank God the doctor relented!"

When I arrived at the stage of life, around eleven years old, when teasing Mom became one of my favorite pastimes, I would bring up the "monkey story." A good time to wind Mom up was at bedtime when she came up to read to me and then we'd pray together, and moments later she would be about to close my bedroom door, having tucked me in. I didn't want to go to sleep.

"Mom?" I asked just as my bedroom door was closing.

"Yes, dear?" Mom answered, opening the door just wide enough to pop her head back into the room.

"Mom, if monkey serum cured me, then maybe it proves we really are evolved from monkeys."

"Don't be ridiculous, dear."

"But would lizard blood have worked?"

"It wasn't blood, dear, and you are just trying to tease me."

"I'm not, Mom. I've been thinking about my polio, and I really do think that maybe this proves the atheists are right."

"I hope you are joking," said Mom, opening the door a little wider.

"No, I really do think that maybe we should change what we believe, because it looks like my treatment proves evolution."

Mom stepped back into the room and turned on the light so she could read the expression on my face, tell if I was serious or not. She gave me a hard look and sighed.

"You might be joking and you might think this is funny, but you are coming awfully close to joking about things we never joke about."

"Monkeys?"

"You know perfectly well what I mean! We *don't* joke about the Things of The Lord! Now *good night,* dear!"

Mom flicked off the light, turned, and took a step back and started to close the door.

"I think this means that Darwin is right."

"I said good night, dear!" Mom said through the door.

"And I think Dad should change what he teaches about creation!"

The door opened. Mom was standing there with her hands on her hips.

"Now you *really* are being absurd!"

"No, I am not. Dad says that Christianity is so true that if anyone can show it isn't true, that he'll give up his faith!"

"Well, the Bible *is* true, and you know that!"

"But I have monkey blood in me, so I've become a missing link!" I said, as I lost my struggle and burst into laughter.

Mom started to smile even though she was trying hard not to.

"Darling, this really is NOT funny! God created us each for a purpose, and I know you might only be joking; but there are some things far too serious to joke about, and this is one of them."

Mom shut the door. I heard a muffled laugh.

"I evolved!" I shouted triumphantly.

"YOU DID NOT!" Mom called back from halfway down the stairs. "Now that is quite enough! *Go to sleep!* You have crossed the line and are perniciously close to taking God's name in vain!"

"I didn't say *God* has monkey blood!"

I heard the rush of her steps back up the stairs, and the door flew open. Mom's face was flushed.

"That's IT! One more word and I'm getting your father! And you know that will put him in a Mood! So don't you *dare* make me!"

6

We were earnest and my parents were sincere. Dad had a vicious temper. Mom was a high-powered nut. But so what? Given the range of human suffering, I had a golden childhood. My sisters remember things their own way. I asked each for her thoughts. Priscilla and Debby responded. Susan declined.

Priscilla wrote:

> 3/1/2007
> My childhood in the Schaeffer family was so different from Frank's. I was 15 years older than my little brother and until age 11 was brought up in the USA. My last years there were in St. Louis where I went to public school and had a regular and routine life. For me there was Sunday School—church—young people's meetings and a huge Summer Bible school. I was surrounded with young people of my own age and I was very involved in school and in the church life.
>
> The one thing Frank and I shared as a Schaeffer child was Daddy's love of art. Daddy would take me and my sisters often to the St. Louis Art Museum and we spent hours enjoying and talking about the art. Later Frank

was taken as a child to European art museums. A couple of years ago Frank and I went through the Metropolitan Museum of Art in NY together and we agreed that what Daddy had given us in enjoyment, appreciation, and interest in the arts was one of the things we most valued in our childhood.

A big difference in our upbringing was that Frank, as a very young child, was surrounded constantly by college-age students who invaded our home—for hours of discussion—table conversations—dealing with intense questions—problems—searching. For me at that time, being in university myself, these were my friends. I was thrilled that I could bring anybody home, no matter how cynical, shocking, blasphemous, and Daddy would be able to sit down and talk to them on their level and would listen to them, and we saw results as the conversations moved forward.

Daddy did change in his view of the Christian life. In his pastorates [in the United States] he tended toward a pietistic view. It was "worldly" to go to movies, to smoke, to drink alcohol, to play cards, to dance, and we could only play hymns or listen to Handel and Bach on Sundays. Coming to Europe and starting L'Abri, Daddy and Mom slowly changed their viewpoint. It really made me proud of him to see he wasn't caught in a box as to what was important in Christian spirituality. He introduced me to art, Sartre, Camus, the Beatles, and modern thought. His book *True Spirituality* shows what he came to see as real spirituality without the earlier pietism. . . .

Susan wrote:

3/2/2007
I wrote four pages for you, [about her childhood memories of the Schaeffer household] that I think would be what I'd want to say. However, now I'm not at all content with them. I feel handicapped too by not seeing more of what you DID experience and feel—obviously so very different from myself. Also, as you have letters from the oldest and youngest [Schaeffer] sisters, that covers a lot. So, thank you for inviting me to have *"un mot,"* but my rather weary granny self has to respond, not at this time or place.

"God bless" and love,

Sue.

P.S. Please don't stop phoning! XOXO

Debby wrote:

3/2/2007
Dearest Frank,

This may not be what you expected! However, I do think it is honest and if you do use it, please use it as a whole. Obviously, if I were writing my memoirs there would be much more to say, but this is stripped down to the core as I see it. I send you this with much love and admiration for your own struggle and passion for life.

My Childhood . . .

Being fully aware that these are my memories, which are highly personal and thus made up of distortions, as well as half-remembered stories, I will attempt to give some clearly recalled events and impressions.

My remembered life begins in a Swiss pension, in Lausanne, with a beloved old man, Monsieur Turrian, sitting in an old-fashioned kitchen, swinging me on his foot. My pneumonia that year, watching the doctor draw blood from my father, to mix with penicillin, so that the injection would hurt less, made a deep impression on my three-year-old self. Being carried on my father's strong shoulders feeling jubilation that I was so high up and, a few years later, the comprehension of the true sorrow of passing time, as he announced that I was getting "too heavy" and that this would be the last time he could carry me, stands out as a milestone. Swinging on his hand and running to keep up with his stride, as well as riding in the child-seat on the back of his bike in Lausanne, in 1948, on the bikes he bought in Holland, stand out clearly. I still feel the soaring joy.

My village life in Champéry was filled with gladness: living in our chalet, walking to school across fields and in the winter skiing every lunchtime. A big part of that period of my life was sleeping at the little school as a boarder, for weeks as my parents traveled [on their missionary speaking trips]. However, though I remember some sadness, mostly I loved the two odd ladies who ran it, Tante Lili and Mademoiselle Huguenin. One was angular and strict, the other puffy and fat and lovely to hug.

My earliest and most abiding memories and view of my father, which never changed, was of a man brutally honest about himself and profoundly humble. The year I was four or five, my father having lost his temper, though not at me, came to me and asked me to pray for him as he had done wrong. Also, that year as we walked home from church, up the village street, he so reassuringly held my hand and said we had two relationships: father and daughter and brother and sister in Christ. Before God, we stood as equals one next to the other.

Thus my parents' often stormy relationship was a factor of strength in my own life, as admission of fault, repentance, and forgiveness was a reality I saw my father practice daily. This relationship of two equal human beings was constantly present, beginning as a very young child all the way to my father's death, as time was always made to discuss and debate the subjects that mattered to me, not only for my sake, but because my father loved to be presented with a new idea. So although my parents were very busy and intensely occupied, I treasure the importance of my person and ideas bestowed on me.

Too many other memories crowd in: of skiing, vacations on the Mediterranean, and most preciously there the afternoon walks alone in the hills with my father, museum visits, and two treasured times in Florence, reading aloud as a family, dinners, so much information and love for history communicated as we walked, ate, or traveled.

The decisions I took alone, that my father felt I should decide for myself, were indicative of what we would today call a "parenting style," that I now feel left too much up to me. However, the legacy of my father was the freedom to look at what I had experienced and reject or change things in my own life, as I was never led to believe by him that these were ideal.

My mother's legacy was in stark contrast, as she single-mindedly pursued her ideals, often blinded to the realities of life or of our lives. As a dreamer and a highly artistic individual my mother created her own life with passion and hard work. I compare her to early discoverers of the North Pole. She pursued her objectives with determination, though bits of bodies all around her were lost to frostbite. The havoc she caused to all around her, as they were dragged in to help her meet self-imposed deadlines and goals, was phenomenal and scarring to me as a child. The force of her personality was such that I, at least, never even thought of refusing. Also, I would say, that though my father taught me the love of the Real, my mother's idealism has taken years to peel away.

Much love,
Debby

7

When I was six, I went to America for an operation on my polio leg. (I turned seven in America.) In 1959 we crossed the ocean on a freighter, the *Coroveglia*. She was owned by the André Shipping Line, a Swiss company that belonged to the André family. They were the wealthiest people we knew, a special subject of awe and resentment. Amazingly for "dark post-Reformation" Switzerland, the Andrés were born-again evangelical Christians. They were rich, and from time to time they gave a gift to L'Abri, but never one large enough to impress Mom. "They could give *so much more* if they wanted to!" she would say. "Are they the richest people in the world?" I asked.

"No, dear, but they are probably the richest people in Lausanne, and some of the wealthiest people in Switzerland, and that is saying something," said Mom.

"They don't seem rich," said Debby.

"That is because they aren't like some rich people who flaunt their wealth."

"Do they have their own plane?" I asked.

"I don't know, dear, but it wouldn't surprise me."

"What else do they have?" I asked.

"Who knows what else, places in South America I think and

offices everywhere for the shipping line, but when you visit them in Lausanne they're just in their ordinary nice middle-class home and Mrs. André is peeling carrots like any Swiss housewife and Mr. André comes home for lunch like anybody else and they don't even have a maid, just someone to help clean. At least I didn't see a maid. It is really admirable, in that Swiss way."

When we traveled on the *Coroveglia,* Mom pointed out that "We *still* have to pay for the tickets, only less than we would otherwise." The idea was that because we were in the Lord's work, any person with a lot of money who was truly discerning would have given us the boat passage and to do less was something like Mary and Martha charging Christ for supper.

We sailed from Hamburg. The ship was carrying coal dust. I rolled in the dust and got covered from head to toe. I remember the crew urging me on and Mom being angry and my eyes stinging.

When I was two, I had traveled to the States and returned on the *Ile de France,* the ship I got polio on. But the voyage when I was six was the first I made where I discovered that life on shipboard, even a small old freighter, is wonderful. The feel of the engine vibrating under my feet, the roll of the ship, the sense of inexorable forward motion day and night, the lash of the moist wind on deck and the stale interior air down below, the dramatic moment each day as we moved our clocks forward: I loved it all, even the ubiquitous yellow linoleum that the cabins and narrow passages were covered with.

The first mate kept a picture of a bare-breasted woman in his cabin. It was a black-and-white photo that had been tinted. Her nipples were mauve. It was my first view of pornography.

I had seen plenty of nude statues and paintings, but I somehow knew this picture was different and didn't mention it to my parents. I knew that if they saw it, my visits to the first mate's cabin would end.

I played on the bridge, went down to the engine room any time I wanted, and appreciatively breathed in the hot oil smell. I wandered all day from stem to stern, scrambling up and down ladders. On the voyage before ours, they had been hit by a hurricane and a huge wave had smashed one of the windows on the bridge. Flying glass sliced open a sailor's face. The first mate told me about how he stitched up the sailor while getting medical instructions, stitch-by-stitch, over the radio from a seaman's medical station broadcasting from Rome.

We sailed into New York past the Statue of Liberty.

"We're home!" said Debby.

Those words didn't resonate with me. Home was our Swiss village. However, I was excited. America was where most of our guests came from. Each Christmas, we got boxes from friends and relatives. In the boxes were candy corn and "trashy American children's books"—slick Golden Books—some with characters like Donald Duck, that gave me a little glimpse into what seemed like an easygoing glittering world of entertainment and abundance.

I had a mental list of treats that I had seen or tasted in small quantities and now wanted to get my fill of: candy corn, root beer, TV, if possible, and a comic book. We headed to Pittsburgh, where I was to have surgery at the children's hospital.

I was taken to a Pittsburgh Pirates game (they won that game and, later, the World Series). I remember the feeling of stepping into the huge stadium in Pittsburgh, and being very embarrassed that I knew nothing about baseball! Was I a real American or not?

Dr. Ferguson was to be my surgeon, and he was going to do a "muscle transplant" to move one less-atrophied muscle (maybe a tendon) from the front of my left leg to the calf where everything was shriveled up. This was to give my foot more mobility.

I remember waking up after the operation as if surfacing from deep under the ocean, and seeing the spreading bloodstain on the heel of my elevated cast. I had the sweet cloying taste of ether in my mouth, nose, and throat and could taste it for days. My leg hurt, in a hot dull way. There were three incisions; a long one from just above my ankle up the side of my leg to my knee, one across the back of my heel, and one along the side of my foot above the arch. I had asked the doctor if I could stay awake so I could watch the operation. The answer was no. On my chart, Mom proudly showed me that in a box reserved for "patient disposition," the nurse had written "cheerful male."

After the operation I had to wear a cast for the rest of the summer. We were to stay in America that whole time, three months until the cast came off. Then we would know if the operation had "taken." Until then I was to *stay off that leg!* I was told that the transplanted muscle was fastened to my heel with a "single stitch" and that under no account was I to walk on my cast because if that stitch came loose, the whole operation would have been in vain.

Maybe this was true, or maybe I was being given extra motivation to stay off that leg. Mom prayed loudly and fervently for that "single stitch, that it may hold, O Lord!" until I could just about picture an angel somehow reaching into my heel and holding the stitch in place. But that didn't stop me from walking without my crutches and often forgetting to stay off the bad leg and then worrying myself sick about the single stitch.

For most of that summer of 1960, we lived on Long Island with "old Mrs. Johnson," as we all called her, the wealthy mother-in-law of Dr. Keyswater. The Keyswaters were a family of "real bluebloods," according to Mom. Dr. Keyswater was a surgeon and born-again. He was a member of our "Praying Family" of supporters and had arranged the operation for me. Some years before, when Susan was seven, she had been visiting their house and had knocked over a four-foot-tall Ming vase and broken it. The Keyswaters had been very gracious about this, Mom said. But I was to touch nothing in the house, because "it is filled with priceless treasures."

I remember begging Mom not to go out one evening but to stay with me. And she did, much to the Keyswaters' annoyance, who declared me spoiled and said that they would have to cancel their dinner reservations as a result.

Old Mrs. Johnson lived on a family estate on Long Island near Smithtown. There were mantraps made of tripwires and spikes to discourage the poachers who came to steal trout from a fish pond in the woods. The gardener gave Dad and I a guided tour while apologizing for the condition of the estate, saying that he was the only person who "she hires to take care of it," so the most he could do was mow the lawns and do some watering. As for the rest of the grounds and the formerly well-stocked fish ponds, well, as we could see, they had "all gone to hell." I glanced at Dad when the man cursed, but Dad didn't seem to care. I knew Mom would have given the man a stern look.

John Sandri and Priscilla came to live with us during their summer break from Covenant Seminary in St. Louis. John built a raft for me and floated it down the small tidal river that ran through the property. I discovered gnats and black flies, something shocking to a boy raised in the Alps, where, except for an occasional horsefly, there are no biting insects. We got incredibly muddy as we made our way up a marshy bank onto some swanky estate's lawn. A woman in a blue striped dress was very nice and let us hose off and telephoned our hostess to come and get us. John had struggled to keep my cast out of the water and mud, but it had gotten filthy. Debby cleaned it off before Mom saw it. I was sure the single stitch was done for.

At dinner, old Mrs. Johnson would treat Mom like a social equal—but only after Mom cooked dinner and served it and then sat down to join us. When we arrived, Mrs. Johnson had let her maid go, since she was going to let the missionaries staying with her provide the domestic help. Mom, Debby, and Priscilla were treated like servants. We were guests but feeling like a family of illegal immigrants stuck without a car, money, or a means to do anything more than work off the room and board. (Susan, barely eighteen, had been left in charge of L'Abri, an experience she described later as frightening.)

"She has *oodles* of money and could get new dish towels instead of making us use these old rags, and all the sheets have holes in them!" Mom would say. "It's the way with old money, very stingy," said Dad.

"She could really do something for the Lord, but this is all she does, lets us live here as her servants! She has enough money so she could buy a whole new chalet for the work if she wanted, *and* keep her maid while we're here so we could get a *real rest* from the Lord's work!"

One afternoon my mother asked Mrs. Johnson why there was only one peeler in the drawer after she had tried to find a second one so Debby could help peel potatoes. "Because," Mrs. Johnson answered, "servants always lose everything and if you have two of anything it just gives them an excuse!" The summer was broiling. It was my first taste of East Coast humidity, and there was no air conditioning. My cast came up to my hip. The skin began to itch. "Something died in there," I said after I noticed that when I'd itch my leg—with a knitting needle—I'd stir up quite a stench. At one point, it itched so badly that I tried to scratch my leg by feeding a fish hook into the cast. Debby spent her summer covering up what I was doing to the cast, taping up the heel I'd broken down walking on it and trying to get the fish hook out and worrying about what the doctor would say when he cut the cast off and saw all the added layers of tape.

Debby would also read to me out loud for hours and hold my legs so I could "swim" in the pool by dunking my head and shoulders into the water up to my waist while keeping my legs out. My one great sorrow was that pool. We had a swimming pool at last, and I couldn't swim in it!

Dad went away on several speaking trips. For once, Mom stayed with us. I was eating my weight in the cereals we couldn't get in Switzerland and drinking A&W root beer. And I was watching TV! I saw *The Lone Ranger* and other programs that had been described to me by American children visiting L'Abri.

It was on that trip that I got a first inkling that our family was pitied by other people. I learned that Dr. Ferguson, "who is not even saved but has a real heart for the Lord's work," donated my operation when he found out Mom and Dad were missionaries. I felt embarrassed.

It was the first time I had met people who said they were believers who had nothing to do with L'Abri. I went along with Dad on several speaking trips to local churches. I was very aware that somehow we weren't like "them." They had ordinary jobs and then were Christians as an added bonus, whereas Christianity was *all* we did. And I would watch how people in "ordinary churches," as Mom called them, related to us and we to them.

I was discovering that we were second-class citizens, some sort of family of beggars. At the same time, from that visit on, I became more and more aware that we were also snobs. I sensed the frosty distance that separated my parents' idea of themselves from "these ordinary American Christians." Unlike them, my parents were aware of culture, good art, and good music. Where these Christians sang hymns that sounded tragically like trashy music, my parents played Bach. We vacationed in Italy, whereas "most of these poor dear simple American Christians don't have your background and have not even *been* to Europe!"

We took a day trip to New York City and spent the day at the Guggenheim Museum, where—to the horror of the guards—I free-wheeled my wheelchair down the winding ramp. On another day, I was taken to Radio City and loved watching the production of sound effects for a radio drama.

It was an odd mix. We were beggars and yet looked down on the culture and the people who made our life possible. They pitied us, donated a place to stay and a free operation, and talked about how hard it must be to "leave home" and "go back to the mission field." And we pitied their narrow existence and compared the genteel sophistication of Switzerland favorably to these "simple American Christians." Sometimes Mom would say "They don't even have real tea rooms here!"

The overall feeling was that we were somehow displaced aristocrats, former royalty reduced to being dependent on less-cultured strangers, grateful yet resentful, sorry for ourselves for the sacrifices we were making for a higher cause, yet envious of those people who could lead normal lives and who owned things, got to eat Grape-Nuts every day, watched TV, and made money from everyday jobs where you were paid instead of waiting for a series of miracles.

We were proud that we were different from other people yet craved acceptance. And we craved this not just for ourselves, but for the Lord that we were living our lives for. Because when people accepted and helped us, when they admitted that we were living lives full of meaning and spiritual purpose that they, too, craved, when they complimented Mom on her clothes and said they didn't know any other Christians who were so stylish, or so smart, or so kind, then we had done our job and had witnessed well for our Lord. But there was also an unintended message that I picked up, which has shaped my life: we were outsiders doing everything we could to be mistaken for insiders, so that we could be accepted by the insiders and then convert them to being outsiders, like us, until *everyone* became an outsider and therefore we got to be insiders forever!

We wanted nothing so much as the respect of the people who found our ideas backward and foolish. In a fantasy world of perfect outcomes, you would write a "Christian book" but have the *New York Times* declare it great literature, so great that the reviewer would say he was converting. And in the Style section, they would say that Edith Schaeffer was the best-dressed woman in the world, so well dressed that this proved that not all fundamentalists were dowdy and that "we have all been wrong about you Christians." And if those reporters visited L'Abri, they would say they had never been served so lovely a high tea, and that they had never heard such clever answers to their questions, and that because of the sandwiches, the real silver teaspoons, the beautifully cut skirt and jacket Mom was wearing, the kindness of the Schaeffer children, the fact Dad knew who Jackson Pollock was, meant that the Very Wealthy and Very Important people all over the world would not only come to Christ, but would, at last, admit that at least *some* Real Christians (in other words, us) were even smarter and better-dressed than worldly people, and that you can believe Jesus rose from the dead, not drink or smoke or dance, and yet be *even happier,* even *more cultured,* better in every way!

What I never heard Mom or Dad explain was that if the world was so bad and lost, why did they spend so much time trying to imitate it and impress the lost? But the single stitch held. And when the fishhook dropped out of the cast as he cut it off, Dr. Ferguson only laughed. God is good.

8

L'Abri swept up many unique and interesting people. Some stayed for a day or two, others for the better part of a lifetime. Jane Stuart Smith stayed for most of her life. *And* she was a great destination! When you cut across the main road, you were looking right down on Chalet Le Chesalet's lichen-splotched tile roof. There was a stone retaining wall right behind the chalet that I would climb down sometimes rather than walking by the path. There were lizards living in moss-filled cracks. If you caught one, the tail came off in your hand.

Jane had been an opera singer until she accepted Jesus, stopped singing worldly music, and stayed on to be a worker at L'Abri. She still practiced every day and sometimes, when I was on the way to her house, I heard her singing scales up and down and up and down to higher and higher notes and then sliding all the way to the bottom notes and starting over.

Jane's father was rich and president of a railroad. Jane grew up in Roanoke. Mom said her father had once rented Carnegie Hall for Jane to sing in so she could have a New York debut.

L'Abri owned all the houses used in the work. Jane and her roommate, Betty, had their own place. And because Jane received money from her family, she heated their house with oil that worked better than our coal furnace. So Chalet Le Chesalet was lovely and warm in the winter. And Jane ate lots of meat, chicken, and sometimes even roasts, and not just on Sundays. In our house, a wing was a big piece of chicken. Mom carved two or three little chickens up for thirty people, bulking out the meals with bread and margarine, rice and gravy, and, in the summer, mounds of vegetables from our garden. Sometimes I'd see a leftover chicken at Jane's that she had shared with Betty, a whole chicken between just two people!

Jane drank wine with her meals. She wasn't bothered by our taboos. At Jane and Betty's house none of my family's many rules seemed to apply. Jane was a L'Abri worker, but she seemed to have diplomatic immunity.

Jane never had guests stay with her but limited her ministry to serving meals twice a week to the guests and giving a monthly lecture on whatever was interesting her just then, from medieval art history to J. S. Bach's theology. Sometimes other workers would complain that she didn't share the workload of having students in her house, but of course no one ever dared to bring this up to her.

I would get a huge welcome from both Jane and Betty. Betty was a writer who had once written a column for a newspaper in Illinois and gave up writing for a worldly paper. Post salvation, she only wrote Christian articles for evangelical magazines and, in later years, several inspirational books.

Betty was diminutive, pale, and quiet and had very tidy hair; Jane was huge and flamboyant. Betty hovered at the edges of rooms; Jane filled rooms. Betty was incredibly kind and sympathetic and used to invite everyone to her birthday and give us all presents. And any time I had a problem, Betty would be the person to go and tell it to. She would make empathetic little growling and clucking noises interspersed with many an "Oh, dear, aw, what a shame. . . ."

Together, Jane and Betty were as much a couple as any of the married workers in L'Abri. After meeting each other at L'Abri, when they were in their late twenties, they lived together for the rest of their lives. Betty once told me that the reason she stayed single was because she suffered from epilepsy and was worried that she might either pass it on to her children or not be a fit mother. Today it would be assumed that they were a lesbian couple, with Jane clearly the "husband" and sweet, retiring Betty the "wife." But I don't think they were lovers, just lifelong companions, and the notion that they could have been mistaken for anything but "godly single Christian ladies" living chaste lives would, I think, have shocked Betty and infuriated Jane.

When Jane would say something unusually outrageous, even for her—say, loudly offering the opinion that anyone who disagreed with her talk on the symbolic meaning found in the art of the Hebrews' tabernacle and Solomon's temple, thereby proved they were not Christians because "Only idiots would disagree with me, and I don't care if they *are* L'Abri workers, and *you know who I mean!*"—Betty would offer a quiet "Jane, you don't mean that." And Jane would yell "Yes, I do!" and flush a deep scarlet but then begin to calm down.

Jane and Betty owned a mid-1950s Mercedes that they drove to Italy several times a year. The car loomed large: It was the only car in the L'Abri community. And between the fact that Jane had a *car* and wore a lot of diamond-crusted jewelry, inherited from her Southern-belle grandmother, not to mention got to eat lots of *meat,* I grew up sure that Jane was almost a royal personage.

"Are those real diamonds?" I'd ask while playing with her big glittering ring.

"Yes, honey, they are!"

"Why, you rich, rich person!" I'd say.

Jane would always laugh uproariously at this little ritual and hug me until I felt as if the breath of life was about to be crushed out of me.

Betty drove the car, and Jane's job was to read out loud to her all the way to Italy and back. When they returned, they would sit me down and tell me about the art they had seen, food eaten, and books read, and would show me the art books they had bought. The way they talked about Italy was as if they had been to heaven.

I didn't need convincing that Italy was the place any sane or lucky person would be if they had a choice. My favorite time of the year was the Schaeffer family holiday we took in Portofino.

A stranger observing my visits to Jane and Betty would have thought I was a long-lost family member returned from war instead of the little boy who lived across the street dropping by for the second or third time that week. Jane told me that her flamboyant manner, her loud—"It's Frankie! Come in! Come in!" greeting—was "Southern hospitality," that she wasn't "cold like you Yankees."

Jane would beam a huge ice-melting smile at me and bellow "MY, HOW WONDERFUL TO SEE YOU!" Her smile would linger and always seemed amplified by very red glossy lipstick.

Mom wore lipstick, too, but she would dab it off with a tissue right after applying it so it was never glossy or red, just pale pinkish, a modest hint of beauty, never an open invitation to stare at her mouth. But with Jane, everything was vivid. She welcomed me with her big greeting while somewhere in the background Betty hovered, making little humming welcoming noises and murmuring, “Now, Jane, invite him in. I’ll bet you’d like something to eat. How nice you came to see us.”

“I have something to show you!” Jane bellowed one morning as soon as I walked in.

“Oh?”

“Come upstairs and look!”

“Now, Jane, do you really think he wants to see that silly thing?” murmured Betty.

“ ‘Silly thing?’ It is NOT silly! Of *course* he wants to see it! Don’t you?” I nodded and followed Jane up the creaking stairs to the chalet’s narrow upstairs hall. Sitting at the end of the hall in Jane’s tiny office was a strange contraption that looked like the scales in a doctor’s office, only it had a thick leather strap hanging in a loop where on a scale the balance bar would be that the nurse moves the marker back and forth on till it tips the scale and shows your weight.

“It’s my new exercise machine! Isn’t it marvelous?” bellowed Jane; then she threw her head back and screamed with laughter.

“How does it work?”

“Look!”

Jane stepped up on the little platform, unhooked the strap, and looped it around the tight black skirt that was clinging to her tree-trunk thighs. The strap slipped neatly under the cheeks of her bottom. She then flipped a switch and the machine began to buzz like a giant mixer and the floor shook under my feet. The strap vibrated violently, and Jane’s bottom and hips began to quiver like a big bowl of Jell-O placed on a jackhammer.

"It is going to reduce the size of my terribly fat *huge* bottom!" Jane yelled delightedly. "Come and try it!"

Jane led me to the contraption, strapped me in, and flipped the switch. My vision blurred, my teeth rattled, and my bottom instantly went numb.

"It just shakes the fat right out of you!" Jane yelled. "I'm supposed to stand here one half hour a day, and if I do, I won't need to wear a girdle any more and still be able to fit into my skirts! Have you ever worn a girdle?"

"N-n-n-n-o!" I said, as I tried to find the switch to turn off the wildly jiggling belt.

"Well, you are *so* fortunate! A girdle is like being wrapped in concrete! And you should see how many layers I have to peel off to even *think* of going to the bathroom! But when your thighs are like *huge* Virginia hams, what choice do you have? Without a girdle, I just *bulge!*"

"Jane, I think that's quite enough," murmured Betty.

"Oh, all right!" snapped Jane, and she flounced back downstairs after giving Betty an angry you-spoil-all-the-fun glare.

After the machine was installed, sometimes when I visited and Betty would come to the door, the whole little chalet would be vibrating and humming as if we were on a ship standing just above the engine room. Jane was upstairs on her machine. Betty would hand me a cookie, smile, and roll her eyes upward in a silent comment about what she thought of "Jane's contraption," while we waited for Jane's exercise to end and the socializing to begin.

Jane was my introduction to American History. She said that the North was the aggressor in the Civil War and that her family had fought for the "dear old Confederacy." I didn't know anything about the Civil War or America, but I could tell that whatever this was about upset Jane. She took "The War of Northern Aggression" so personally and made her vivid declarations about it so passionately that I assumed that this war had been fought when she was a little girl.

Jane would string a whole series of declarative statements together about many subjects. The South, opera, "colored people," all got mixed into the short sermons she would preach to me. Jane was loyal to the South and to opera and said her family's "colored people" had been happy and well cared for way back when "my family owned slaves," before "everything was stolen and burnt down by those damned Yankees!"

Jane gave me a Confederate flag and a replica muzzle-loading flintlock pistol and talked about the magnolias in her front yard "back home" with tears streaming down her cheeks. And Jane told me about her "mammy," the "dear, dear colored lady who raised me." She said that her mammy was a saint, the best person in the world, and that she was in heaven now. And to hear Jane tell it, her father, Robert Hall Smith, was the greatest and probably the most important man who ever lived, and his presidency of the Norfolk and Western Railway was the major event of Southern history. He was at his office at eight each day, seven days a week. No matter how much he traveled, he always came home to go to church. When a lady who lived along the tracks wrote to Robert Hall Smith that the train whistle was waking her grandchild, Robert Hall Smith made sure that it was never sounded again near that woman's home. And at the annual Railroad Night dinner in 1958, the president of the Pennsylvania Railroad said that "The Norfolk and Western is one of the best-managed railroads anywhere." As I understood it, these were the main points of American history, and I've never forgotten them.

Almost every time I visited, Jane played me parts of Bellini's opera *Norma*. She showed me black-and-white photographs of herself in costume holding a spear, as well as many other glossy black-and-white photos of herself in other roles.

"Why don't you sing any more?" I asked.

"I sing in church every Sunday!"

"You know what I mean."

"I gave it up for the Lord! The world of opera is a wicked place! You have NO IDEA about the TEMPTATIONS I faced!"

"Was it terrible?"

"NO! It was marvelous! THAT was the problem! I LOVED those temptations!"

Then Jane would launch into descriptions of her opera adventures, about how a tenor's beard was coming unglued in a performance in the Palermo opera house, and how she saved the day by slapping him during their duet so the beard stuck back on. And she told me all about how Maria Callas was evil, how she would bend other singer's hands when they all went out to take a bow and held hands in front of the curtain, so only Callas could raise her head and smile at the audience. Jane told me how in Venice she was taken from her hotel to the Venice opera in a gondola, while in full costume for the role of Tosca. And she had pictures to prove it.

I spent hours trying to imagine what those temptations had been that had made her leave such a wonderful life. Once I drummed up the courage to ask, and Jane snapped, "Never you mind, honey, never you mind!" and glared at me. Another time, I said, "Will you please sing some opera for me?" Jane answered, "No, honey, I won't. My voice is too big for this little chalet living room! Why, if I was to sing in here so close to you, it would probably kill you!"

When the Chalet Les Mélèzes living room got too small to hold our church services in, or rather when L'Abri grew too big, and we built a chapel, Jane gave the money for the construction from the sale of her costumes. She also had a Flentrop organ built for us in Holland, a "genuine baroque instrument" so that when Bach was played, it was on the "right kind of organ." And of course Jane had a bronze plaque screwed to the side of the organ dedicating it to the memory of her father.

Jane gave me apple juice and cookies and hot chocolate and all the other "Southern hospitality" that made me see that what she said was true: Southern hospitality *was* best. And I came to believe that she was right: it really was "a tragic shame" that the North won the Civil War. I agreed that Jane's colored people must have been happy, seeing as how she was so welcoming and seeing how if her slave-owning ancestors had shown their "dear negroes" this kind of hospitality, it must have been really nice for them.

Jane would conclude every history lesson with "So don't you go believing all those lies those Northerners tell!"

"I won't, Jane."

"Now we're coming to the Casta Diva, the greatest aria Bellini ever wrote. And in this recording, Joan Sutherland is singing the role. Maria Callas was more famous, but Joan's voice is far, far better! So don't ever believe anyone who says Maria Callas could sing!"

"I won't, Jane."

"Hush! Just listen!"

"Yes."

"Isn't that *marvelous?*"

"Yes."

"She will die in the flames! She will go to the pyre and DIE!"

"Yes, Jane."

"Would you like some more hot chocolate?"

"Yes, please."

"So you go on back up there to all those Yankees in Chalet Les Mélèzes and tell them you have seen REAL Southern hospitality!"

"I will."

Jane had chickens, too. I killed my first chicken at Jane's. And later, in imitation of Jane, my mother got chickens, too. But Jane had them first and would say how good the eggs were compared to anything we ever got from the store. Many of them were double-yolked. I knew because Jane fixed me fried eggs and bacon and sometimes let me take eggs home. But one chicken got sick and Jane decided I should cut off its head.

"In the South, real men hunt! My brother is a great squirrel hunter. You *must* kill something! He began to hunt when he was seven, and you're ten!"

"Oh?"

"When we all get to Heaven the lion will lie down with the lamb. But right now, regretful as it is, killing is part of life! I'm GLAD for the Fall! I couldn't live without meat! Have you ever tasted roasted squirrel?"

"No."

"It's *marvelous!*"

Betty held the feet and Jane counted to three. And with my heart pounding, I swung the hatchet and did the deed and the chicken really did run around with its head cut off.

"Now you are a Southern gentleman!" Jane declared, as the chicken bled out at our feet. "A lady asked for assistance, and you gave it!"

"My pleasure," I said, hoping that my response was sufficiently gallant and that my voice didn't sound too shaky.

"I am going to give you a marvelous book as a reward." Jane marched up to the chalet, and I followed her to Jane and Betty's book-lined bedroom, where Jane took a little hardcover copy of *Black Beauty* off a shelf.

"This was one of my favorite books when I was your age."

"Thank you."

"In another year or two, I will give you an even better book!"

"What will that be?"

"Never you mind, honey, but it's called *The Decameron,* and it is filled with stories *some people* don't approve of, but they're wonderful! They are *art!* They are about Italy, and Italy is the best place on earth! A very great man wrote them! He was a fine Christian! All Italian artists are fine Christians!"

"But they're all Roman Catholics, aren't they?"

"Oh, dear, you just don't understand! That is just what they have to say they are, but underneath they are all *real Christians!"*

"Oh."

"Do you think Bellini could have written something as wonderful as the Casta Diva without the love of Jesus in his heart?"

"I guess not."

"Well, don't you ever believe anything different, honey! Italians are *all Christians!"*

"Oh?"

My mind would reel delightedly at Jane's heresies. And sometimes I wondered how she was allowed to say things that were just not right at all, things that were the opposite of what my parents and the other workers said. But Jane wasn't like anybody else. And when Mom talked about Jane, even she made excuses for her.

"Jane has some confused ideas, dear, but she is a wonderful person," Mom would say. Jane's personality seemed to overwhelm any criticism. There was nothing right or wrong about Jane; she just was Jane, a force beyond all the normal categories.

Jane may have "left the world" to serve the Lord, but thankfully she brought a lot of the world with her. With her love of art, music, and literature, not to mention her eccentricities and flamboyance, visiting Jane was something like taking a bath in a carwash, *sans* car. I would tumble out of her chalet, my ears ringing with opera, full of expensive food, dazzled by Rubens and Dali or an illuminated Book of Hours, or Lorenzetti's frescoes in Siena. And my mind resounding with Jane's anti-Yankee propaganda.

Jane's way of rationalizing who was saved and who was lost was very personal. If you knew about art and loved it, or loved music or the South, everything was forgiven. If someone painted "wonderful pictures" or composed "wonderful music," they suddenly had become "Real Christians," no matter what they said they were. In their hearts, Jane knew that they knew the Lord. It was a lovely and circular argument. Jane would have made a great goddess, terrible in her wrath and forgiving of all sinners, as long as they created something beautiful.

I wrote to Jane recently. She is very old and back in Virginia, caring for Betty, who has Alzheimer's. I wrote to tell Jane what she and Betty meant to me. I thanked her for being one of the people who shaped my life and made it so much richer than it would have been. Jane wrote me a lovely letter back, and she enclosed a fistful of yellowing clippings. They were of articles I'd written over the years and reviews of my novels. Jane had been watching over me even though we hadn't been in touch for more than twenty-five years. She said she was proud of me. It meant a lot.

9

Chalet Les Mélèzes—big as chalets go—was originally built to comfortably house a family of eight, maybe with a spinster aunt or two thrown in, or a maid and cook tucked away in one of the smaller back rooms. It was not like the older small squat peasants' chalets clustered in our village.

Our chalet had been built by some upper-class Swiss in the 1920s, probably as a big summer home. Chalet Les Mélèzes sat about a quarter mile from the village center, out in steep open fields with just a couple of other houses nearby. It had a "Venus II" woodstove on every floor, as well as a big old coal furnace that almost warmed our ineffectual radiators. Sweeping balconies wrapped around each floor, and every room facing the mountains had large multipaned windows and/or a glass door that opened onto the balconies. And every window and door had thick wooden shutters that we closed at night during the winter, to provide a little insulation from the cold.

When the shutters were closed, my room was completely dark except for one small shaft of light that, once the sun was up, would pour through the tulip-shaped cutout that decorated the shutters. Everything was beautifully made and fit snugly, with all the doors and windows exquisitely crafted. The tulip pattern was repeated on the pine boards that provided a solid railing for the balconies.

When I opened my curtains, if the sun was shining at a certain angle, a brilliant beam of light shot through the cutout tulip and across my bedroom, picking out glittering dust particles. If I smacked my pillow a couple of times, I stirred up a dazzling explosion of dust and it seemed as if a whole universe had suddenly sprung to life, complete with galaxies, suns, and worlds swirling and twinkling in the light that cut through the thick dark.

I'd wedge myself between my bed and the wood-paneled wall—my bedroom was very small, only about five feet by ten—on the narrow patch of faded blue linoleum. I stared up at the mote-filled light. Maybe, I thought, our Planet Earth is nothing more than a dust mote floating in some huge bedroom.

What if on one of my dust planets there was a boy lying on his back watching dust glitter in *his* sunbeam? What if his mother was downstairs preparing to lead the Monday Morning Bible Study and telling her young people—assuming other universes had lost people, too—that God was watching over them and had a wonderful plan for their lives?

By the time I was seven or eight, on any given weekend there were about fifteen guests packed into our house. By the time I was eleven or twelve, L'Abri had "grown so wonderfully" that there were twenty or more guests staying with us all week. In summer, there were even more, with the overflow sleeping on the balconies that ran around the second and third floors, protected by the wide eaves.

If I got up in the night to go to the kitchen downstairs to grab a snack, I'd be stepping over young men and women spread out in sleeping bags all over the middle-floor hall, filling our chalet with the intimate musty flesh-smell of warm breath and bodies that mingled with the faint scent of pine.

Pine paneling covered the thick solid squared timbers from which the chalet had been constructed according to the old custom, wherein the wood walls were solid, much like a log cabin, only the beams were squared into magnificent six-inch-thick perfectly interlocking timbers. In the winter, I could hear our chalet "breathe" when it changed temperature outside and those timbers creaked. In the summer, I could smell the pine.

Many years later, when I moved to America and tried to hang up my paintings, I was stunned to learn that I could not just nail anywhere. The idea that I had to find where the stud was under the sheetrock was like being told I was living in a cardboard box, a fake building, a swindle. "What would the Swiss think of this?" I'd mutter, as a nail disappeared into a wall with a hollow thud.

By the time I was fifteen, there were eighty to a hundred guests with us year-round, though no longer just in our chalet. Over the years, other chalets were added through a series of "miracles," each one part of the growing list of proofs of God's hand on us, each with its own inexplicable list of attending coincidences as to how the money came in so amazingly that "even a New York atheist couldn't explain this away," as Mom would say.

All the L'Abri chalets had married couples running them. About half the time, those houseparents were my sisters and brothers-in-law. When my sisters married, they roped their husbands into serving the Lord, or rather "God put His hand on them." By the time I was on the cusp of my teen years, my three sisters were all back and living in chalets near ours, receiving L'Abri guests in their homes and raising their children as we had been raised: child missionaries press-ganged into the Lord's work.

Priscilla met her future husband John Sandri at the University of Lausanne, and more or less started L'Abri by witnessing to him. John was one of our first guests. My sister invited him home for a weekend to ask Dad all those questions about God that she couldn't answer. Maybe John was also interested in spending the weekend with us, then another and another, due to the fact that Priscilla looked like a fortunate blend of Grace Kelly and Jackie Kennedy.

John was a tall, handsome, olive-skinned Swiss-American and had been a basketball star in high school in Scarsdale, New York. After he moved back to Switzerland—his Swiss-American industrialist father brought the family home when John was eighteen—John played for the Swiss national basketball team. John always treated me like a favorite little brother, and I would eagerly wait all week for his weekend visits. By the time he married Priscilla, John had graduated from the University of Lausanne. Then he was offered a job in the Swiss-American company his father ran. He followed the Lord's call instead, gave up his worldly ambitions, and went to seminary.

My sister Susan—home from Oxford, where she was studying occupational therapy at Dorset House—met her future husband Ranald Macaulay when he visited L'Abri after hearing Dad speak. This was while Ranald was a law student at Cambridge. Ranald was a tall, athletic, piano- and rugby-playing South African-Scot, with bright red hair and a scar on his face where a wild dog had bitten and almost killed him as a child. Ranald's father was a QC in South Africa, and then later a judge in Rhodesia.

My mother was thrilled by "Cambridge converts" like Ranald. How could what we believed be ignored or called stupid when people from "the top universities" were coming to Christ though us?

Debby met Udo Middelmann at L'Abri when he came as a guest for a weekend, then came back several times. Udo, also tall, handsome, and extremely bright and accomplished, was the son of a German diplomat. He was a law student in Germany when he first visited. By the time of his later trips to L'Abri, he had graduated. He met Ranald, and Ranald "led Udo to Christ."

All three brothers-in-law got their theology degrees. And all three thereby went against the wishes of their families. John and Udo graduated from Covenant Seminary in St. Louis. Ranald went back to Cambridge for his theological degree.

My future brothers-in-law had to become *our* kind of people before my sisters could marry them. My sisters were very good at training their husbands, just as Mom had trained Dad.

After my brothers-in-law had converted, the ultimate power struggle with unseen and far-away "non-Christian" in-law parents was won. My brothers-in-law chose us over their own flesh and blood, in the ultimate in-law rivalry victory. The Schaeffer clan's grandchildren would be raised "in The Work." They would be spending every Christmas with us. When they went to a family reunion, it was to the Schaeffer reunion. And at those times when my brothers-in-law would visit their families, we would pray for them that the "difficult time" would soon pass and that they would come home unscathed.

Everyone working at L'Abri was a disciple of my parents, including my brothers-in-law. Theoretically they could have been led to another Christian work—my parents grudgingly allowed that *some* "other Christians" did good work—but in practice we all knew that anyone *really* hearing the Lord's voice would never settle for a lesser calling than L'Abri.

Mom got to have her cake and eat it, too. Her daughters had married "truly cultured and refined men," and then they joined L'Abri and denied their worldly standing that had made Mom so pleased to fold them into our family. The more successful in the world you were *before* you got saved, the greater the triumph when you "turned from these worldly things to serve the Lord."

There was some awkwardness at my sisters' weddings that I remember noticing even as a child. Mom and Dad were in charge, so no alcohol was served. I could see our new in-laws visibly withering under the strain of being in close proximity to the Schaeffer family without any benefit of the fortification provided by what must have been a dire need for several stiff drinks.

Dad presided at the weddings, except for Priscilla and John Sandri's. Another famous evangelical, Dr. Martin Lloyd Jones, preached at their wedding. This meant that Dad, and/or Dr. Jones, had the opportunity to "clearly preach the gospel." In other words, the parents of my brothers-in-law were treated to hour-long sermons about how, without a faith in Christ, a personal faith, a real faith, a faith like ours, no marriage could last. Of course there was no dancing.

The families my sisters married into were headed by bon-vivants. There was Ranald's dad, the South African judge, a whiskey-and-soda man. (Some years later, when this lovely man stopped by and visited us while we were on vacation in Italy, he surreptitiously poured me a glass of Chianti, my first taste of wine.) There was John's dad, the Swiss industrialist with his fondness for chamber music and first-class alcoholically well lubricated ocean travel. And there was Udo's cigar-smoking, schnapps-drinking German diplomat father, more at home in the halls of UN power politics and embassy parties than any church.

At the weddings, our new in-laws looked somewhat distracted as the full weight of just what their sons had married into sunk home while my mother prayed at them and Dad preached at them, literally. And they were surrounded by earnest pale "seekers" and theologians, all of whom were exuding an unctuous concern for the wedding guests' souls. It must have been a tough day.

10

The mountains were beautiful, the conversation all about everlasting life. Our guests' parents or wives or husbands, sisters and brothers, were far away, and we were right there with the new member of our eternal family, embracing them with an all-encompassing love that outshone anything they had ever encountered before. When someone who got saved was headed back to a "hostile situation," say to "secular parents who will not understand" or to a family of "nominal very social Christians, you know, Episcopalians," or to "a very anti-Christian secular Jewish mother, you know, dear, typical of New York," we would gather around the soon-to-depart convert and pray that the Lord would give them the strength to withstand the "very real persecution" they would be facing. We could not have been more fervent if we had been sending them off to the lions. There were many exchanges like this:

"She will have to face her difficult mother," Mom said, shaking her head sadly.

"Her mom isn't a Christian?" I asked.

"Oh, no, darling, far from it! Joan comes from a VERY secular background. Her father is a top lawyer, a top Harvard man. And Joan went to Wellesley."

"But is she going to be able to stand for truth at home?" asked Debby.

"We'll just have to pray she does," said Mom.

"I'll bet she'll face all sorts of temptations," Susan said with grim relish.

"They are VERY worldly, aren't they, Mom?" said Debby.

"My dear, they are top Harvard New England sorts. And they have real money, old money, very New England."

"If they all got saved, then they could really do something for the Lord, couldn't they?" asked Susan.

"Yes, dear, but you know it is almost impossible for Episcopalians to trust Christ as their Savior. They think they're already saved."

"But how can they be?" asked Susan. "They drink and smoke, don't they?"

"Yes, dear. They also have a very Roman Catholic view of communion."

"And Joan said that they even allowed her to go to dances!" said Susan.

"Well, we need to pray very hard that she is not lured back. And then there is the boyfriend," said Mom with a significant grimace.

Debby and Susan moaned. A non-Christian boyfriend or unbelieving girlfriend was the worst lure to backsliding.

"Well," said Susan with a shudder, "we can only hope she breaks it off right away."

"And we can pray that the Lord leads her to a boy who *is* saved!" said Debby.

In Joan's case, I hoped the Lord would do no such thing. I had a big crush on her. She had been taking me swimming down at Lake Geneva several times a week during the summer.

I was always in love. I can't remember a time I didn't have my eye on one or more L'Abri women. In early childhood, it was about generating more of that warm feeling I got in their presence. By the time I was eight or nine, it was about marrying them. By the time I was thirteen, it was about wanting to have sex with all the women in the world. And by fifteen, it was a matter of finding a place in the woods in summer, or attic in winter, where I could fumble to get the clothes off my nineteen-or-twenty-year-old "date."

Long before I got anyone's clothes off, but well into my crush-of-the-moment phase, sometimes Mom would help out by giving one of the young women the job of taking care of me, tutoring me, taking me to swim, going for a walk with me. Some of this related to therapy for my polio leg, or to being homeschooled, or to just keeping an eye on me. I made sure that if I liked the girl she had an easy time. If I didn't, she was soon begging my mother to be allowed to do other work.

In Joan's case, I liked her a lot. And she looked fine in that late-fifties one-piece bathing suit! It was navy blue with tiny white polka dots and had a little skirt fitting tightly around her slim hips. Joan would change on the pebble beach at Villeneuve, modestly managing to shed her swimsuit from under a towel. It would fall wet and mysterious to the pebbles and leave a mark when she picked it up.

Joan had tanned, freckled breasts, and her cleavage was plumped up above the rigid corsetlike support. She had been a competitive swimmer in her women's college and walked smoothly like the athlete she was. She was sweet, breezy, and easy to get on with. I was absolutely besotted by her, and very put out when a British friend of my brother-in-law-to-be, Ranald, showed up and soon was engaged to "my" Joan.

They were an "ideal L'Abri couple," Dad said. They were both saved at L'Abri, and she had gone to Wellesley! And he had gone to Cambridge! "Top people!" Mom declared, "top people serving the Lord!"

They became L'Abri workers, and Joan's husband later went on to teach at a famous evangelical seminary and was a fearsome one-man bastion of the most severe brand of Reformed theology, a firebrand anti-Catholic and antiliberal defender of truth. And when I left the evangelical world and wrote about my departure obliquely in *Portofino* (my first novel) though I had not heard from him for years, he wrote me several furious and personal letters denouncing my "apostasy."

Mom would often talk about the fact that people like Joan and her husband, not to mention my brothers-in-law, were so accomplished, such "top people." They had gone to "top universities"; they each could "be anything"; but they had "given it all up to serve the Lord." And this affirmed Mom's ambition for her daughters, both socially and spiritually. But for all my mother's addiction to winning "top people" for the Lord, she could also be found every day in the kitchen cooking up huge meals for the guests.

Mom was often on her hands and knees scrubbing the floors, rising at four in the morning to pray and then to type up the dictation she'd taken from Dad as his secretary the day before, or spending hours talking to and counseling the guests and students. She always paid as much personal attention to whomever she was with, from a hotel chambermaid to some new guest, as to the President of the United States, when, in later years, she became an evangelical "star" and was a guest in the White House.

My parents' compassion was sincere and consistent. And

they never allowed belief to make them into bigots. I grew up in a community where homosexuals (the term "gay" was not in use) were not only welcomed but where my parents didn't do anything to make them feel uncomfortable and regarded their "problem" as no more serious (or sinful) than other problems, from spiritual pride—a "much more serious matter," according to Dad—to gluttony. And I never heard any of the nonsense so typical of American evangelicals today about homosexuality being a "chosen lifestyle."

My parents weren't given to calling their friends liars. So when our friends who were homosexual—Mom was always open, as was Dad, about which students were or weren't gay—told my parents that they had been born that way, not only did they believe them, but Dad defended them against people who would judge or exclude them.

Dad thought it cruel and stupid to believe that a homosexual could change by "accepting Christ"—or, for that matter, that an alcoholic could be healed by the same magic. Dad often said "Salvation is not magic. We're still in the fallen world."

Dad always counseled gay men and women against getting married to a heterosexual if they were doing it in the expectation that it would change them, let alone to impress their parents. This was in the late 1950s and early 1960s, when few people in secular circles, let alone evangelical circles, would even admit that there *were* gay people.

There were guests of all races at L'Abri. We had a steady stream of African students and African-Americans, Asians, Chinese, Japanese; representatives of every nation. My parents spoke hotly against racism and practiced an all-encompassing love for every human being.

Dad went out of his way to tell his children that if we ever wanted to marry a black person, he would support us. He didn't say that in response to a specific question but spelled it out as a matter of principle; again, this was in the late 1950s and early 1960s.

The best friend I ever made who was a L'Abri student was Mus Arshad, a Malaysian who came to L'Abri, converted from Islam to Christianity, and was therefore completely cut off from his family. (His family let him know that—in accordance with Islamic law—if he ever came home, they would have to kill him.) Mus was like a big brother to me. (Many years later Mus worked as a cameraman and photographer on several of the documentaries I made.)

Dad and Mom were tough on intellectual ideas they disagreed with, but not on people. Ideas interested Dad, not theology per se. If he was lecturing on art, music, cultural trends, he stuck to the subject. He hated circular arguments that depended on the Bible when used against secular people who didn't acknowledge biblical authority. He believed that you should argue on a level playing field, where both people stay on common ground.

"What's the point of quoting the Bible to people who don't believe it's true?" Dad would say.

In later years, when he started to argue for the pro-life cause, Dad always disagreed with the Bible-thumping approach that quoted verses (usually out of context) about the sacredness of life. He believed that you argued on the merits of ideas that both sides could agree on—for instance, on what the genetic potential of a fetus was, or what direction we all can agree that we want society to go in.

Above all, Dad's sensitivity was disarming. Bishop Pike, the famous self-proclaimed liberal minister and writer, told me that my father was one of the most compassionate men he ever debated. And after Timothy Leary had several long discussions with Dad, he said, "If I thought your father is typical of other Christians, I'd reconsider my position."

There were many sincere conversions at L'Abri that had a life-changing effect. There were drug addicts who got off drugs. There was a prostitute who converted, married, and settled down, and sent back baby pictures. There were African students who converted during their holidays from various European universities, and went back to Africa; and the last I heard, a few were ministers and even bishops in several growing denominations. And there were intellectuals who converted, and remained in the academic community and became leaders in their fields.

When I was about fifteen, I asked Dad how come he was so good at turning people's lives around, particularly in his one-on-one sessions of counseling. Dad answered very matter-of-factly, "It isn't what you say to someone that matters, as much as the fact you are listening. Knowing how to listen to people is what helps them."

During a discussion that left, say, some clever Yale philosophy major breathless, or a young English artist wondering how it was that this preacher knew more about the surrealists than he did, Dad's sparring partner of the moment would be stunned by my father's kindness. Guests often left L'Abri loving Dad even while disagreeing with him. But I also know quite a few people, for instance an old friend of mine, a Harvard comparative literature graduate and master furniture maker who converted and then, later in life, began to wonder if he had been brainwashed.

I have sometimes wondered, when my parents "converted" people, if those people really accepted Christ, or if they had just fallen under the spell of my energetic and attractive parents.

There were many converts who "fell away" after they got out of my mother and father's powerful orbit. For many, the Christian world they went back to never measured up. They had a hard time finding churches they liked. It left many wondering if L'Abri was the only place where "true Christianity" was being put into practice. If so, what did that say about the claims that Christianity was universal truth?

My parents perpetuated this problem with often-repeated (not so subtle) hints that when you left L'Abri, there would be few other places as close to ideal in both theology and daily Christian practice. My parents were always talking about this or that student who wrote back saying they couldn't find a "good church." Dad warned converts: "Look for a good church. But I'm afraid you'll have a hard time finding one. There aren't many."

11

My parents took three weeks of vacation each year. In the summer, we spent two weeks in Portofino, Italy, at that time an inexpensive place to go on holiday. In the winter, we went to Zermatt to ski for a week. We went to the same places year after year and got the "off-season" rates.

We stayed in the Pensione Biea in Paraggi every year till I was twelve, then switched to the Hotel Nazionale in Portofino. The Hotel Nazionale was on the main square of Portofino, overlooking the horseshoe-shaped harbor and side-by-side pastel buildings accented by green louvered shutters that lined one side of the bay. The buildings provided a stage-set-like backdrop for the yachts, the fishing boats, and the jet-setters.

The Pensione Biea was on the beach at Paraggi. Paraggi and Portofino were a twenty-minute walk apart in adjoining bays, separated by a spit of rocky coast. We took a walk between Portofino and Paraggi every day to and from the beach, when we were staying in Portofino; and to and from our evening ritual stroll around the piazza in Portofino, when we stayed in Paraggi.

We walked up a narrow path paved with Roman brick some of the way, tile in places and cut from the bedrock the rest of the way, over the hill that separated the coves. The hillside was covered with a mix of Scotch pine; live oaks; and, above those (and out of sight), olive groves. Below the path, the almost-vertical hill fell precariously to the one-lane main road. Below that was the glittering sea.

As we walked along, we got tantalizing glimpses of the turquoise water. The air was filled with the scent of basil, arugula, and wild thyme, as well as the perfume of gardenias wafting over the walls of several fabulous old villas. These I-wonder-WHO-lives-*there?!* villas were surrounded by shady gardens replete with huge terra-cotta amphorae and fountains.

The Paraggi Bay (where the beach was that we sat on all day) was framed by high hills. The air was filled with the smell of the pines, gnarled and misshapen, looking like giant bonsai trees that hung at odd angles over the water. There were black powdery pine nuts strewn in the alley behind the changing cabins, which I smashed between rocks to get at the sweet tangy white flesh. The smell of cooking wafted out of the pensione kitchen and got progressively more delicious all day.

We breakfasted on rolls, apricot jam, and hot chocolate and dined on fabulous pork and veal roasts, fresh green salads, huge vine-ripened tomatoes striped with green and yellow and still warm from the sun, grilled fish rubbed with minced sage, big creamy slices of cheese, and grated Parmesan on pastas and risotto. But no wine for us!

We had church on Sundays up in Mom and Dad's room and had to sing hymns. Mom said grace at our meals, which made everyone else on the terrace stare at us, a daily and mortifying event. When I was twelve or so, I drummed up the courage to press Mom on this point.

"Mom, *why* do you have to pray out loud?" I asked, after supper one night while we were taking our stroll around the main square in Portofino.

"Why would I change what we do just because we're on vacation?"

"But everyone always looks at us!"

"And I hope it reminds them that they should be thinking about eternal things."

"Can't we just eat?"

Dad was walking next to Mom and had said nothing. He surprised me when he spoke up a few moments later.

"Edith, you know you *could* pray a shorter prayer. I don't like watching my soup get cold every night."

Mom gave me a oh-how-could-you? look. Then she shook her head sadly at our worldliness and said nothing more. After that, I noticed her prayers were a bit shorter for a few days; but soon she was back to saying a long nightly grace.

Most of the time in Italy, I was free of being born-again. The vacation was a time when I was as "normal" as I ever got. I was free of my polio leg, too. Italy was the one place where I never had to wear my embarrassing and uncomfortable brace. I was barefoot most of the day and spent two thirds of each day in the water. And the only time I really had to think, rather than just BE, was because of the deliciously agonizing daily choice of what to spend my fifty-lire-per-day vacation allowance on—one slice of pizza, an ice cream, or a lemon soda?

Italy was where I first got to hear "jazzy music," actual jazz and even rock and roll! The one catch was that in the early years, before she relaxed, I had to be careful not to let my mother see me hanging around the jukebox by the snack bar; I had to pretend that I was just watching the snack-bar lady making pizza. The key was to not tap your foot to the "demonic rhythm."

Dad didn't become a famous and Evangelical leader (awash

in book-royalty money) till I was in my late teens. So during my childhood, I was haunted by the big question: Is there enough money in the vacation box this year? There always was, although some years there was no money for the extra treats like ice cream.

Even when giving was down, Mom somehow saved the money for the train tickets and the cost of the pensione and/or hotel. (Of course, the great exchange rate between dollars, Swiss francs, and lire helped.)

Italy was where I got to know Lino, an almost-famous surrealist painter. He was probably in his late thirties when I first met him. Lino was slender, olive-skinned, quiet, and polite. He was also very "typically Italian-looking," according to Mom. He dressed impeccably in a suit, even when he was painting

I would take Lino my paintings and drawings, which I was always working on while in Italy. He talked to me as a fellow artist, not as a child. I also got to know his debonair middle-aged homosexual lover and manager—a tall aristocratic man who dressed in gray wool slacks, pastel knit shirts, and loafers with no socks and a sweater draped over his shoulders, perpetually tan, and smelling faintly of exotic cologne—and several other artists who let me hang around their studios in Portofino.

I'd known Lino and his lover since I was six or seven—"forever"—and had always hung around Lino's studio watching him paint. It was my favorite after-the-beach-before-dinner place to visit.

Lino told me that his first big break as an artist was being commissioned to paint a large mural on the ill-fated SS "*Andrea Doria*," the famous Italia Line ship that sank off Nantucket. He once showed me a postcard of his mural, then shrugged, and said, "And now it is all at the bottom of the sea!"

Mom and Dad seemed to thrive in Italy, too. They would slip off in the evening for the walk from Portofino out to the lighthouse that sits at the tip of the peninsula protecting the harbor. The path was lit by small, beautifully concealed lights that cast a soft romantic glow over the flagstone path. Mom and Dad would leave me playing in the main square, or up in my room with Debby reading to me, and slip away. If I was up when they came back, I always noticed how happy they were. They would seem so relaxed and so in love. Mom's eyes were bright. Dad was smiling. They would always be arm in arm and head straight for their bedroom.

If two lines were forming—one headed to the L'Abri chapel, the other to Portofino—I always knew which line *I'd* be in! Portofino was paradise! You'd walk past a small gallery where there were Salvador Dali's for sale and sometimes Salvador Dali himself. I saw Rex Harrison, Jackie Kennedy, Princess Grace, mob bosses, and probably most of the ever-changing Italian government, and everyone else who drifted in on a yacht or came over from Santa Margarita in a slick power boat of a late afternoon.

This was the Riviera as portrayed in the first thirty minutes of *The Talented Mr. Ripley* (before the movie's story turns dark). It truly was *La Dolce Vita.* It was warm air, and the smell of fresh pizza coming from the chimney of some little trattoria or the aroma of leather goods wafting out of shoe stores. It was the glittering window displays of boutiques that sold belts and sweaters too expensive to bother putting a price tag on.

I absorbed a vision of a verdant existence that somehow was bigger than everything else. This fleeting vision left me happy and wistful, longing for something I could not pin down. I still feel it.

My unnamable longing has to do with sex, and living forever, and the freshest food, and best smells, from wild arugula to spilled red wine, to the distant sounds of motor boats and the scratchy whisper of lizards' claws scampering over sun-baked walls, and girls in bikinis, sultry mothers breast-feeding babies, cobblestone back alleys full of stores smelling of the glue used to repair shoes, and the stale blood of butchered rabbits on sawdust in the tiny shops that lined the alleys where we would walk in the nearby town of Santa Margarita, cigarette smoke and thick dank air of the bars we'd duck into to buy a fresh-squeezed orange juice now and then. Mostly it has to do with beauty, and wanting . . . what? I can't name what it was or is. Perhaps it has to do with wanting to live well and never getting there, because "there" is to be unself-consciously Italian and you have to be born that way, and I wasn't.

The smell of Italian leather still evokes those glorious shoes and belts with no prices and still makes me feel dreamy and luxurious, as if I've been transported to a world of perpetual warm water and the distant sound of boat engines, the smell of oil paint and linseed oil, that easy feeling of all being well in a world where the colors are bright, the people happy, cats are scrawny, girls are pretty, men are polite, children numerous, dinner is late, ice cream is dark and impossibly chocolatey. Many a saleswoman on Madison Avenue probably wonders why this middle-aged man will step into their shoe emporium, sniff the leather-scented air, close his eyes, sigh, and then head back out to the street in a blissful trance.

And my parents God bless them, let me be! Italy was where they proved themselves to be so much more than their fundamentalist beliefs. It was as if they *wanted* me to somehow grow past the constricted world they had fallen into.

I think Mom and Dad were a lot more comfortable in Portofino, too, than they were in L'Abri. Mom dressed like a movie star; Dad looked like one of the more intellectual faculty-members of some Italian university. And Mom always looked so elegant. She had taste and was extraordinarily creative. She could combine her few simple pieces of silver jewelry, a silk skirt she'd made, and a blouse bought on sale for a dollar or two, into an outfit that made people do a double-take, as in "who is she?" Besides, in Europe, that intellectual craggy look of Dad's was always "in."

My parents certainly did not look American. In fact, Mom would often say, with a disgusted shake of her head, "They look *so* American!" as a put-down to visiting missionaries who came thorough L'Abri, or, heaven forbid, if we saw Americans in Italy, or during our ski vacations in Zermatt. My sisters would hiss: "They look American! Stop speaking English until they go away!" And we'd clam up or speak French. Mom and Dad always went along with this, although, because Dad never learned French and Mom spoke it incredibly badly, they would just sit silently until the danger passed.

12

In the winters, we went to the Hotel Riffelberg. It was perched above a cliff overlooking the Zermatt Valley and a range of jagged peaks, including the famous Matterhorn. To the north, the hotel faced a steep snowfield perfect for skiing, which swept up for a mile or more to the top of the Riffelhorn and beyond that to the summit of Gornergrat Mountain. We stayed at the Hotel Riffelberg because it was less expensive than the hotels in Zermatt, and the skiing was better.

The trip from Huémoz to Zermatt began at the front door of Chalet Les Mélèzes with my mother running down the stairs while Debby acted as a kind of relay team whose duty it was to both relate information about Mom's progress to my father and to hurry Mom along out of the chalet.

At last my sister bundled her down the icy steps, along the path cut through the snow, through the gates, then down the steep stairs to the road. Mom's descent was watched by my exasperated father, the furious driver of the yellow postal bus, and the angry passengers who—mostly heavyset and malodorous peasant women on errands to Aigle, our "big town" in the valley—were by now ready to make good their threat to drive off and leave Mom and the rest of us *"Américaines"* to find another way to get to the station.

"Tell Edith," Dad yelled, "that if she's not here in ten seconds, everyone in this bus will miss their connections in Aigle! Tell her we've probably already missed the ten-forty to Visp and the connection to Zermatt! Tell her that if we miss the twelve-ten to Zermatt, there isn't another one until five-eighteen and we'll miss the Gornergrat train and won't get to Riffelberg tonight!"

"Yes, Dad," I said.

"And tell that woman that if we miss the Gornergrat connection, she can just forget the whole thing!"

The driver added a sour comment, *"Non, mais! C'est pas possible! Je pars en trente secondes! Nom de Dieu! Non, mais! Merde!"*

On the cog rail line that was the last step in the four-hour journey, I'd be staring at the snow-covered pine trees. Their branches were weighed down so heavily that the snow formed an almost straight white sheath, making the trees look strangely narrow. Through the trees, the high peaks could be glimpsed, dazzling white and towering above everything as the view unfolded. My heart always raced at the thought of what the slopes were going to be like, judging by the amount of deep powder piled in tall sparkling drifts along the track.

Riffelberg was only a mile or so above Zermatt as the crow flies, but the cog railway slowly meandered for twenty minutes through dense forest and over several high bridges, as well as through various glistening icicle-crusted tunnels, before it ground its way out into the open above the tree line. The forest suddenly ended, and the splendid twilit view of the town of Zermatt below and the pale mountains above exploded around us. Stars were visible in the darkening arch of sky.

13

Mom used two trees to illustrate a major point in her "Talk on Prayer." She had several standard talks. There was the "L'Abri Story," her "Girl's Talk," and the famous "Talk on Prayer."

Ours was such a "special story," right up there with the biblical narrative of the struggles of the People of Israel, that when a new guest arrived at L'Abri, the first thing that happened was that Mom, or one of my sisters, would sit them down and tell them "The L'Abri Story." (In later years, Mom wrote *L'Abri,* and it became a best-selling book, her first of many that led to a huge following of evangelical readers.) The new guest would learn about what mighty deeds God had done to raise up The Work that they might be led to us. They had stepped into an ongoing miracle. And they could become a part of it, too—or, as Mom would say, "Another thread in the tapestry." With every new chalet added to The Work, every new brother-in-law, every new step—for instance, when Dad and Mom published their books—the "L'Abri Story" got longer.

I forget the point Mom made with her two trees in the prayer talk. I only remember that she spoke at length about going up into the woods and putting her feet on the trunk of one tree, then switching her feet to the trunk of the other tree while praying, something she demonstrated while lying on the living-room floor. (Mom liked to wear slacks when she spoke, because that way she could prance around, get on the floor, do whatever it took to illustrate her points.) Anyway, the trees illustrated something or other about how one trunk represented our requests to God and the other trunk was something to do with how he answered us—or, rather, answered Mom, because she was our number-one prayer warrior, the rest of us not even being a distant second.

It was amazing how everything Mom did in her personal life had such spiritual significance, even Mom's favorite spot in the forest above our chalet where those trees were folded into the ministry. Mainly what Mom's talk on prayer proved was that she prayed for hours and hours every day and just loved it! Sometimes I wondered if she did protest too much. Who was Mom trying to convince that she was having so much fun up there in the woods with God?

Mom drove me crazy with her pietistic spin on just about anything. She also drove my sisters and myself crazy by folding the most personal moments of our childhood lives into her talks as further illustrations of God's hand on us, or to make points about how to raise a family.

14

As L'Abri grew, it became more formal. Guests were called "students." Then students had their stay limited to three months, after too many people were being turned away and/or were trying to stay for very long periods. At some point (in the early 1960s), the students were asked to pay a minimal amount per day to stay, whereas at the beginning of the work they were considered houseguests and of course everything was free. If you wanted to stay longer than three months, you could become a "helper" and stay up to six months more. And if you felt led by the Lord (and, more importantly, if Mom and Dad really, really liked you), you could become a "worker."

The workers were the permanent staff. Some workers would be elected to become "members." But the members—who were supposedly our independent board—pretty much did what Mom and Dad wanted. I never knew of a decision the members took during Dad's lifetime that went against his wishes. And this whole network of people, past students, workers, and friends were all bound together by my mother's "Family Letters" that she sent out every few months.

Cynthia was a L'Abri worker when I was a small child. She was in and around the L'Abri work for years. Later, she became a member. Cynthia was also my homeschool tutor for a time.

Mom didn't put me in the village school with "all those rough peasant children," for fear that they would make fun of my polio leg. Besides, Mom wanted me in a Christian environment. So I was homeschooled, but most of the time I did little more than struggle to sound out a page or two of words then head for the forest or village. Out of sight I was also out of mind for whole blessed days at a time.

Cynthia had "a special heart" for the Chinese, with Japanese and Koreans coming a close second. Her plan was to heed God's call to her to be a missionary to the "millions of lost souls of the Orient." Cynthia felt that the Lord was leading her to follow in the tradition of Hudson Taylor, the pioneer missionary to China, who grew a pigtail and dressed like a native, the better to "reach out to the lost Chinese." (He founded the mission my grandparents were in.) Cynthia planned to go Hudson one better; she planned to marry "an Oriental."

Cynthia suffered from bad breath; at least she thought she did. I thought her breath was fine. Nevertheless, she brushed her teeth six or seven times a day and I used her imagined affliction to avoid learning to read. I pretended to be sickened as we bent our heads together over the page. Then she would excuse herself and go brush her teeth—again.

I'd never say anything, just pull away and take a deep breath as if about to charge through a smoke-filled room, then read out loud till my breath ran out, then lean way back and take another gasp of air. With any luck, when she went down the hall to brush her teeth, she would get distracted by Mom, who needed help in the kitchen making lunch for thirty guests. Cynthia wouldn't come back for a while, and I could just stare out the window. Of course, this was when there were no Japanese, Chinese, or Koreans around. If there were, then Cynthia was fully occupied and homeschool was indefinitely postponed while she gave the current Oriental Bible studies.

Would God answer earnest, sweet, pretty Cynthia's prayer and provide her a husband so she could return with him to some far-distant land as a missionary with access to the "indigenous people"? I would daydream about Cynthia's future husband out there somewhere, if only he'd marry Cynthia before "the change."

Mom would comment, "Poor Cynthia, you know time is really running out for her! I just *pray* that the Lord brings her someone . . . *before the change!*"

There was so much to worry about: God finding the man in time, God preserving a few good eggs in Cynthia's aging insides, the man being "God's choice for Cynthia," and keeping the lost millions from getting sick and dying before Cynthia could get there and do her stuff and save them. All sorts of clocks were ticking: biological, spiritual, eternal . . . *and* she'd have to learn the language first! Between the babies, learning the language, finding a man—and this didn't even address the issue of the funds to get out there—how could God do it all *before the change?*

The quest for Cynthia's husband and the state of her withering ovaries became a major obsession of my childhood.

"Have you found anyone yet?" I would ask.

"No, but there are two Koreans coming up next weekend from the University of Lausanne," Cynthia said.

Cynthia picked up the reading book and thrust it in front of me.

"But tell me," I added hurriedly, "how do you know that the Lord wants you to marry one of them?"

"I don't know who the Lord will lead me to, but I have a very special heart for them. And there are signs."

"What signs?"

"Well, for one thing I'm naturally good at languages. I've been learning Japanese and Chinese."

"But now it looks like it may be a Korean."

"Never mind that."

"Or two of them."

"Don't be silly."

"Okay, what other signs?"

"Well, by God's grace I'm small. I couldn't marry one if I was towering over the poor little chap, now, could I?"

"If they're really short, they can stand on a box to kiss you."

"That is quite enough! Now open your book and read from: 'Kate has a ball to share with Jack. . . .' "

"I just want to know one other thing. Are you going to have children with them?"

"Of course, if the Lord wills."

"Mom said it will have to be soon because of the change."

Cynthia, always slightly pink, sometimes blushed as only pale Englishwomen do, turning strawberry-red. And I was cruel the way only little boys can be cruel, especially one who knows far too much about female anatomy and uses this knowledge to distract his tutor from doing her job.

With three older sisters and a mother who liked to talk "frankly" about sex to her children, I had been swimming in a sea of female secrets and absorbing titillating inside knowledge since I could remember. Mom skipped the birds and bees and cut to the chase. By the time most boys were just beginning to wonder if girls were different from them "down there," I was awash in menstrual cycles, ovaries, the inside dope on my sisters' urinary tract infections, Mom's diaphragm—"We're not Catholics, and spacing your children is a *good* idea!"—even intimate knowledge about how sex could help Dad's Moods.

"Your father insists on having sexual intercourse *every single night!* That's why I can't be with you and *have* to go on this trip to England with him. He won't be away from me even for *one* night, darling."

The thousands of young women and men who passed through L'Abri between, say, 1957 and 1980 (when I moved away to America) may assume that every single private and deeply embarrassing conversation they ever had with my mother was "shared" in vivid detail with my sisters and myself, not to mention with other L'Abri workers. There was the airline stewardess whose husband said he would leave her unless she had breast augmentation surgery. She did, and he still left her, and, "on top of that, her breasts were ruined!" And there were all the single pregnant women. I knew the details of how each one got pregnant. "And she was a *virgin!* And they were in his car, and you know what, she said all she felt was *pain* and didn't even enjoy it! And she never saw him again! And now she's pregnant!" The average guest at L'Abri was a pretty girl in her early twenties, full of questions—"deep questions" were even better—about God, about life, and about relationships—above all, marriage. And Mom's talk on marriage kept her female audiences spellbound. Mom told me what she was telling them, and about their "private" questions.

"If you get sent out as a missionary to darkest Africa," Mom would say, "it's just as important for you to bring a see-through black negligee as to bring your Bible, if you want your marriage to be good and keep your husband happy."

The more Mom talked about how amazingly God had made

our reproductive organs, and the more she told me how I was to save those organs for marriage, the more I wanted to try them out. I was like a starving child given an endless restaurant tour by an expert chef while being commanded not to touch or taste anything until I grew up!

What was happening to my body was also monitored by Mom. Years ahead of time, I was forewarned about the "changes about to take place." I was on the lookout for the pubic hair Mom said would soon grow and the wet dreams Mom said would soon trouble my sleep. When *at last* I spotted the first fuzz of pubic hair—I was about twelve—it was as if I was witnessing some biblical prophecy being fulfilled. And the so-called wet dreams Mom loved to tell me that God would some day "send as His way of relieving your desires until He brings you the girl he has chosen for you to marry" never materialized, probably because I never gave God the chance. I had been taking care of my needs for years on my own.

Life had two huge demarcation lines, a cosmic *before* and *after,* from which everything else flowed. There was salvation, the crossing of the line from light to dark. And there was marriage, and life *before* "the wedding night" and life *after.*

Life before the wedding night was a constant battle to resist temptation; life after, a nonstop romp wherein you could become "one flesh" as much as you wanted, look up the skirt of your beloved, see her naked all you wanted, and all she had to worry about was yeast infections and urinary tract infections, "common to newlywed young women."

I kept thinking that every pretty girl who got off the bus in Huémoz and walked up the front steps to L'Abri was maybe The One. That was one obsession; the other was that I worried that I could not remember a *specific moment* when I'd accepted Jesus.

I just always believed in him. But wasn't that like being a Roman Catholic? They didn't get born-again; they just trusted in men's traditions and sacraments. I would ask Mom, and she said that we could make sure by praying right then and there, again.

I would pray the sinner's prayer quite often: "Dear Heavenly Father, we just come to you to say we are sinners and that we are trusting in the saving grace of Jesus, who died for us on the cross. . . ." But I never got that feeling of "inexpressible joy" that other people, former pagans and Catholics and Jews and liberal Protestants and deflowered fallen women, got, or said they got, when they were saved.

When a pagan accepted Jesus, my sisters would rush down to the living room and play the scratched, much-abused "Hallelujah Chorus" from the Handel's *Messiah* on the record player. And everyone would run around talking about how the angels in heaven were rejoicing over this or that lost sheep. Then the newly redeemed gave up smoking, or married the girl, or quit studying to be an architect and went to Covenant Seminary in St. Louis instead.

I may not have had a dramatic conversion, but I had no intention of letting the second of life's big moments pass me by. I might not know the *exact moment* I passed from dark to light, but I was on the lookout for the right woman from the time I was about eight.

15

I believe that my parents' call to the ministry actually drove them crazy. They were happiest when farthest away from their missionary work, wandering the back streets of Florence; or, rather, when they turned their missionary work into something very unmissionary-like, such as talking about art history instead of Christ. Perhaps this is because at those times they were farthest away from other people's expectations.

I think religion was actually their source of tragedy. Mom tried to dress, talk, and act like anything but what she was. Dad looked flustered if fundamentalists, especially Calvinist theologians, would intrude into a discussion and try to steer it away from art or philosophy so they could discuss the finer points of arcane theology. And Dad was always in a better mood before leading a discussion or before giving a lecture on a cultural topic, than he was before preaching on Sunday. I remember Dad screaming at Mom one Sunday; then he threw a potted ivy at her. Then he put on his suit and went down to preach his Sunday sermon in our living-room chapel. It was not the only Sunday Dad switched gears from rage to preaching. And this was the same chapel that the Billy Graham family sometimes dropped by to worship in, along with their Swiss-Armenian, multimillionaire in-laws, after Billy—like some Middle Eastern potentate—arranged for his seventeen-year-old daughter's marriage to the son of a particularly wealthy donor who lived up the road from us in the ski resort of Villars.

Did the followers of Billy know that he'd plucked his seventeen-year-old daughter out of her first semester at Wheaton College to marry a man almost twenty years older than her whom she had never met until Billy introduced them? Would they have cared?

Every human being has a dark side. But when you are being hailed as a conduit-to-God, the fact that you are a mere human—or, in the case of Billy Graham, just plain bizarre—has to be ignored by your followers for the same reason that the tribes of Israel really and truly had to keep on believing in Moses' abilities as they wandered lost in the desert. Believing in "things unseen" is tough. That cloud must be a "pillar of fire" right? And the coincidental windstorm or earthquake has to be some sort of "parting of the Red Sea." Believers tend to grasp wildly at anything that gives them hope, including clinging to religious leaders who throw things at their wives, then preach on love or run out of food on a pilgrimage to some promised land.

In his "year of doubt"—as Mom always called it—Dad had spent the better parts of several months pacing in our old Champéry chalet's hayloft. He was considering giving up his faith. Things no longer made sense to him. Somehow he convinced himself to still believe. And in 1949 (at about the same time Dad was pacing), Billy Graham was also suffering from doubts and had a similar re-conversion. Billy walked into the woods, laid his Bible on a tree stump, and prayed for more faith. Suddenly he just *knew* it was all true!

To an outside observer, these self-fulfilling miracles of renewed faith might be open to question; they *might* even seem to have something to do with the fact that Dad and Billy, and many others, had a vested interested in their belief, belief through which they found meaning, the respect of others, and also earned a living. But since Billy mentioned to Dad—at least half a dozen times over thirty or so years of knowing each other—that he was terrified of dying, maybe Billy's moment of sublime revelation hadn't quite done the trick. As for Dad, his temper and violent rage at my mother lessened with time but only disappeared altogether when he was dying of cancer. God might have given Dad faith, but he never did manage to get him to be polite to his wife.

Flimsily based as Billy's reason for faith was, it did not stop half a dozen presidents accepting at face value the received wisdom that God had "called" Billy to be "America's chaplain." And when it came to how Dad sometimes treated my mother, other L'Abri workers looked the other way. They must have heard the screaming, and some must have known there was abuse. They did nothing. And to the faithful, Dad was, in the words of *Christianity Today* magazine, "a great oak" of Christian leadership, something they called him when he died. That the great oak abused his wife was beside the point.

Even presidents need to believe in something. And since the something in question is invisible, the worldly qualifications of the prophet and soothsayer don't count. So it makes perfect sense that Billy became a religious leader. Billy had his flash of faith at the tree stump, and successive presidents had Billy.

Falling in faith and falling in love can be understood the same way. People fall in love with no evidence of how a relationship will work out and no real knowledge of who their partner is, let alone who they will be ten, twenty, or thirty years later. There are no good reasons. And people get "saved," and pick a religious leader to follow, in about the same way.

We never have any real information about anything important. It takes a lifetime for the ramifications to be worked out. Billy always worried that he had never been to seminary. But a Bible on a tree stump is as good as a hundred years in a seminary studying invisible "truths." And the fact that my dad was called Dr. Schaeffer, when his doctorate was an honorary one, made no difference either. The most ridiculous thing in the world is a PhD in theology, an oxymoron if one ever existed.

The irony is that we all—secular or religious people alike—make our biggest life-shaping decisions on faith. Life is too short to learn what you need to know to live well. So we make a leap of faith when it comes to what we should believe in, who we will marry, and our careers. Who we happen to meet, one conversation when you were eighteen, the college course you happened to sign up for, the teacher you liked, the elevator you missed and the girl you met in the next one, decide whole lives. You would have to live a lifetime to be qualified to make any big decisions. And since we can't do that, we trust to luck, religion, or the kindness of strangers. Only the trivialities—say, buying cars, washing machines, or airline seats—are chosen on the basis of good information. I've always known I like aisle seats, but what does one really want in a wife? And spiritual leaders are selected like spouses, not like airline seats. There is never a good reason, just a feeling, just that fear of death that must be overcome somehow by something—by religion, or orgasms, or art, or having children, or politics—by anything that interrupts the contemplation of oblivion.

The paradox is that sometimes the less it makes sense, the

better it works. And the less one knows about the "holy" people we follow, the better. One of the mysteries of human need is that religious leaders must become more than the sum of their fallible, sometimes awful, parts, because other people *need* them to be more. This does not make the religious leader a hypocrite; it just shows that the rest of us are desperate.

So when Billy preached, no one wanted to know why he'd gotten his daughter into an arranged marriage with the son of a very wealthy donor. And when my father stepped up to preach at a multitude of Christian colleges, few knew, or would have wanted to know, that my sisters and I sometimes huddled in our beds listening to the dull roar of his voice as he screamed at my mother and occasionally abused her.

16

In some marriages, a husband and wife are said to complete each other. In the case of my mother and father, they also competed. Each was such a powerful force that they sometimes seemed to eclipse the other. Dad was abusive at times, but my mother was in no way intimidated. In fact, she seemed to relish her martyr status. And she loved him, as he did her. In some ways they had a very good marriage, with some horrible moments. In other words, they were like most people.

Where they were perhaps different from most was in their fierce competition in the arena of "Christian work," especially as fellow evangelical authors. And what they never intended, but was also part of their legacy, was that they drove their children crazy.

Mom always let us know not only how hard she was working but how many demands Dad was loading her with. And Dad always let us know how depressed he was at having to face "all those people." So their competition began as a competition in martyrdom. Serving the Lord was tough, a "spiritual battle." They both gloried in all they gave up for God.

Mom was best at the martyrdom game. When she wrote to me, as she did almost every day while on her many L'Abri speaking trips with Dad—when he was lecturing and preaching all over Europe and later all over the United States of America—she would sometimes include a story about her long suffering, the way she did in this typical letter she wrote to me in 1961 from Holland, when I was nine, which is reproduced here in full including the use of capitalization found in the original:

> Dear Frankie,
> I had a special blessing from the Lord today. Fran had to spend the night over in Rotterdam so I was here at this lovely little hotel all alone. I was able to sleep for an hour and a half last night, then got up to type all the letters Dad dictated as well as write to you. The special blessing was that with Fran away I had time to get all my work done and also to wash and iron Fran's clothes. You see before he left he said, "Edith, you make sure you have ALL my clothes clean and pressed BEFORE I get back tomorrow!!!" Well, I had been praying about how I could wash and iron all his clothes AND type up all his correspondence. And the Lord showed me because with Fran away for the night I didn't have to accompany him to the dining room and eat. And so I was able to skip all my meals and not sleep till 3 AM and was able to wonderfully use those extra hours the Lord gave me to do all the work. Then when Fran got back the next day since the Lord had provided me with a room with a bath I took a really relaxing twenty minute bath! And do you know what? In spite of the fact I'd had practically no sleep, had been doing Fran's laundry in the hotel tub and typing up his letters, and had not eaten for 24 hours and had also found time for 3 hours of uninterrupted prayer, in spite of all this,

> when Fran came back I felt and looked as fresh and rested as if I had been on a nice long vacation!!!
> Love Mom.

Dad would write short postcards, like this one he wrote from that same trip to Holland:

> Dear Frank, Today the canals here are frozen. Kids your age are skating on them from town to town. Be good and obey Susan till we get home. I love you, Dad.

I'd be home with Susan and Debby. (Priscilla was married and in St. Louis, teaching French to put John through seminary.) And Susan was in charge. Susan loved to play doctor, nurse, psychologist, mother, spiritual guide, and teacher with her little brother, practicing on me for all the roles she imagined herself playing later in life. And when Mom was away, Susan was, at last, able to do all those things I needed done to me under the heading "If I was your mother. . . ."

When I was five, Susan was sent to bed for a year after she was diagnosed with rheumatic fever. From her bed, she provided a dayschool. I would sit and color and play at a little table next to her bed in her tiny chalet room. Susan was fiercely patriotic, and before "class" each day she would lead me in saying the American pledge of allegiance, something my parents never did. It is thanks to the fact that Mom was away so much, and to Susan's experiments in child-rearing, that I learned to read at all. Mom was not lax, she was just nonexistent during the day. All her time and attention was given to L'Abri. And therefore I was gloriously free to roam my mountainside, follow any of the students around I liked, invent endless games, visit Jane and Betty, play in the village, watch rabbits and chickens being killed, fields being cut, hay turned, cows being milked—and avoid schoolwork.

With Susan in charge, I'd feel as if I had been living in some carefree Italian village that had just been taken over by the Germans. I'd have to sit inside for hours on sunny days actually working! And Susan had been told she could discipline me. Her method was to slap me, or do the dreaded "Indian wrist burn" where she clenched my wrist in her hands and rubbed my skin back and forth between her fists till she raised welts, or roll me up in a bedsheet, making a full-body strait-jacket out of it. She would pin this down the back and leave me face-up, lying entombed on my bed. I could struggle free by wiggling around for a while but when Susan came back, if the sheet was loose, say after the one-hour sentence was done, then the time I'd have to stay imprisoned would be doubled.

In another family, Susan would have grown up to be the first woman bishop of some denomination, a prison guard, an astronaut, or the first female general in the United States Army. In our Reformed Presbyterian denomination, Susan could never be a minister, teaching from the pulpit being reserved for men. But she did become a zealous missionary when she followed my parents into L'Abri.

It was Susan who kept trying to remind my forgetful parents to "do something about Frankie!" And she tried to teach me as best she could. And once Susan was married to Ranald, they showed me a great deal of kindness. Ranald would take me camping, wrestle with me, and take me on hikes. When they came back from their honeymoon in South Africa, they brought me a real elephant's toenail, an African spear, a drum, and a piece of ivory.

Susan was a gifted (if somewhat terrifying) teacher, and in later years she wrote several books on education inspired by the work of the education pioneer Charlotte Mason. And of course my childhood "memory" of Susan's draconian discipline looms large. She probably only wrapped me up once or twice, slapped me rarely, and maybe she was just showing me *how* to torture someone while demonstrating the Indian wrist burn, not punishing me. Although when Susan knocked me down by smashing a colander full of wet spaghetti over my head, that was real enough.

17

Since I learned to read with the threat of Susan's winding sheet and/or a solid slap hanging over me, I deeply resented Dad's need for nightly sexual intercourse. If *only,* I thought, he could have gone for a week or two without Mom and let her stay home!

It never occurred to me that perhaps it was somewhat strange that, by age seven or eight, I had been told by my mother that Dad wanted sex every night. (Dad never, *ever* talked about his private life, so I only have Mom's version of this.) Nobody I know had a mother who shared this sort of Kinsey report on her bedroom activities with her children, although, when I saw the movies *Running With Scissors* and *Almost Famous,* I felt a great sense of solidarity with the protagonists who survived strange childhoods, nutty mothers, and in their youth lived as if on another planet.

What Mom never explained was how her saying that she wanted to be at home with us, rather than on the road with Dad, fit in with her wildly enthusiastic reports about how the Lord used her so mightily when she gave her talks. She would blame Dad for forcing her to go with him yet seemed to relish life on the road nonetheless. As a matter of fact, after she hadn't been on the road for a while, Mom got downright bored and would sometimes look up at airplanes flying high overhead and say "I really want to travel again!"

Mom spoke to evangelical groups as much as Dad did and would often tell me that the women, or the organizing local missionary, or this or that lost person who had gotten saved at the meeting told her later that while they enjoyed Dad's talks, it was Mom's talk on marriage, or the Bible, or prayer, or Mom's telling "The L'Abri Story" that had *really* moved them. "Fran's talk just went right over their heads," Mom would say; "fortunately, the Lord used *me* to really reach out to them!"

It seemed that more was happening on my parents' speaking trips than daily sex, or Mom typing up Dad's letters and doing his laundry and helping him with his Mood. Mom loved becoming an evangelical star. And so the competition between Mom and Dad became intense.

It was Mom who wrote the first book (*L'Abri*). She would always say that she was the "real writer," whereas "your father just dictates his lectures and calls *that* writing!" Dad let it be known that her spiritual books served a "real purpose," but that his books, like *Escape from Reason* and *The God Who Is There,* were in an altogether different category, "the foundation of our ideas." Mom would sometimes say "Fran has written more books, but I've written more pages. Fran's books are *so very short!*" (My parents' twenty-plus books are mostly still in print, have been translated into more than forty languages, and have sold millions of copies worldwide.)

My parents also would not brook much editing. I grew up hearing about the evils of editors, who just didn't understand that Mom was a much better writer than them, so how *dare* they tamper with her inspired words? or Dad explaining that editors didn't really understand his work, as they tried to make it conform to "all those stupid evangelical books that don't reach anyone."

It was Dad who depended on Mom, though, not the other way around. After he died, Mom often said "I'm glad he went first. He never could have managed without me." She was right. Dad could hardly boil water for tea, and he never booked a boat or plane ticket or planned a vacation. Mom was in charge of our finances. Dad got in Moods, became discouraged, suffered bouts of depression. Mom never showed any weakness. She could do everything, and she let us know it, including mentioning the fact, again and again, that although it might say "From Mom and Dad with Love" on a birthday or Christmas present, *she* had bought the present, wrapped it "at two AM," and decorated the tree it was under and/or baked the cake, because "you know poor Fran can't do anything."

Except when on vacation, my parents never paused to take a breath. My mother was a whirling dervish of activity, a perpetual-motion machine who was aware of her superhuman energy and very proud of it. And my father literally did nothing but work. (Dad only subscribed to magazines that he could quote from, and even on vacations he brought his "reading matter": articles and periodicals he'd saved all year to "catch up on.") He only took breaks in his normal routine to hike. Mom rarely hiked; in fact, she hated it. Mom's idea of a good time was to sit in some lavish Swiss tearoom dressed exquisitely and being seen, while talking to some person she admired.

Outside of our annual vacations, my parents never took a day off. And of course, Sundays were the busiest day of the week, from Dad preaching, to Sunday lunch and the interminable lunch discussion with the students and Sunday visitors, to Mom's lavish high teas on Sunday nights for the students (and the day visitors who stayed all day after coming to church to hear Dad preach).

If someone mentioned taking a nap, Mom would invariably scoff, "I *never* take naps!" My sisters sometimes turned into quivering wrecks from trying to keep up with their mother, both as young women trying desperately to help bring people to the Lord in the early days of L'Abri, and then again once they officially joined the work as grownups.

When we were children and someone "came to the Lord," Mom always made a big point of telling us when that person had said something about this or that Schaeffer child having played a part in their journey to salvation, through us children having been kind and understanding or through the answers we offered to that "seeking person's" spiritual questions. "You played a real part!" Mom would exclaim, and, at other times, "The Lord has called us *all* into this work, and Dad and I couldn't do it without you!"

I have a photo album Mom made of my childhood pictures. Mom wrote many odd captions that have a lot more to do with her spiritual ambition for her children than with reality. Almost every caption has a strange spiritual twist to it. For instance, next to a picture of me playing with a friend when I was seven or eight, Mom wrote: "Frankie sitting with his friend, explaining Christian Basics." I'm positive I was doing no such thing: we were playing cowboys and Indians.

Mom's spiritual pride, mixed with fierce spiritual ambition for her children, mixed with a willingness to be a doormat to her overbearing husband—as a further example of her piety and her ability to be the perfect wife for the Lord's sake, while Dad was so far from perfect—left my sisters and me with a lifetime of conflicted emotions. Whose side were we on? Whose side *should* we be on? How much Christian service was enough? Should we try to live up to Mom's spiritual fantasies about us? How could we ever live up to Mom's expectations on the one hand, and to her absurd claims about her children's spirituality and zeal on the other?

I was not a child when I was a child: I was Mom's secret agent for the Lord. A lovely sunrise was an illustration of God's love. A tragedy was a reminder that we depend on God. If someone died, say my Mom's mom, the first thing we did was reassure ourselves that they were with the Lord, or not, as in the case of those people like my Dad's mother, who passed away when we were not sure that she had accepted Christ. In that case, we could only hope that she "came to know the Lord before the end."

The superspiritual pietistic grid through which Mom saw life was a heavy load for her children to bear. *Should* I have been explaining "Christian Basics" to that friend? *Was* the only point of playing cowboys and Indians to get to the moment in a friendship where I could try to convert him? If he didn't convert, was that *my* fault?

The implication was that whatever you were doing for the Lord, more was required. Normal life was just a series of interludes between bouts of evangelical zeal. And the spiritual pride that underlay Mom's zeal made her children grow up with the feeling that no matter what we did to serve the Lord, it was never enough. Mom had gotten there first, and the rest of us weren't even in the race.

18

I think what drove my parents was their reaction to the theological battles in which their early faith was forged. Both Mom and Dad were traditional Protestants trying to come to terms with the theological liberalism that was sweeping through the seminaries and mainline denominations starting in the early 1900s. There had been doctrinal differences between Baptists, Methodists, and Presbyterians; but prior to this time, the denominations shared an orthodoxy that today would be called fundamentalism. All Protestants had believed in a literal Bible and the divinity of Christ, not to mention the virgin birth and Christ's resurrection. But Darwin's theory of evolution challenged the Bible, and the academic discipline of "higher criticism" claimed mere human authorship for scripture.

Traditional Protestants such as my mother's missionary parents, or my newly born-again father, inherited the enthusiasms—and the paranoia—of the counterattack by fundamentalists against the so-called modernists. By the 1920s, the modernists were taking over the seminaries and the bureaucracies of the big denominations. New York's most prominent Baptist minister, Harry Emerson Fosdick, converted to a new kind of orthodoxy—the belief in a liberal progressive vision of mankind. And he began to preach that the Bible was not literally true, but that God would save the world through human progress. (After the horrors of the World Wars, his ideas about utopian progress fell out of fashion, but the liberal deconstruction of the scriptures continued.)

J. Gresham Machen, a theologian at Princeton Theological Seminary, opposed Fosdick. Machen published a book called *Christianity and Liberalism* and argued that any theology that denied Christ's divinity or doubted the Bible was not Christianity. But Machen lost the battle. Princeton Theological Seminary was taken over by the liberals. And Machen was fired for being too conservative, a last hold out for the old literalist view of the Bible.

Machen was my father's hero, mentor, and friend. Dad kept a big black-and-white picture of him taped inside his bedroom cupboard. When I was very young, I heard Machen's name a lot. As I got older, Dad talked about him less.

I think my father lived with a tremendous tension that pitted his growing interest in art, culture, music, and history against a stunted theology frozen in the modernist-fundamentalist battles of his youthful Christian experience. Dad took Machen's firing from Princeton personally. My father's theology was formed in a particularly bitter moment and never evolved along with the rest of his thinking. The theological battles of the 1920s and 1930s shaped Dad in the same way that political battles would shape the Vietnam generation in the 1960s. Passions forged in those battles became part of a personal identity that was difficult for people who did not share the passionate and polarizing experiences to understand.

When Machen was kicked out of Princeton, he founded Westminster Theological Seminary in Philadelphia, where Dad went. But once fundamentalists left or were kicked out of the "mainstream" denominations, their habit of searching for theological error turned inward. Groups separated one from another even over such issues as whether the King James translation of the Bible was the only translation that contained God's pure word. And within months of Machen's founding a new denomination, even his new church suffered a schism. And Dad was part of a split from Westminster and helped form the new Faith Seminary. (The disagreement was over the timetable and order of events regarding the "return of Christ.") Dad and Mom then became part of several more Presbyterian splinter sects and the founding of ever more "pure" groups.

Dad spent the rest of his life trying to somehow reconcile the angry theology that typified movement-fundamentalism, with a Christian apologetic that was more attractive. He maintained a rather fierce enthusiasm for an absolutely literal interpretation of scripture that I believe he held on to more as emotional baggage (out of loyalty to Machen and others) than for any intellectual reason. On the other hand even in the early days of his ministry my father had cultural interests far beyond those of the usual fundamentalist leaders.

Even though Dad often denounced what he termed the harsh side of fundamentalism, old habits die hard, and for the rest of his life Dad was critical of all "compromise" on interpretations of the Bible. Who had "compromised" and who had not remained a big topic, just as what side you were on during the Vietnam War still divides and embitters aging former hippies and aging former soldiers.

During my childhood, I was very aware of who had compromised and who hadn't. Machen had *not* compromised. Billy Graham *had,* when he invited liberal theologians, even a Roman Catholic, to participate in his New York 1957 crusades.

(Dad had little good to say about Billy until they became rather close in the 1960s, after Billy's family began to visit L'Abri.)

Mom and Dad were in an awkward place. Theologically, they were fundamentalists, but they were also compassionate and wanted fundamentalism to have a more humane and less embarrassing face. Other people were struggling with the same problem. One was an acquaintance of my father's, Dr. Harold Ockenga (the pastor of the famous Congregationalist Park Street Church in Boston). In later years, Harold sent his son John to L'Abri in a last-ditch effort to get John "back on track" spiritually. It worked for a while, before John left the faith, but not before he introduced me to smoking pot.

Dr. Ockenga had been a student of Machen's at Princeton University and followed him out. But then Ockenga, like Dad, became a critic of the fundamentalist's endless civil wars and started looking for a new way to present a friendlier evangelical faith (and face). He helped invent a movement called the New Evangelicals. Their mascot was Billy Graham.

Other figures like Carl Henry, founder of *Christianity Today* magazine (and a man who became bitterly jealous of my father in later years), criticized fundamentalism's failure to address the world's intellectual and social needs. A movement was born—modern evangelicalism, a fundamentalism-lite where everyone could more or less do their own theological thing, as long as they "named the name of Christ" and paid lip service to the "inerrancy" of the Bible.

On the fringe of all this activity, almost forgotten and buried in his little mission in Switzerland doing the "Lord's work in the Lord's way" during the 1950s and 1960s, my father developed his apologetic wherein he reversed the priorities of fundamentalist dogma. Instead of spouting Bible verses, Dad talked about philosophy, art, and culture. Only when he had gained his listener's interest would he slip in a more traditional "Jesus saves" message. In a way, Dad became the answer to one of the questions Carl Henry asked over and over again in his early writings: "When will evangelicals get involved with their culture?"

Dad went one step further. He got interested in the secular culture, not as a means to an end but for its own sake. In the early to mid-1960s, my father's focus slowly changed. He slipped into a second career as an art historian, pop culture analyst, and futurist.

I sometimes wonder what would have happened to my parents if, at that point, they had followed what were obviously their most heartfelt interests instead of continuing to try to bridge the widening gap between their aesthetic appreciation and their former theological passions, forged in the fundamentalist-versus-modernist controversy of the 1920s and '30s. What began as Dad's attempt to find a way to preach the gospel to modern young people turned into a lifelong interest in culture.

In evangelical circles, if you wanted to know what Bob Dylan's songs meant, Francis Schaeffer was the man to ask. In the early '60s, he was probably the only fundamentalist who had even heard of Bob Dylan.

19

How much faith was enough? The answer was that you didn't need much faith, only as much as a mustard seed. We didn't have any mustard seeds, but Mom said they were very small. So how much faith was that? It was a tough equation, like trying to measure love by the pound or fear by the yard.

Well, judging by how hard we had to pray just to get some Swiss peasant on the Ollon communal town council to stamp a piece of paper approving a building or residency permit, we didn't have much faith. If you can't even get a perpetually drunken farmer to sign his name, how far are you from saying, to a cripple, "Take up your bed and walk!" with any expectation that they will?

I tried this a few times with my bad leg. I commanded it to grow, and it didn't. So then I tried it on Jean Pierre over at Chalet Bellevue, the home for cerebral palsy sufferers next door. I was twelve at the time and home from English boarding school during the summer holidays. Jean Pierre was tall, angular, and a year or two older than me. He had short hair, a big long nose, and big hands that sometimes were clenched when he had spasms. He had been rescued from an abusive home and sent by the Swiss authorities to Chalet Bellevue.

There were lumps on his face from scars where his mother had beaten him with a stick.

Jean Pierre liked it when I visited, because most of the other CP kids next door were girls. (The home was started as a sister mission to L'Abri, by some like-minded American evangelical women—"The Ladies"—who were fans of my dad.) I was the only boy Jean Pierre knew who could walk well enough so we could play army.

After fighting our wars all over the Bellevue property, sometimes we shared an underwear ad and masturbated under the Les Mélèzes hedge. (In *Saving Grandma,* I put in a story about a spastic who needs help with masturbation. In real life, Jean Pierre managed just fine.)

Jean Pierre had accepted Christ after being led to the foot of the cross by Rosemary Sperry, one of the American ladies who ran the home. So he was ready to try out the healing idea. In the scriptures, various methods were used. We decided we'd try the anointing of oil that the apostles were said to have used in the New Testament church. So I went into Chalet Les Mélèzes.

"Mom, can I have some oil?"

"What for, darling?"

"I just need some."

"How much oil, and what for?"

"Just regular oil, just enough for some anointing."

"What?"

"I'm going to play King David, and I want to do some anointing."

"I suppose that's all right. Here," said Mom, taking an empty yogurt cup out of the cupboard; "you can pour in a little of that sunflower-seed oil, but don't spill any on the floor."

We had our oil, though I'd lied to get it since playing King David sounded less strange than saying I was planning to heal Jean Pierre. Dad said that we *did* believe in healing, so I knew I would not be struck down or anything. But Dad said we did *not* believe in healing like those confused Pentecostals who didn't seem to realize that in the New Testament, the point of all those miracles wasn't the miracles themselves but to prove who Jesus was so that people would believe and the church could get started. It was started now, so healing was rare and usually unnecessary.

We believed that God still could do miracles, but that there had to be a bigger reason. For instance when he saved certain missionaries in the China Inland Mission, it was so more Chinese could hear the gospel and be saved. So that was why the missionaries were miraculously delivered from various bandits, warlords, Boxer rebels, and communists. It was for God's greater glory, not just to save the missionaries, who, after all, were perfectly willing to be martyrs, just like Stan and Betty Stam, co-missionaries with my grandparents who had "gladly" died singing hymns as the Boxer rebels beheaded them.

I didn't say what the oil was for because I couldn't think of any good reason to heal Jean Pierre, except that he didn't want to jump at loud noises. And we all already believed in God, so we didn't need more proofs because we were like the people—in fact, we *were* the people—Christ spoke of when he said that Thomas had believed in him because he had seen him and touched him, but that certain people in the future would believe without seeing, just by faith alone. Those believers were going to be particularly blessed. That was us.

But I had doubts. It always seemed to me that what Mom and Dad assumed were answered prayers sometimes had more mundane explanations. For instance, Mom always said: "We never ask for money. We just take our needs to the Lord in prayer." But I also knew that she "shared" our needs in her "Family Letter" with our "praying family," who then sent donations. I knew that Mom paid very special attention to wealthy visitors and also shared our needs with them, sometimes by mentioning the current need in one of her long prayers. I kind of had an inkling of how the living-by-faith trick worked. Perhaps this was why, when I prayed, it was with very little faith. So I thought, if Jean Pierre *is* healed, then I for one will gain greater faith and believe even more, so *that* might be the greater purpose. Anyway, it was worth a shot.

"Jean Pierre!"

"*Oui?*"

"Stand still and think about how much you believe."

"*Bien.*"

"How much faith do you have right now?"

We were standing up on the back road behind Chalet Bellevue. The day was perfect, hot sun, crisp cool air, and the mountains looked so close and sharply detailed that they seemed unreal. No one was around. We were hidden by the pine hedge, so if someone did come along, all they would see was us standing there with me holding a small plastic yogurt cup. There was nothing suspicious about that: For all they'd know, we could just be collecting slugs or worms. And if it worked, then who was going to get mad once Jean Pierre began to jump for joy and thank Jesus?

"I have *le* much faith," said Jean Pierre.

"Do you solemnly promise that you are sure this will work?"

"*Bien sur*!"

"So you're sure that you'll be healed?"

"*Oui.*"

"Okay. Then in the name of Jesus . . . stand still!"

"I am nervous."

"But you have to *stop* twitching! You made me spill some oil!"

"*Je m'exuse.*"

"Okay; now are you going to stand still?"

"*Oui.*"

"Okay, then. Now in the name of Jesus. . . . Wait. Do you think I should do it like Dad does when he baptizes new believers in the name of the Trinity?"

"*Pardon?*"

"You know what the Trinity is, don't you?"

"*Non.*"

"What?!"

"What it ees?"

"Well, how can you say you accepted Jesus if you don't know who the Trinity is?"

"Nobody deed tell me thees."

"Dad will be furious with the ladies. How on earth can they lead people to Christ if they aren't telling you guys that he is the second person of the Trinity? Why, you don't even know who you believe in!"

"I am tired and must sit. Heal the oils *tout suite,* Frankie!"

"Okay. But if it doesn't work, it's because you have a theological problem. But here goes. In the name of the Father, Son, and Holy Spirit . . . by the way, THAT is the Trinity."

"*Bien. Je comprends.*"

"In that name and of course mostly in Jesus's name, I command the spasticness to depart and that you be *healed!*"

I reached up—Jean Pierre was a foot taller than me—and

poured the oil over his head. There was more in the cup than it had seemed. It looked like a little but as it ran all over Jean Pierre's shirt and stained his maroon corduroy pants a dark blotchy black-red, I realized that this anointing business was a lot messier than as advertised in the Scriptures where it only said it ran down over people's heads, shoulders, and beards, and nothing about really messing up their clothes.

"Are you feeling better?"

"*Non!*"

"Well, then, you didn't have the faith after all."

"*Mes oui,* I have the faith! It ees *you* who did not have the faith! *Salaud*!"

"What are you going to tell the ladies happened to wreck your shirt and pants?"

"*Merde*!"

"See?! We're in the middle of a healing and you are using profanity and you expect God to heal you? I'm wasting my time!"

"It ees *you* who have no faith! It ees because you are play with your pee-pee that *Jesu* no heal me!"

"You're blaming *me* because we touch ourselves? What about you?!"

"Oui, you are feelthy, so God he don't hear your prayer, so he don't heal me."

"Fine, then find somebody else to do it!"

I marched off in a huff. And it was a week before I went back over to Chalet Bellevue, and I only went then because Jane Stuart Smith was doing her weekly Sunday hymn-sing with the children and I liked to hear her sing. After the hymn-sing, Jean Pierre and I made peace behind the hedge, aided by several bra advertisements.

20

Two old ladies—rather one old lady and one middle-aged lady who seemed old—arrived. First, Gracie Holmes came to stay, and then Grandmother Schaeffer, Dad's mom. Gracie lived in a little room at the end of the middle-floor hall, two doors down from the kitchen and next to a girl's dormitory. Grandmother got Susan's old room at the end of the upstairs hall.

Gracie came to live with us when I was nine or ten. She was an Englishwoman with the IQ of an eight-year-old. She had had a stroke when she was in her twenties that left her paralyzed on the right side of her body. She walked with a limp, dragging her right foot, and her right arm was almost useless. Gracie's face was asymmetrical. She had false teeth and pink babylike skin and watery pale blue eyes. Her tongue would loll out of her mouth when she was thinking hard. Gracie had somehow gotten stranded in a Swiss home for mentally retarded adults. Susan met Gracie (where, I don't know) and brought her for a visit to L'Abri so she could meet other people who spoke English—and, of course, have the chance to accept Jesus. Gracie came to visit every weekend after that and accepted Jesus as soon as Susan told her to. Then one day Mom asked Gracie if she would like to stay. Gracie burst into tears and said yes.

After Gracie moved in, she would lug a big Bible to church

every Sunday and sit there smiling at everyone with her Bible open and upside down. Gracie and I became good friends. It was as if she was my little sister. I teased her but never about her condition, only in the sense that she was easy to fool. She would accept anything I said at face value, either believing it or pretending to. For instance, Gracie and I prepared in various ways to meet Jesus.

"Jesus is coming back in a few minutes Gracie," I said barging into Gracie's room one morning.

"Very nice, darling," Gracie said, very matter-of-fact, except she pronounced it "dalin."

"So you better get ready."

"Yes."

"So get up and get dressed. You don't want to meet the Lord in that old nightgown, do you?"

"No, dalin."

"Okay, then hurry."

A few minutes later, we were standing in front of our chalet. Gracie was looking up into the sky expectantly and clutching her oversized handbag, while I was trying not to burst into laughter. Gracie was in her best dress. A few minutes passed.

"Where is he, dalin?"

"I think he took the bus from Ollon."

"Oh?"

"After he gets here, he'll take us all to heaven."

"On the bus, dalin?"

"Several buses."

"Good, dalin."

Ten minutes later. . . .

"Where IS he, dalin?" asked Gracie with a petulant edge in her voice.

"He's late."

"I must do the ironing, dalin."

"We won't need anything ironed when Jesus comes back."

"But I MUST DO IT!"

Gracie's tongue was protruding and she was turning a bright pink. She got upset if something kept her from her duties. Her eyes, always larger than life as seen through her thick glasses, seemed to get bigger.

"Okay, but don't blame me if you get left behind. What will Jesus think if you aren't waiting?"

"Well, dalin, you tell him I'm upstairs doing the ironing for Mr. Schaeffer, because he wants his nice white shirt for Sunday."

"I will, but Jesus might be angry."

"Never mind him, dalin."

Mom looked over the top-floor balcony. "Frankie?"

"Yes, Mom?"

"What are you and Gracie doing?"

"We're waiting for Jesus, but I must go iron, dalin, mustn't I?"

"Yes, Gracie, you go do that, but maybe you'll want to change out of your Sunday dress first."

"Yes, dalin," said Gracie, and she marched off.

"Frankie!"

"Yes, Mom?"

Gracie would hide the shirts she scorched. She would also count the silverware and follow guests around asking them where a missing spoon or fork was until everyone was so exasperated that people would drop what they were doing and help her find the fork. And then Gracie would beam at them and/or mutter darkly about how she knew they had been stealing

"Mrs. Schaeffer's forks." Sometimes I would hide silverware under a student's pillow and then hint to Gracie that I suspected the girl or boy of theft until she searched their room. Then it would take Mom half the afternoon to get Gracie to stop following the suspect while mumbling darkly and calm the accused "thief" down. The possibilities were endless.

After a few years of being "in charge" of the house, Gracie would routinely hide all the silver, the napkins, and even the toilet paper. That way, no one could do anything without going to her and begging for whatever they needed. My parents never made her change her strange and squirrel-like habit. "She just wants to feel important," Mom would say. "There's no harm done."

Grandmother Schaeffer came to live with us in 1962 (or thereabouts), after she broke her hip. She was my bad grandmother, as opposed to my good grandmother. (Our "good grandmother" was Mom's missionary godly mom who had passed away many years before, though Mom's dad went on living till he was a hundred and one years and three days old.)

"Grandmother Schaeffer believed nothing when she was raising poor Fran," Mom would say. "She wasn't even a *nominal* Christian. And now, look, we're stuck with her!"

Grandmother Schaeffer had always been small and now was shrunk down to a barely-four-foot angry troll. She had a tough little wizened face and a perpetually sour frown. I resented her. We had no privacy in our home anyway, and now what little there was evaporated with my grandmother's coming to haunt our top-floor apartment.

Grandmother had never been outside of Philadelphia until the day she flew to Switzerland. It was her first and last ride in a plane.

Years later, just after she broke her hip a second time, Genie and I visited Grandmother in the Aigle hospital on our wedding day. She glared and snapped: "How can that fool boy be married? He's only twelve!" She wasn't demented, just being her usual insulting self. I had it coming. I had teased her—a lot.

When Grandmother died, Birdie, a L'Abri worker who was a retired nurse, washed and dressed her body. (There were few undertakers in Switzerland in those days.) But Grandmother's mouth kept falling open. I found the solution in my art supplies and sprayed fixative, the liquid spray glue used to "fix" charcoal drawings, into her mouth, over her false teeth and lips. It worked very well. My only problem was that I couldn't figure out what expression to give her. To make her smile gave Grandma a false look, different than she ever had in life. On the other hand, to give her the frown that was so familiar seemed a mean thing to do. So I settled on flat, pursed lips, a quizzical what-now-in-the-afterlife? expression.

Knowing Grandmother Schaeffer explained a lot about Dad. For one thing, Mom wasn't lying when she said that she had more or less saved Dad. His mother's idea of a good time was reading the obituaries and muttering gleefully, "Outlived him, too!" She hated any food she was not familiar with, and Grandmother was familiar with two dishes: chicken soup and corned beef hash. She hated the classical music Dad played all day to create a wall of sound to block out the voices of the guests and—after Grandmother came to live with us—the sound of Grandmother talking to herself, often about the wrestling she had loved watching on TV and now missed.

Grandmother Schaeffer provided some unintentional insight into my family history in another way. Priscilla said that when she was a little girl (back in America), that her best times were when Mom and Dad dropped her off to stay with Grandmother Schaeffer. If being with Grandmother contrasted so positively with life at home with Mom and Dad, it told me a great deal about the quality of life in the early, oppressive strict fundamentalist days of our household. Priscilla always said how free she felt with Grandmother.

Gracie had been living with us for several years before Grandmother arrived. And there was an instant rivalry between them that extended to them both trying to cheat while playing Pacheesi, arguing loudly, and my grandmother occasionally throwing Gracie out of her room with a "Git outta here, ya damned moron!"

Gracie called Grandmother "the bad lady." And after my Grandmother broke her hip again and spent the last three years of her life stuck in bed or in her chair, Gracie would walk into Grandmother's room clutching a pile of freshly ironed laundry in a triumphant show-and-tell, demonstrating how she was living a productive life while Grandmother was stuck. Grandmother would stare down at her paper and pretend she didn't see Gracie. And of course I'd play one off against the other.

"Gracie?"

"Yes, dalin?"

"Grandmother says you don't iron very well."

"She is a bad woman! I iron lovely, dalin."

"I know you do, but she says you should not be allowed to iron any more."

"She is wicked."

And: "Grandma?"

"Git outta here, ya brazen brat!"

"Okay, but Gracie said you cheat."

"I don't care what some retard says!"

Gracie was my coconspirator. When I was fourteen and got a Super-8 movie camera, Gracie was my main actress. The dramatic scene where Gracie got hit by the car worked fine, except that the blood mix accidentally got in Gracie's eyes, and since it was red oil paint thinned with turpentine, I had to abandon filming, though her initial reaction fit my plot well since she was screaming very realistically. But that ruined her ability to "die" because she kept yelling at me that I'd blinded her and to "take me to Mei Fuh," and wouldn't lie still. Mei Fuh was what Gracie called my mother. (It was Mom's name in Chinese, and for some reason Gracie learned it and always called her that.)

When the spastics next door got a small swimming pool installed on their property, The Ladies forbade anybody but the spastics to use the pool. This seemed grossly unfair. The pool was ridiculously small, but it was the only pool anywhere near us, and being banned disappointed me. So I would sneak over at night to swim. And once I took Gracie.

It was about 11 PM. Gracie didn't have a bathing suit, so she went in her underwear; a large white bra and a pair of bloomer-type panties. Gracie panicked once I got her in, though the pool was barely four feet deep. Her bloomers floated up around her and seemed to suddenly have the volume of a parachute. She began to shriek. I tried to haul her out. She slipped on the ladder. When she came to the surface, she let out a loud yell followed by "You are so naughty, dalin!" repeated furiously at increasing volume. Then her false teeth came out and I had to dive to look for them in the dark.

Lights went on in Chalet Bellevue. I tried to tug, push, and pull Gracie out, but her wet soft flesh, her limp leg and arm, and my panic made it impossible. So I bolted and hid under the hedge. Moments later, Rosemary, one of the fiercest of the three ladies, found Gracie more or less naked and spluttering incoherently in the pool. Rosie demanded explanations and didn't get any, because Gracie was being loyal to me. Rosie had to go back inside to wake one of the other ladies up to help her fish Gracie out.

They got her back to our chalet and, of course, moments later Dad was looking for me. By then I was in bed pretending to sleep, but Dad knew. I told him what I'd done and he laughed. And Dad refused to punish me, other than making me promise not to endanger Gracie again. Dad was as resentful of the ladies as I was for not allowing me to swim in their pool.

21

Most L'Abri students were bright balanced people. A few were not. People with mental problems were the minority at L'Abri, but they found a welcome. I grew up experiencing a series of friendships with the sorts of people living in our house (or in the other L'Abri chalets) that most boys would only meet in the street when accosted by a homeless man or woman. There was Mr. Hamburger from England, who had been lobotomized and who would periodically throw himself down the mountainside in a half-hearted suicide attempt. There were the several students who were convinced that they were demon-possessed and heard voices. There were some who would sit and cry for no reason, or yell out in church. A few had done time in prison. So it seemed normal to have Gracie and other less-than-perfect people in our house, just as it seemed normal to have the occasional unwed mother stay with us.

Our "single mothers" were sometimes accompanied by Mom, or another worker, to the hospital in Aigle for the delivery. Sin was sin; but since we were all sinners who had fallen very short of the glory of God, there was no stigma attached to pregnancy. Nor was there a stigma attached to mental retardation, or mental illness.

I saw that my parents' compassion was consistent. Their idea of ministry was to extend a hand of kindness, and to truly practice the rule of treating others as you would be treated. It was such a powerful demonstration that it gave me a lifelong picture of what Christian behavior and love can and should be.

My parents were not advocating compassion that someone else would carry out with tax dollars, or at arm's length, but rather they opened their home. The result was that those gathered around our table represented a cross-section of humanity and intellectual ability, from mental patients to Oxford students and all points of need in between. My mother and father marshaled arguments in favor of God, the Bible, and the saving work of Jesus Christ. But no words were as convincing as their willingness to lay material possessions, privacy, and time on the line, sometimes at personal risk and always with the understanding that if they were being taken advantage of, that was fine, too.

Between my sisters' pregnancies and the several unwed girls' pregnancies, not to mention many of the workers' wives' pregnancies, baby-making was something I was completely familiar with. For a woman to be pregnant seemed normal and wonderful. I loved being allowed to place my hands on those huge bellies and feel the babies kick. I never heard a judgmental, unkind, or even condescending word spoken about our unwed mothers. In fact, my parents would express fury when they talked about "some Christian parents" who were "ashamed of their daughter" and sent them to L'Abri to be out of the way during an embarrassing pregnancy. Dad let it be known that if anyone in L'Abri had a problem with his nonjudgmental attitude, they could leave.

I remember one young woman in particular. Jan was a

lovely breezy twenty-year-old. She had long brown hair and a freckled face and was an old-fashioned tomboy. She used to sit with her long tan legs splayed wide open and frankly push her cotton print dress down between them to be modest but never even pretended to cross her legs.

I was about eight or nine when she came to L'Abri. She stayed the better part of a year. Jan spent hours telling me how she had installed a truck engine in her car and used to race boys from the one stoplight to the crossroads in her small Michigan town. She loved the fact that she could always "blow them off the map" with that truck engine.

Jan was a mechanic, and her dad was, too. Jan was at L'Abri because her father was also an elder in their local Reformed Presbyterian church and didn't want to be humiliated by his daughter's pregnancy. Mom and Dad were enraged against her father on her behalf. Jan was one of the best people, and certainly one of the most attractive people, I have ever met.

After Jan came home from the Aigle Hospital—Mom went with her for the delivery—she stayed with us for about six more months. I would help bathe the baby, watch Jan breast-feed from hugely swollen breasts, and I noticed that she leaked milk. She always laughed about the way her blouse would stain. Jan would tell me all about how she planned to raise her son.

Jan became a helper. There were some evangelicals visiting who said they were a bit shocked that a L'Abri helper would be a single unwed mother. What kind of example was that? Dad went ballistic, as did Mom.

22

Dad could be screaming at Mom one minute, or just bluntly muttering "I'll kill myself one of these days," and ten minutes later he would be down in the dining room earnestly answering questions from the guests. They never had any inkling about his state of mind—except when, once in a while, the yelling could be heard or when a tea tray or vase would be hurled down the stairs or over the balcony. But people pretended nothing was happening, except of course for Mom, who would work a sanitized version of her interminable fights with Dad into her talks as a demonstration of the way God was working in their lives "in spite of Fran's weaknesses."

I once thought Dad's ability to present two very different faces to the world—one to his family and one to the public—was gross hypocrisy. I think differently now. I believe Dad was a very brave man.

Suffering from bouts of depression, I have come to understand that the choice is to carry on or not, no matter how I feel. And since my dad literally had no close friends, let alone a confessor or therapist to talk to, his suffering was in near-total isolation. When that bleak grayness envelops everything for a few days or hours and sucks all the joy and air out of a day, as a writer I can just shut the world out, if I want, and retire to some inner cave and nurse my depression. Dad craved privacy, too, but his work *was* people. And Dad never sought counseling.

I was lucky enough to go to the same therapist (once every two weeks for about a year) who had helped my son Francis cope with, then overcome, his severe childhood dyslexia. I've also been fortunate to have several very close male and female friends about my age—not counting family and work-related friends—who have stuck with me through all the twists and turns of what feels like a long life. And even with the luxury of that support, I've found many days hard to get through.

Dad was incredibly alone. I can't think of one nonwork-related friend, let alone a contemporary, who he kept up with. Dad had adoring followers, co-workers, and family, but no equals, no one who knew him who he had stayed in contact with, no friend from school days, no one to pour out his troubles to, no one to tell him he was full of shit from time to time.

The only private space my father had was in his bedroom. And he spent every moment he could cloistered there. If he stepped out and went downstairs, a group of guests would instantly gather around him and follow him.

"Dr. Schaeffer, I have a question. . . ."

Dad sat in a small rocking chair pulled up to his bed, which he used as his desk. He worked on a tray, hunched over his papers. There were ink stains on the thick yellow wool bedspread. (Dad used three different colors of ink to mark his Bible and make notes in the margin.)

Dad's bedroom/office was invaded by the voices of the students talking in the rooms below. The more students there were staying at L'Abri, the louder Dad turned up his music. I grew up thinking that classical music always has be played so loud that the speakers bounce and that it is normal to play blasting music ten, twelve, or fifteen hours a day. My room was next to Mom and Dad's bedroom. Dad's wall of deafening music turned my room into a concert hall. It is rare for me to hear a piece of classical music I can't hum along with. (Even today, whenever I hear classical music played at anything below full blast, it sounds wrong.) "Dad's music," as I will always think of the classical canon, became part of me, as if it had been surgically embedded in my head. I still feel close to him whenever I listen to any one of his hundreds of "favorite pieces."

We always knew what to give Dad for birthdays and Christmas. The trick was to sneak into his bedroom to try to find what pieces he didn't already have or, sometimes, to check on what records were so scratched that he might like a replacement. (Dad's method of putting a record on a turntable was to slap it down like a pancake being flipped in a skillet, then drop the needle wherever it happened to land.)

The music would shelter Dad from students' voices, but it didn't lift his depressions. However, I don't recall Dad canceling any appearances in his daily routine or on a speaking trip. But I do recall many a day when he became so grim and silent that he seemed to be dead.

Dad did contemplate suicide. He sometimes spoke in detail about hanging himself. I went through my childhood knowing that there were two things we children were never to tell anyone. The first was that Dad got insanely angry with my mother; the second was that from time to time he threatened suicide.

Mom was naturally gregarious. But Dad's idea of what he had to do with his life was horribly at odds with his introverted personality. And the fact he carried on doing what he believed to be right—opening his home—was a brave and wholly admirable thing.

Dad's dedication took a toll. His basic demeanor was one of being chronically annoyed, as if his world was filled with buzzing flies he wanted to swat. He "swatted" them by being a habitual complainer. He would never go anywhere, from a vacation to a speaking trip, without a litany of moaning and groaning about how tired he was, how he would never make it, how "I just *can't* do this, Edith!"

But later, when it counted most, Dad proved that he was made of brave material. In his midsixties, after my father was diagnosed with lymphoma, he suddenly quit all his petty complaining. For the six years he was fighting for his life, Dad never said a word about the discomfort and pain caused by the interminable chemotherapy sessions, bone-biopsy punctures, lung-fluid draining, weight loss, collapses, emergency procedures, nausea, and diarrhea. His stoic silence surprised us. And Dad never once talked about suicide during his illness.

My father met his death fearlessly, clear-eyed and with no self-pity. Dad didn't become any more or less spiritual than he had always been. He had never laced his speech with the-Lord-this or the-Lord-that jargon. (My father always dismissed such typical evangelical pietisms as "all that superspiritual stuff I hate.") And Dad never expressed any fear of death. He apologized for the wrongs he remembered doing, put his affairs in order, and was less demanding than he had ever been.

23

When I was about nine, Dad and I started taking hikes together. He reserved one Monday a month as "my day with Frank." (Everyone called me Frankie but Dad.) I loved those times.

At home, it was as if Dad was an actor on stage, always performing for the students, always "on," always certain, always bold. I had almost never been alone with my father before. Who he really was—when not around the students—came as something of a shock.

Out of the limelight, Dad was quiet. He was sweet. Above all, he was humble and considerate. And what moved him wasn't theology, but beauty.

"Look at the light!" he would exclaim, as a ray of sun broke through the clouds above some high valley. Or "Stop! Listen!" as we stepped over a stream, and Dad would pause to enjoy the sound of the water splashing into a rocky pool.

Dad is clearest in my mind plodding steadily ahead on a trail, his sturdy pistonlike legs passing over the steep path effortlessly. He would turn, stop, wait for me to catch up, and sometimes hug me or tousle my hair before we walked on.

We would set out on misty mornings when the mountains were shrouded in fog. Dew clung to the twigs; the mud on the trail would be slick. Water dripped from the pine branches, and Dad always led. I followed mile after mile as he kept up a steady pace, the same uphill as down. Years later, when Dad had cancer and told me he was getting out of breath just walking up stairs, I knew the cancer was going to kill him. Dad never broke a sweat, never gasped for breath, no matter how far we walked.

We'd hike from about seven in the morning until five in the afternoon, then take one of the many narrow-gauge trains that crisscross the Swiss Alps, or one of the many postal buses, back to some town, then the train to Aigle, then the small train to Ollon, and finally "our" bus up to Huémoz. Or sometimes we'd use the same network to take us twenty or so miles from home, then walk back. Once in a while, we'd stay out overnight in some clean little room over a café.

Dad always carried maps and laboriously marked where we had walked by tracing over the trails on the hiking maps with ink. One of my most treasured possessions is my collection of Dad's tattered and heavily marked-up hiking maps. When I look at them, I sense my father much more clearly than when I open one of his books and read a few lines.

On our hikes, we would talk about Dad's childhood in Philadelphia, or his bitter mother and how difficult it was having her live with us, or his weaknesses and how sorry he was for them, perhaps after he'd been fighting with Mom the day before and knew I knew he had been. Left to himself, Dad never talked about theology or God, let alone turned some conversation into a pious lesson the way Mom did. Left to himself, reality seemed enough for Dad. Besides, this was a day off, and God and the Bible were work.

We talked about the Second World War and how the Swiss mined all the tunnels and bridges so that the Germans didn't invade. We talked about Dad when he was a Boy Scout troop leader. Dad told me about shooting rats with his .22 rifle at his college, Hampden-Sydney, about getting in a fight there with a huge drunk student and banging his head on the ground to knock him out, about the deal he cut with the "unsaved" students in his dorm: Dad agreed to put them to bed on Friday nights, after they passed out on the way back from bars, if they would go to church with him on Sunday mornings.

Dad taught me the Hampden-Sydney football fight song, which we would sometimes sing together so loudly—"I'm a tiger born and a tiger bred, and when I die I'll be a tiger dead! Rah-Rah Hampden-Sydney, Rah-Rah Hampden-Sydney, Rah-Rah Hampden-Sydney, *Rah, Rah, Rah!*"—that our voices echoed from the cliffs in many a high valley. Sometimes we'd stop for a rest and Dad would show me wrestling holds, like the half-nelson, chokeholds, or where to hit someone so they would go down, or how to get in close, grab, twist, break bones, and incapacitate someone bigger than you (a lesson in fighting dirty and for keeps that came in handy several times later in life).

We talked about the Depression and how, as a teen, Dad had worked in an RCA factory and was part of a strike when the foreman kept speeding up the conveyor belt and forcing them to work faster and faster, and how he was paid twenty cents an hour and felt lucky to get that. We talked about the Soviets, and if America was strong enough to stop them taking over the world. But most of the time we hiked for many miles without speaking a word.

When I was fifteen and on a hike with Dad, I confronted him over how he treated Mom. Years later, Mom said that after that he began to behave better. Maybe this was true, or maybe she was just being kind to him and to me.

Sometimes I meet former L'Abri guests who tell me they went on a hike with my father. (He would occasionally take a student.) They tell me about the deep, long philosophical or theological discussion they had with Dad on this or that memorable hike. They say how privileged they feel at having gotten "so close to him." I want to tell them that if Dad was talking about his usual subjects, they never did get close to him. They only saw him when he was "on."

Once in a while, I could tell that Dad was waiting for the right moment to instruct me. Then he would act serious and reserved until he got it off his chest.

"Mom says you aren't trying very hard in your schoolwork."

"Yes, Dad."

"Are you trying at all?"

"Yes, Dad."

"Well, try harder, or I'll have to spank you."

"Yes, Dad."

And that was it. His duty done, Dad seemed relieved. He had of course been put up to this by Mom, who sometimes would say "You have to speak to Frankie, Fran." And Dad would wait until we were on a hike to do his duty.

After that, he'd relax. And the mountains would seem to slowly roll past, subtly changing shape, narrowing or fattening depending on the perspective from wherever we were on the trail.

Sometimes we had adventures.

"Dad, that looks like a bull."

"I don't think so. They wouldn't put him here in an open field."

"Okay."

Moments later: "Frank! It *is* a bull! Get behind me!"

Dad waving his walking stick, back to a tree. Me, hiding behind him.

"We'll need to work our way to the fence, then dive under the barbed wire!"

"Okay, Dad!"

Running, slipping in the wet grass, noticing a cloud of flies rising from the cow shit I've just landed in, the young bull running around us in circles bellowing, Dad turning to yell at it, holding his cane out like a saber, me picking up a stick and also waving it, Dad and I laughing hysterically after we get under the fence and, moments later, both getting the shakes.

I'd count the hours until we'd stop to eat the wonderful sandwiches Mom had made with crusty fresh bread. In the summer, she always put in big slices of peeled cucumbers from our garden, or peeled carrot slivers. They had just been picked by her, and the bread had still been warm when she sent a student to the village bakery that morning to get it.

It was a big moment when Dad opened his little leather backpack and pulled out the sandwiches, along with the salt and pepper he always carried in two old aluminum film cans with twist-off tops, and his small sheath knife with the antler handle. If we were near a village, we'd stop at the café and order apple juice for me and a coffee for Dad, and eat our picnic while some old farmer eyed us suspiciously and sipped his white wine.

24

Lynnette accepted Jesus. She became one of those great salvation stories, a "true testimonial to the power of God," because later that night, the same night her name was written in The Book of Life—presuming that she was not going to backslide and thereby prove she wasn't of the Elect after all—Lynnette, who was a ballet dancer, danced before the Lord.

Actually, she danced before the Lord and us on the terrace in front of the chalet, the place we had hot-dog roasts every Saturday night in the summer and outdoor discussions. Lynnette danced in the moonlight while we stood on the second-floor balcony above and watched. She danced for joy at her newfound faith in Christ. My sisters, several guests, and Mom wept.

Usually when someone got saved, Susan just played the "Hallelujah Chorus" part of Handel's *Messiah* on the record player. But in this case, Lynnette danced to the strange and disturbing music from Stravinsky's *Firebird*. (Dad had the record in his collection, though it was not one of his favorites.) This piece was chosen by Lynnette because she had danced in the *Firebird* ballet in London. Her interpretation was particularly moving (at least to Mom and my sisters), because Lynnette announced that now that she had accepted Jesus, she was feeling led to leave the ballet and to go into "full-time Christian work," maybe at L'Abri, or perhaps back in London where she might use her flat (an apartment with a rather swanky address at Sloane Square) as a "L'Abri base" for my dad to hold discussions in.

"I'll never dance again," said Lynnette.

"But oh, Lynnette," answered my Mom with tears streaming down her face, "the Lord says that what we give up for Him will be returned to us tenfold! Someday you will dance again in Heaven before the Throne of God! And you will dance *forever* with your new incorruptible body, and you will fulfill all that talent He gave you!"

Lynnette and my sisters wept some more. It was one of those many beautiful moments my mother shared with the Praying Family in her next "Family Letter."

Lynnette's use of her London flat was the beginning of another chapter in the Lord's work. Lynnette was a wounded and desperate young woman when she came to L'Abri. Her mother had committed suicide. And that was how Lynnette got her lovely flat at the good address: She had inherited it. And so that was also another example, as Mom explained of how everything, even tragedy, seemed to help our work in God's great plan.

Mom and Dad's English trips became more and more frequent, and I collected a whole album of postcards from all over the British Isles. And Lynnette teamed up with Cynthia—my sometime tutor—and Hillary Schlesinger (the pretty younger sister of the famous English movie director John Schlesinger) to organize discussions Dad would preside over. And a few years later, Susan and Ranald moved to London and opened a branch of L'Abri at 52 Cleveland Road. Then, a few years after that, they moved to a country manor house in Greatham, an hour south of London, and started a full-blown English L'Abri and soon had almost as many students staying with them as there were in the original Swiss L'Abri.

In the early days of the "English work," Mom and Dad always used the same method. They would go to the home of a L'Abri convert like Lynnette. The convert would then "open their home" and invite their friends to talk with this remarkable American Christian. The result was that Mom and Dad were setting up what amounted to cells of followers all over England. And because there was always someone opposing the Lord's will in these matters, an anti-Christian parent, a scoffing academic community, a Church of England liberal priest, who tried to undermine someone's faith after Mom and Dad left, these forays into England had a somewhat clandestine air about them. Mom and Dad would come home and report as if bringing news from behind enemy lines.

Englishmen and Englishwomen began to "become Christians." And looking back at that time, I am amazed at how little I knew about the fact that maybe, just maybe, there were *already* Christians in the British Isles, *before* my parents got there. As a child, the way I took what was being said about my parents' English trips was that before my parents went to England, there were no Real Christians there. In the misty past, there had been Puritans and some notable martyrs, when the evil Roman Catholics killed people for believing right; but today, in the present, we and we alone were taking the Truth to lost England.

The people who "got saved" were not just any old kind of English people. I never heard a Cockney accent until I was in English boarding school and I talked to Peg and Fred, the embittered, downtrodden and perpetually angry working-class caretakers. The only British accents I heard at L'Abri (at least in the early days) were the plumy upper-class tones honed in Oxford and Cambridge, where Mom and Dad often went, as well as to London, to conduct discussions hosted by students who wanted to share what they had learned with their friends.

25

My parents would begin or end any conversation of any length or seriousness, any event, meal, or get-together with prayer. They would meet people on trains and buses, or just in the hall of the chalet, talk for a while, perhaps learn of some problem, and, nine times out of ten, suddenly exclaim "Do you mind if we take this to the Lord?" or "Would you like to pray about this?" or just issue a declarative "Let's pray!"

Then they would launch into a prayer that was earnest and full of theological content, and in Mom's case unbelievably long, so long that Dad would often shoot her annoyed glances. People would shift from foot to foot, and if there were several people standing with Mom when she was praying, and I was lucky enough to be on the fringe and not stuck next to her, I might sidle away.

Mom sometimes would hold forth in prayer for—*literally*!—forty-five minutes or more. And sometimes, if I kept my eyes closed the whole time the way I was supposed to, when I finally opened them and looked up, I was dizzy.

The excuse for the prayer, for instance the information that someone was ill, would get briefly mentioned. Then a lot of solid theology would also be mixed in. And since presumably my parents believed that God already *had* correct theology, and *didn't* need instruction, it was clear that they were praying *at* the person with them, not *to* God, because God didn't need to be told he was sovereign, the Creator, loved each of us but hated sin. Nor did he need to be reminded that we are all sinners, and that only his son's "finished work on the cross" could save us.

Prayers began "Dear Heavenly Father" and continued with a litany of requests. When prayed out loud, the prayers were often a not-so-subtle vehicle for sermons. These sermons (masquerading as prayer) were for the good of those here on earth who were eavesdropping on what was purporting to be a conversation with God but was really a way to say things to Dad, that Mom didn't dare say out loud, or a way for Dad or Mom to preach *at* an unbeliever.

Praying out loud was also a way of advancing one's case, the advantage being that no one dared interrupt you or argue back. Moreover, prayer was a way to tell God to behave, to stick with being the God we said he was, and a way to remind God of his "many promises" so he wouldn't try to do anything odd or theologically inconsistent.

"Dear Heavenly Father, we just come to Thee to thank Thee for the fact that Thou art a Sovereign Lord Who has seen from before the beginning of time who You wouldst ordain to save. We just thank Thee that Thou art a good and loving Father Who has chosen us to serve Thee and to demonstrate Thine existence to an unbelieving world. . . ."

All the basic precepts were right there in my parent's prayers. Now God knew what he was supposed to be doing—predestining each individual to be saved or lost and doing this from before creation—so we could relax. Prayer was a way to remind God not to let his attention wander or forget that we, and we only, really understood what he was supposed to be doing. So we prayed *at* him, too. The logic of those prayers, if one was reading between the lines, was something like this:

"Dear Heavenly Father, in Your Word You say that when two or three are gathered together, You will be in the midst of them. Well, we're gathered here, so do what we're telling You to do because we have You over a barrel and can quote Your own book back at you! And in case You're thinking of weaseling out of this deal, we claim Your promises, and because You can't break any of those since You wrote it all in the Bible, You'll do what we say, and You'll do it NOW! Amen!"

On days of prayer (Mondays), Mom signed up for several hours, but Dad only put his name on a half-hour box on the prayer chart posted in the kitchen. Mom would dismissively say "Poor Fran just prays from his little list, but that is certainly *not* enough for me! I mean, my dear, I *really* want to *TALK* to the Lord! Would you only want to have half an hour of conversation with your best friend?!"

I sometimes wondered if God ever tried to duck out of the room when he saw Mom coming. We each took at least a half hour; Susan and Debby took more than me, more like a whole hour. The workers signed up, and some of the guests did, too. That way, someone was constantly praying from seven AM to seven PM. But during my half hour, I just sat in my room and stared at the wall and couldn't figure out why it was a good idea to tell God stuff he already knew.

Theologically speaking, we believed in an absolutely powerful omnipotent and sovereign Lord. But in practice, our God had to be begged and encouraged to carry out the simplest tasks, for instance to keep moving the hearts of the local Swiss authorities to renew our residency permits.

How exactly was this supposed to work? God was in charge, but he wouldn't do anything for us unless we believed he would do it. But if he didn't do anything, what reason was there to believe?

We lacked the faith to pray effectively and make God do stuff. So we prayed for the faith to make God give us faith to make him do stuff. But getting enough faith was the biggest problem, so we prayed for the faith we needed to pray for faith. But how much faith did it take to pray to have enough faith to pray for faith? And if God knew you wanted faith, why didn't he just give it to you? It was like spending all your time calling directory information for phone numbers that you aren't allowed to call unless you can guess the number right without asking.

What is strange is that today, in my totally "backslidden" state and long after I rejected the faith of my youth, or rather the faith I was supposed to have had in my youth, and have become "horribly secular" and write for "liberal publications" and have "questioned everything," I *do* pray a lot. The habit of faith can't be rejected so easily. Mom won.

It doesn't matter what I think. It is a question of what I am.

PART II

EDUCATION

26

When I was ten, my parents despaired of trying to homeschool me. Susan pushed them to send me to school, any school. And since it was far too late to put me in the rigorous Swiss public school system, they sent me to a local private school, the ludicrously misnamed Gai Matin (Happy Morning).

I went there because the school offered a class taught in English. The school was owned and run by Madame Moraz, a robust tweed-clad, child-hating, wide-hipped French woman married to a small subservient Swiss husband who trotted at her side, the way a worried pilot fish accompanies a shark. The school was in Chésières, a village a couple of miles up the road from Huémoz next to the ski resort of Villars. Chésières was mostly chalets and barns, but my school was a five-story stone-and-stucco building with big picture windows and a stupendous view of the mountains. An old red tram ran from Villars to Chésières and made its final stop in front of the school.

There were about forty or fifty of us. The student body was mostly made up of the absentmindedly conceived offspring of globetrotting euro-trash, children of Milanese businessmen who once a year drove up to Switzerland from Milan to visit their mistress's sons or daughters and check on their Swiss bank accounts, and half a dozen or so Arab oil-sheiks' children, as well as a few French and Swiss boys and girls too dim to succeed in the Swiss or French public schools. There were also the sons and daughters of a few American diplomats and international businessmen, and some kids who had been institutionalized virtually from birth, when they were dumped into local homes for children at the age of six months and later "graduated" to Gai Matin. (There was even a school in Les Ecovets, half a mile from Chésières, that took kids as boarders from three months of age.)

Unlike the boarders at Gai Matin, I lived at home and walked the thirty minutes up the road every morning, or sometimes hitchhiked. It took fifteen minutes to walk/run down the mountain on the way home. And in winter, I'd bring my sled and careen home in about five minutes, using the footpath that ran steeply down our mountain cutting a straight line through the big lazy hairpins of the main road.

The best part of going to a "real school" was that we got to ski in Bretaye above Villars every afternoon, from mid-December through late April. From Bretaye, on clear days, which, at least in golden memory, was every day it was not snowing, you could see Mont Blanc peeking up over the range of mountains that sat directly across from our chalet, dominating the lower part of the Rhône Valley. There were almost always several meters of fresh powder, a dazzling blue sky, hot sun that would burn you faster than summer sunshine, and no lift lines because we were skiing on weekday afternoons.

Except for the whirr and jingle of the cable running over the lift's pulleys, the silence was almost complete. If the lifts stopped, which they did from time to time if someone fell and was being dragged by a T-bar or had trouble getting into a chairlift, all you would hear was the cry of mountain ravens, skiers' voices floating up from below, and far distant sounds from the Rhône Valley, maybe a train whistle if the wind was right, but so faint that it sounded as if it were coming from another universe.

On some days I wouldn't bother to ski back to the school but asked permission to head down through the forest and skied right up to my front door, through new unbroken snow, absolutely alone for a blessed hour, completely free. Sometimes I would play a little game with God. I would radically alter my path, make illogical and sudden turns and stops, just to see if I could momentarily get ahead of predestination, do something God wasn't expecting. But I always had the feeling it wasn't working. And out in the wilderness I was glad enough to believe that the Lord was watching over me. I knew that if I fell and broke my leg, I might be stuck outside for a night or worse.

Skiing was a great equalizer. On skis I was very fast, didn't limp, and never even thought about my bad leg. In fact, I always hated to take off my skis and take that first step, feel my left leg stomp down on the heel, earthbound after I had been flying down the mountain free as if I was already in my perfected resurrected body that Mom told me I'd have some day.

When I was four and just beginning to recover from polio, Dad, against doctor's orders, took me skiing before I could balance again on my atrophied left leg and walk. I literally learned to ski before I could walk, at least the second time around. Dad gave me confidence. From then on, I assumed that I had no disability, just a nasty-looking left leg and a limp, something I could overcome with a little effort.

When I taught my daughter Jessica to ski, and we were snowplowing our way down the slopes above Villars, the memory of Dad teaching me flooded back. I actually couldn't remember his teaching me to ski, but the feel of holding three-year-old Jessica and placing her skis inside mine, and guiding her down the slope while I gripped her between my knees, revived a kind of kinetic memory. Suddenly I knew just how my father had felt, teaching his little boy. I could sense the tenderness as he held me up, bracing me against his legs, showing me how to compensate for a leg that wouldn't work, to put my weight on the right leg, turn, and pull the other leg around by shifting my body weight.

At Gai Matin, I took ski lessons with the advanced class. I won several downhill and giant slalom races against other schools. I also learned to skate and played ice hockey, the only drawback being that my bad ankle would wobble even in a specially reinforced skate boot.

Except for a couple of miserable and exceedingly fat Saudi brothers, I got on well with the other children. As for those fat Saudis, they would sometimes spit. Why they spit on me and the other children, I have no idea.

I cured their nasty habit after they had been spitting on me every time they passed while we were skating at the Villars rink. I cornered them in the locker room and punched each of the Arabs in the solar plexus, hard. They looked surprised, as if it had never occurred to them that anyone would do more than yell back. They both landed with a plop on the floor and began to wail like babies.

The sports-master-hockey-coach-math-teacher, a tall, forty-something bald and cadaverously wiry Frenchman, asked the fat Saudis why they were crying. When they told him, he grabbed me, spun me around, then kicked me in the bottom as hard as he could, sending me flying into the lockers as if I had just been drop-kicked through a goal. Then he asked for my side of the story. I told him that the boys had been spitting at me. He lit a cigarette and sucked down a huge drag—he was a chain-smoker and even smoked when coaching hockey, and in class—and stood staring down at me and blowing smoke through his enormous and widely flared nostrils that looked like the blackened openings to twin train tunnels. He asked several other students for their account and they said yes, the fat Arabs spit at everyone. Then he gathered about a dozen of us in a circle and told us to spit on "*Ces sale Arabes*" (these filthy Arabs), and after we all did, he kicked them hard in their fat behinds—they, too, went flying—and that was that.

The private Swiss "schools," tucked away by the dozen in practically every valley and on every mountainside, were crazy little fiefdoms with their own laws and were completely off the map as far as any normal discipline went. Madame Moraz played favorites. If you were on her good side, you could do anything you wanted. If you were on her bad side, she would organize elaborate public humiliation spectacles and laugh a barking grim laugh at the child being punished. One good way to gain her favor was to mock the offender as loudly and gleefully as possible.

The most routine punishment was to have to sit cross-legged outside Madame Moraz's study door while balancing a big Larousse dictionary on your head while every student who walked past was encouraged to jeer. Then there were the more extravagant public executions, including standing on your chair to show the class—in the case of the very little children—your wet pants, if you had wet yourself. Or she would make you stand up in the dining room and eat food you hated like liver or sauerkraut that you hadn't finished. Then she would ask the other students to take whatever food was left on their plates—the favorites, of course, didn't have to eat anything they didn't like—and pile those leavings on the offender's plate, while he or she tried to eat it all and got sick. And, of course, slapping, kicking, and pulling hair was par for the course, though ironically there was no formal spanking and in the school brochure—printed in at least a dozen languages, accompanied by lovely pictures of the mountains and wide-angle photographs of the school's interior that made all the rooms seem three times bigger than they were—it stated that corporal punishment was "against the founder's principles" and never used because she was "a follower of Gandhi," something my mother read to me by way of warning me to be on the look out for "Hindu influences."

The free-for-all of abuse that I saw was usual for the private schools in our area. When Debby was a child, she had learned about local private school "discipline" when Mr. Fausto, the gym teacher at Beau Soleil (Beautiful Sunshine)—another misnamed "school" a little way up the road from Gai Matin—broke her little finger by flinging a twenty-pound medicine ball at her repeatedly as a punishment for not catching it.

As for actual education, I didn't learn much more than I had in the old days with Cynthia and Susan. (Cynthia had moved back to London to do more language studies; and then, several years later, she did find her Korean and went to Korea, where she and her husband started a mission.)

All the classes at Gai Matin were in French, save one taught by Miss Spink. Miss Spink was a pink, curvaceous, Rubenesque young woman who wore tight bright pink sweaters, or jumpers as she called them, over wonderfully huge and bouncy breasts, tight knee-length tweed skirts, white blouses, and shiny black Wellingtons (rubber boots) on school walks, and little silver-colored slippers with roses painted on them when indoors, it being the rule that inside the school no one wore their outdoor shoes. She was probably twenty years old, had full lips, the creamy coloring of a Victorian English milk-maid, and thick strawberry-blonde hair, spoke lovely high-class English, and smiled all the time. I was in love with her.

Miss Spink came from a born-again English family who had recently left the weirdly cultic Closed Plymouth Brethren (the English version of the same group my aunt Janet had joined in America). One reason Miss Spink took the teaching job was to be near L'Abri, to strengthen her shaken post-Closed Plymouth Brethren faith. She came to Saturday night discussions and Sunday church. On one occasion, Miss Spink visited our chalet for church with her parents, people my mother later declared were a "real English gentleman and real lady."

The Spinks were wealthy art dealers and had been in the news for discovering a Rembrandt that Mr. Spink bought for twelve pounds and sold for a fortune. Miss Spink had a little brother my age who was in a boy's British boarding school. Miss Spink would tell me about how wonderful that school—Great Walstead—was in comparison to Gai Matin, and that it was a pity I could not go to a "real school, instead of this foreign sham."

Miss Spink played a big role in my life. She wasn't much good as a teacher and let her students more or less just mess about in her class, where those of us (about seven children) who were studying in English spent our days. But Miss Spink talked to my parents about Great Walstead. She said her brother was happy there, as was his cousin from the other branch of the Spink family. That other branch was even wealthier than Miss Spink's family and had also recently escaped the Closed Plymouth Brethren. The David Spinks—my teacher was one of the Robin Spinks—were gem, antique gold, silver, and rare coin dealers whose company, Spink and Sons, bore the impressive "By Appointment to Her Majesty the Queen" insignia.

Miss Spink talked to Mom about the fact that a boy of nearly eleven should be able to read and write a lot better than I could and that she thought boarding school would do wonders for me. Mom asked me if I wanted to go.

27

The idea of going to England fascinated me. I had never been there, but I had received a steady stream of books, postcards, letters, gifts, candies, and glowing accounts about the wonders of English life from Mom and Dad, as well as from the English guests who came to L'Abri. My room was filled with postcards of the Tower of London and the Queen and her guards at Buckingham Palace. And my favorite books were by English authors. Our greatest heroes were the English martyrs killed by the Roman Catholics and described so glowingly in Fox's *Book of Martyrs*, wherein there were grim and wonderfully descriptive accounts of our Protestant saints' excruciating deaths, as Protestants went willingly, even joyfully, to the stake and were burnt to a crisp because they would not bow to the pope. Latimer was the best. As the flames licked off his skin, he declared himself to be "a candle lit that will never be put out in England!"

And I would get to ride on a jet airplane! Maybe I would even eat at Lyon's Corner House Restaurant, where Dad had once had supper just after the end of the war, when the only meat you could order was whale steak that tasted of oily blubber. I would have proper English afternoon tea with crumpets, a food I'd heard about in books but never tasted. I would eat kippers and real marmalade and Devonshire cream, and all the other literary delicacies that everyone from Bertie Wooster to E. Nesbitt's children heroes in the *Would Be Goods* seemed to love so much, washed down with tea or ginger beer, a drink that the children in the books craved and that Mom said she tasted once but that was hard to describe. *And* I would be in a country where they all spoke English! I would be in a country where they played cricket, and if I played cricket I would look just like the young Prince Charles as featured on a postcard Mom had sent me. *And* I would be in a schoolboy's uniform also just like the young prince, with a school cap, and wearing shorts and a blazer as well as a shirt and school tie. Best of all, I would be doing something normal, be like other boys my age. Mom said that someday I might even be able to wear an old school tie.

"What is an old school tie, Mom?"

"Men who have been to the finest schools wear them."

"Why?"

"That way, when they meet another man who went to Cambridge or Oxford, they recognize each other."

"Oh."

"You see, dear, with the Lord having opened this door through the Spinks' offer to pay for your tuition—at least for the first year, then we'll just pray the Lord meets our needs—you are going to be able to go to a school where you will meet boys from fine English families. And who knows but that there will be a future Hudson Taylor there [founder of the China Inland Mission my grandparents had served in] or a future Winston Churchill!"

"Oh?"

"And someday, after you have gone to English schools and then on to Oxford or Cambridge, you'll be wearing an old school tie and will be moving in those sorts of circles. And the

Lord will really be able to use you. And you will be the sort of Englishman that. . . ."

"I'm going to become *English*?!"

"Well, not actually, you will have an American passport still, but having gone to the best English schools you will be one of them, be part of what they call an old boys' club."

"What is that?"

"It's the association of men who come from the upper classes who naturally know each other and are able to use those contacts in a way that benefits them. And those contacts you'll have with the finest English gentlemen will last you a lifetime. And who knows how the Lord will be able to use you."

"I might want to be a doctor."

"That would be fine, as long as the Lord leads you into that field. You want to be where *He* wants you. In any case, you'll be moving in the right circles. You will not be like poor Fran."

"Why?"

"Your father has had to make do. But you will be able to begin life with all the advantages and the good manners of an English gentleman and the contacts the Lord gives you and the education that your father never had. But when you get there, begin as you mean to go on and be a witness to the other boys. The Spinks say the headmaster is a real believer. The Spinks speak very highly of him."

I was excited, terrified, and homesick even before I left. What would the other boys think about my polio leg? And how would the school uniform, shorts and knee socks, look on me? Would the knee sock on my left leg fall down because the calf was atrophied? Miss Spink said not to worry. "There is no bullying allowed at Great Walstead. You'll love it."

28

After the first term, I always traveled alone to and from Switzerland. But that first afternoon, Mom and I were driven over to the school from the David Spinks' farm a few miles away in Seven Oaks, where we had spent the night.

It was a bright sunny day. The lawn had just been cut and smelled good. The main house of the school seemed huge. I was seeing everything through a blur of tears. I felt as if the sights and sounds belonged to someone else, that somehow this was just *not* real. What had I done in agreeing to leave home? I burst into tears and, feeling ashamed, dragged Mom into the cover of the rhododendrons next to the school.

"Please don't leave me, Mom!" I was saying between sobs.

"I won't if you really don't want me to. Dad will be furious if I bring you home now that it is all arranged, but if you really don't want me to, I won't."

"I guess I do want to stay, but I wish I didn't have to."

"I love you so much, darling," said Mom, wiping her tears. "I'll write every day, and you write to me, too. The term will fly past; then you'll be home for the vacation. And you'll have so many wonderful stories."

Mom left me crying in the rhododendrons. Eventually Spink One—since there were two Spinks in the school, they were designated "Spink One" and "Spink Two"—my appointed "new-boy's shadow," found me, and we went in to tea. I hoped my face wasn't too puffy. But no one was looking at me. A new boy was the lowest form of life.

During my first term, I was often in Matron's small sitting room huddled over her single-filament electric heater while she offered words of comfort. She sat at a tidy rolltop desk filling in health certificates or folding mountains of laundry along with the two assistant matrons who would periodically march back and forth to the various dormitories where we boys would later find our socks and underwear neatly piled at the end of our beds, ready to be put away in our lockers.

Matron must have been in her late twenties. Her assistants were probably in their early twenties, perhaps even late teens. They wore pale green housecoats and were pretty and unfailingly kind. When our nametags came off, the matrons sewed them back on. When we missed our mothers and cried, Matron gave us tea and digestive biscuits. When we were ill, she nursed us in sick bay or drove us in her little red Mini-Minor up the road to the Lewis cottage hospital to get stitched. Matron also referred boys to the headmaster for punishment when she felt the need, say after repeatedly catching one of us talking after lights out.

During my first term, my favorite place in the school, besides Matron's sitting room, was the library. I sat at a huge oak table that covered half the floor, and at which Prime Minister Lloyd George had once presided over meetings during World War I when he occasionally used our school as one of many secret meeting places. I would pore over the huge atlas. Actually, what I pored over was the double-page fold-out map of Switzerland. I traced the road from the Rhône Valley up to where I knew our chalet's front door was and fell into homesick daydreams.

Mom wrote to me every day, and the desperation of my homesickness during my first term can be measured by the fact that I even read her pages and pages of spiritual advice and her litany of martyrdom, wherein Dad was always the ogre, L'Abri such hard work, and she always the long-suffering heroine. Dad wrote postcards about once a month, but sometimes he would scrawl a hasty "I love you, boy" at the bottom of Mom's seven-or-eight-page letters.

I was the only American at Great Walstead, an outsider who had never even lived in his own country. I had grown up in a Swiss mission, a place even less explicable to the other boys than America. At first I felt as if I were walking around in a cage, peering through the bars at the other boys' normal lives. But Miss Spink had told the truth about the no-bullying ethic of the place.

Great Walstead (GW) reflected the character of its headmaster, Mr. Gordon Parke, and his wife Eunice. Mr. Parke was fair, kind, decent, friendly, open, and admired. Where Madame Moraz had played favorites, Mr. Parke was impartial, treating each boy with a firm respectful kindness that was the best example of leadership I have ever seen. Where my father hid a deeply flawed character and huddled reclusively in his bedroom-study, Mr. Parke lived out in the open.

GW was the place where I discovered who I wanted to be. I wanted to be like Mr. Parke. He had a handsome, symmetrical, square-chinned face with deep frown lines, perhaps from his time at sea as an officer in the Royal Navy. He was usually smiling. His idea of being a headmaster was to be unfailingly cheerful, play riotous games on the school lawn with us boys on Sunday afternoons, get sincerely angry when provoked—his face would flush, and he would yell. He was not just the law, but a god. And his wife Eunice was a goddess and, in her way, even more feared and loved.

Mrs. Parke was small and athletic and had birdlike sharp pretty features, bright dark eyes, and a natural authority, but with the added threat of Mr. Parke's wrath if anyone showed his beloved wife the least disrespect. Together they ran the best and happiest school I was ever in or have ever seen or heard about. The boys did not ask about my bad leg. And even though I was an outsider, most of the boys either left me alone or were kind.

At Great Walstead, no one knew anything about me. I never talked about the Bible studies or endless prayer meetings or the fact that the other boys had fathers with real jobs while we Schaeffers were living off God. My dad was a teacher, I said, which was almost true.

I also ignored my polio leg, never wore my brace again, and, by my second year at GW, even made it onto the First Eleven football (soccer) team as right back, a position that I played so fiercely that I helped take our team to an undefeated season one year. Mr. Marsh, our sports master, told me I was the "most dogged" defender he'd ever coached.

When I made the team, I felt as if I had just won a gold medal at the Olympics, joined the human race, been vindicated in some cosmic way, was declared normal for the first time in my life, and now was "just like other boys," as I thought of it. The joy was right up there with getting my first novel published, actually better.

When I was fifty years old and Mr. Parke had just read one of my novels, he wrote to me out of the blue and said he remembered me as being "a very courageous boy." I hadn't heard from him for many years. His compliment meant more to me than anything anyone else has ever said, as if God decided to show up unexpectedly and say something nice.

When an attacker would break through and leave the rest of our team scrambling, and there was no one left between the goalie and the attacker but me, and the whole school was on the sidelines yelling while Mr. Parke called out "It's up to you, Schaeffer! Stop him!" and I did, took the ball away, then managed to land on my left leg, so my wickedly strong good leg powered the foot I used to clear the ball, and I cleared it the length of the field while the masters and boys cheered and Mr. Parke called out "Well done!"—every problem, sorrow, or setback evaporated.

29

Great Walstead School sat at the end of a long, oak-lined driveway. The grounds covered 294 acres of fields, woods, ponds, a small river, playing fields, and lawns set in gently hilly landscape, midway between London and Brighton, about an hour train ride from each. You passed the school's small farm while on your way up the drive. Next to the farm—it consisted of two tumbledown cow barns—sat Walstead House, the cottage the older boys lived in, which I moved to after my first year at school.

Walstead House was an Elizabethan farmhouse built of brick and crooked oak ship's timbers. The boys said it was haunted. And we thought that several stains on the ancient oak floors looked like blood. The low oak doors, string-pull latches, and steep creaking stairs had not changed since Elizabeth was waiting for news of the Spanish Armada. The place smelled of shoe polish.

After passing Walstead House and a massive half-acre cluster of rhododendrons, the main school building appeared on the edge of a close-cropped lawn. It was made of brick, with ornate white trim around the roofline. It was four stories high, topped by many tall chimneys and a steeply gabled slate roof. It had been built as a manor sometime in the 1800s and turned into a school in 1925. Wings had been added, jutting in several directions behind the original building.

The main house had fifteen- to twenty-foot ceilings, a wide and stately staircase descending to a marble-floored front entrance hall, large common rooms, a library, an oak-paneled headmaster's study, and many dormitories on the upper floors. Behind the main house was a series of decaying huts linked by rickety half-covered passages. The huts had been bought from a nearby Royal Air Force base at the end of World War II. These served as our classrooms, as cold in winter as they were hot in summer. In winter, the huts were heated by portable kerosene stoves. The windows had to be opened when the eye-watering fumes got too intense.

The huts were always dusty and almost impossible to sweep clean, no matter how hard the boys assigned to sweeping duty worked. The good news was that most of the hut classrooms, propped on cinderblocks a few feet off the ground, had loose floorboards. We would pry one up and just sweep everything through the hole.

There was a large dining room that had been added just a couple of years before, in 1960. It smelled powerfully of some sort of tar-based disinfectant, a smell that sometimes overpowered the taste of the food. The dining hall provided an object lesson in the postwar decline of the Empire. Its doors were made of hollow plywood, its walls of flimsy sheetrock, and the floors were covered with thin linoleum. The shabby new wing included the tuck room. That was where we kept our all-important tuck boxes, miniature trunks about the size of a case of wine. Our tuck boxes were filled with "tuck"—jams, potted meats, squash (bottles of concentrated fruit syrup), and any other little treats from home that we'd bring out at tea time.

GW was a prep school—in other words, a private boarding school for boys aged five to thirteen. "Prep" stood for preparatory. What we were being prepared for was entrance into a select public school. And everything came down to the Common Entrance (CE) exam.

A public school was a private (usually all boys or all girls) boarding high school. Most of the boys in public schools would have attended prep schools since they were five. Home for them was where you visited during the "holls." By age eighteen, they had spent less time with their parents and siblings than most American children spend with their families before they're eight.

The aim of the staff at GW was to make sure that we passed the CE exam with marks high enough to be admitted to the public school of our parents' choice. In the case of most of the boys, this meant they would go where their fathers had gone. The well connected, rich, and lucky few would attend schools like Eton, Rugby, or Harrow; the rest of us would head to lesser schools. The public school you went to determined what university you got into. That would decide your fate.

The "brainy boys" would some day get "firsts" from Cambridge or Oxford; the lesser mortals would get lesser degrees from lesser colleges, and some might even be relegated to trade schools. A lack of seriousness about one's studies could always be cured by the oft-repeated phrase "You won't be so pleased with yourself when you get those CE results!" The twice-yearly mock CE exams, taken by all the boys in fourth, fifth, and sixth forms, loomed large.

While looking at other boys' confident faces as they bent over their mock CE exam papers, I felt the vastness of my ignorance spread out in front of me like a dark toxic pool. I had just turned eleven and was just starting real school for the first time in my life. I could read and write—haltingly—but not much else. The only subjects I was any good at were history and geography. Mom's reading out loud, the discussions I heard, and the living tableau of human geography that came and went through L'Abri paid off when it came to general knowledge.

I could not spell anything in English correctly, let alone in French, let alone comprehend anything Mr. Rouse was trying to impart in Latin class. And math was a closed book. I *was* good at French, or at least the Swiss Canton of Vaud-accented French spoken in our village, but, of course, not the grammar.

"It's a verb!" Mr. Marsh, the French master (and soccer coach) said.

"Yes, sir."

"Well, get on with it, lad."

"Yes, sir," I answered, while staring into the distance and waiting for inspiration.

"Well, Schaeffer, what's the problem?"

"Nothing, sir."

"But you haven't written anything. As I said, it is just an *ordinary verb*!"

"But, sir?"

"Yes, boy?"

"What *is* a verb?"

In 1962, there were many thousands of prep schools like GW feeding many hundreds of public schools. There were rumblings that the Labor government would someday shut down "elitist" private schools in favor of government schools; but, other than that, the whole system seemed secure and as much a part of the English landscape as the local pub. Some prep schools were miniature hells reminiscent of something out of Dickens, where bullying and brutal caning were facts of life. Sometimes when we visited another school to play them at soccer, the place would seem grim and the boys looked a "sorry lot." We always stayed for tea after the match and sometimes heard whispered stories about what had happened to this or that boy or cousin at this or that prep school where bullying was allowed, perhaps even encouraged as a rite of passage by sadistic masters. But there were also many places like Great Walstead, solidly middle-class, with a distinctive religious character of one sort or another ranging from Anglican to Roman Catholic, Baptist, and all points in between. Most of them seemed like happy places, at least the dozen or so I visited from time to time as a member of the First Eleven.

At GW, our religion was Mr. Parke's religion, a sensible low-church Anglicanism. A jolly local Church of England priest, Father Sheldon—the father of Paul Sheldon, a tall, gangling bespectacled boy who was our best cricket bowler and one of my best friends—came to the school to conduct chapel on some Sundays. The rest of the time, Mr. Parke and the teachers led our short and lighthearted Sunday and daily chapel services. They tended to reflect the theology of the master taking them, or, in the case of "Bubble," his cantankerous atheism.

The only remnants from the school's founding were Mr. Alban and Mr. Brabey, both of whom had fought in World War I. We called Mr. Alban "Bubble," because of his snuff habit that resulted in congested breathing that sounded disgustingly like a kettle bubbling. His snuff-taking gave us opportunities to watch in delighted disgust as noxious brown juice trickled out of his bulbous red nose and stained his upper lip, before Bubble would wipe his nose with the brown-stained handkerchief he kept shoved up the sleeve of his ubiquitous, shapeless, and patched navy-blue cardigan.

Everything about Bubble reeked of nicotine, and everything on or near him was stained yellowy-brown. His thinning hair was always greasy and his sallow skin the color of putty. He was short and had bad teeth.

Bubble taught us to make Molotov cocktails, which we threw on the old tennis court, sending fireballs up into the air like miniature nuclear mushroom clouds. He showed us how to bayonet an attacker. He told us stories about the Home Guard of WWII, "not my war, mind you, but they had me organizing the local chaps."

Bubble would gleefully try to turn us against God. He raved about the wonders of evolution, more as a personal manifesto than as science. He also made a big point of advertising his far right political sympathies.

Once Bubble put some boys in detention, including me, who argued with his assertion that anyone who believed in God was "thick as mud." When he put us in detention for believing in God, we appealed to Mr. Parke, who upheld Bubble's right to punish us unreasonably, but who also told us he thought it was "jolly unfair," but that we, like the "martyrs during Bloody Mary's reign, should suffer gladly for your faith." Mr. Parke laughed when he said this, and detention was not so terrible. All we did was sit at our desks doing a bit of extra studying.

Bubble was one of our favorite teachers, and the ruder he was, the more we liked him. Mr. Parke knew that we knew that his allowing Bubble to be unreasonable was some huge game, and we were all in on the joke.

Both Bubble and Mr. Brabey were past retirement age and had become as much part of the school as the massive oaks and cedars towering over the lawn. They puttered around "teaching" and generally being the sorts of characters that only the English have a way of nonchalantly putting up with, the sorts of eccentrics who send a boy to half an hour of detention for saying God exists.

Mr. Brabey was assigned to tutor me in extra math when, about halfway through my first term, it became apparent to Mr. Parke that I was so woefully behind in every subject that I'd have to undergo extra tutoring in just about everything. "It's as if you've had no education at all. What *have* you been doing?" asked Mr. Parke during one of our many "My dear chap, this just *won't do*!" meetings.

Old Brabey was living in a damp, closet-sized room next to the school kitchen that smelled of mildew and the glue from the lifelike models of animals he made out of plastic wood, then carved with files. Brabey was bald, short, and fat with a kindly face, a pudgy triple chin, and a fringe of yellowing white hair around his shiny pate. He was easy to distract, and we did very little extra math.

Brabey had been a stretcher-bearer in World War I. His face and hands were the color of boiled lobster, a bright reddish-pink that only the perpetually chilly English seem to be afflicted with, along with cold- and damp-related ailments like "chilblains." "Old Brabey" (as we boys called him) dressed in baggy heather-colored tweeds and sometimes smelled of undergarments past their prime.

I spent many a gray afternoon listening to harrowing tales of life in the muddy, rat-infested trenches. Each lesson in trench warfare ended when Old Brabey would shout furiously that I was distracting him from teaching me math—or "sums," as he called it.

"But, sir, I have not tried to distract you, sir."

"Wipe that grin off your silly face! Do you think this is *amusing*? I weep for you, boy! I *weep*!"

"Yes, sir."

I'd sit staring out the high window at the lawn and distant sodden cricket pitch soaking up yet more drizzle, the view made wobbly by the wavy Victorian glass panes while visions of men on stretchers, brains blown out, mingled with the view of the English countryside.

"He died the worst death there was, lad: *gas*!"

"Yes, sir."

"Choked his life away before me, me a *helpless* stretcher-bearer and not one thing I could do for my *own brother*!"

"Yes, sir. Sorry, sir."

"Have *you* ever seen someone die in a gas attack, lad?"

"No, sir."

"Well, I did! My own brother! Clarence, poor Cla—"

Brabey dabbed at his puffy eyes with his inky handkerchief. A tear would roll down his cheek and hang trembling from his yellowing nose whiskers, then splash on my notebook and make the pale cheap ink run.

Boys with parents close by went home for one or two weekends per term. I went with friends or to my sister Susan, who had just moved from Huémoz to live in London. Once per term, I took the train from Hayward's Heath to Victoria Station and then the tube to Ealing for a long weekend. Susan and Ranald provided a home away from home. Margaret, their daughter, was born before they left Switzerland, and soon they had another daughter, Kirsty.

Ranald made it clear that at the English L'Abri, he was going to do things *his* way. "We will not be as disorganized as The

Work in Huémoz," he would say, and "We will put more emphasis on study." Ranald was going to be a L'Abri missionary, but not like "your loud father who shouts when he preaches."

I learned that the British, including Ranald, felt rather superior to everyone else, especially to Americans. There was a right way to do things, the British way. I learned that when a woman walked into a room, you stood, and that you did not talk to an adult with your hands in your pockets. I called my school masters "sir." I addressed women by their last name, as in "Yes, Mrs. Parke." I did not "sneak" (tell on people). I did not lie, or when I did I made sure never to be caught; and, when confronted, I learned to admit what I had done in an "honorable English way," by raising my hand quickly and "owning up" to having been the boy to have done whatever it was I had done.

I was doing my best to rise above my embarrassing shouts-when-he-preaches father. I had cricket whites and a fine bright pink blazer and school cap. When they sang "God Save the Queen," I stood. I not only knew who Gilbert and Sullivan were, I sang in *HMS Pinafore*. (I also played the Count in the *Marriage of Figaro*.) I could even quote a little Shakespeare and was studying Macbeth. I had wealthy English friends whose fathers would pick me up in their Jags and Bentleys for a weekend. I would hang around on the David Spinks' farm with Spink One and shoot starlings with his air gun, or at the posh Robin Spink house with their heated pool and little dog that would hump your leg.

There was only one problem. My passport to this pleasant club could and would be revoked unless I passed the Common Entrance exam. And I knew that if you peeled back the top layer of my polite English schoolboy veneer, you would find a horribly ignorant young man, one who could talk without putting his hands in his pockets—Mrs. Parke only had to remind me once—but who also did not understand the first thing about geometry, spelling, and Latin and never would. I knew I was doomed.

30

I had grown up with the idea that God wanted me to be strange, perpetually weird, perpetually different. For the first time in my life, I encountered people like Mr. Parke who seemed to share my parents' evangelical faith but didn't set themselves apart from the world. The thought that you could be a normal person and still believe was new to me.

At GW, it was good enough to just show up in chapel, be polite, and let God do the worrying about how sincere other people were. There were several teachers besides Bubble who were unbelievers, and they were all in good standing.

When Bubble took chapel, he once had us sing some odd ditty he'd written, set to Wagner as the "hymn" and smirked while he read the scripture passage of the day. Mr. Parke bore this with a good humor that only served to make his faith seem unassailable. Mr. Parke believed what he believed, and Bubble believed what he believed, and there was room for all of us.

GW was actually a rather humble little place, with minimal facilities beyond a wonderful natural setting. The fees were low, the classrooms bare, cold, and ugly. But Mr. Parke's philosophy of education—it was about finding something each boy could be good at, opening doors beyond mere exams, about learning basic rules of politeness that would serve you all your life—was wonderful. And most of the teachers were highly eccentric, and therefore interesting. That was all that mattered.

Mrs. Parke was a particularly magnificent teacher. She understood *exactly* how to make history come alive for little boys by describing torture, mayhem, battles, murders, plots, heroic deeds, imprisonments, voyages, the Black Death, all in glowing Shakespearean detail. Sometimes she would demonstrate how the rack had been used and lay on the teacher's table, arms stretched above her head, her gray wool knee-length skirt tucked neatly under her trim body, and she would describe in detail just *how* Guy Fawkes or other traitors felt as bones were pulled from sockets, and then how they would be hanged, "just for a bit," then taken down, revived, and quartered.

Dates, names, and places, the whole shape of history, stuck, glued into our little brains.

"And then the ax fell!"

"*Please,* Mrs. Parke, where did the king's head go?"

"Into a basket, or onto the straw put there to soak up the gouts of blood!"

"Do you think he *knew*?"

"Certainly. I expect the brain stayed alive for several horrifying seconds. And, of course, the body would twitch a good bit."

My world got bigger. Instead of saving men's souls, my days consisted of learning history from Mrs. Parke, learning to play cricket (badly), being surprisingly competitive at high jump (my right leg was three times as strong as any other right leg at GW), and joining the rifle club and discovering that I was a good shot. I also discovered that other boys shared my interest in women.

It didn't take much in those days. The "naughty postcards" were hardly explicit. They were drawn somewhat in the style of the early Vargas pinups, usually of a young woman in some suggestive pose with a witty caption. There was a girl on a swing, with the breeze lifting her skirt to reveal stocking tops and tight panties molded to her figure. A farmer was walking past with his rake over his shoulder, the inference being that the handle was going to penetrate where all we boys—passing the card around—longed to go. The expression on the girl's face was shocked but pleased, her mouth frozen in a startled "O!"

When we "wanked," we didn't think of it as sex—at least the other boys didn't, to the extent they talked about it. (I did not advertise the amateur gynecological training that Mom had given me!) "Sex" was that far-off thing they dreamed about doing to girls. And our dreams were not terribly specific: just addled, and usually somewhat romantic, thoughts about "girls," or "a girl." Real girls and actual sex seemed farther off than Mars. (Matron and the other females in the school seemed to be living behind a thick sheet of glass.)

When we wanked in a group from time to time—usually in the forest while taking a break from building a camp, raft, or fort—it was a game, something like armwrestling but where everyone could win. We sometimes compared the distances we could shoot sperm. It was matter-of-fact and jovial, a community undertaking.

Mr. Parke advised us against all forms of "abuse." However, he only mentioned this once in the context of the Sixth Form (eighth grade) facts-of-life talk. The rest of the time, no one said anything about wanking, pro or con. Since everyone teaching at the school knew everything there is to know about boys, I'm sure it was no mystery to them that there was some "bashing the bishop" going on. No one seemed upset. We were never lied to and told any of the mythology that I've read other boys were told, stories about masturbation driving you mad. It just wasn't that important. Privacy was respected.

Every other week, Mr. Parke rented a movie and showed it on Sunday evening on a rickety old 16-mm projector that clicked along so loudly that if you were sitting next to it, you couldn't hear the dialogue. We watched patriotic war epics made in the 1940s, or comedies, mostly from the 1940s and '50s, the Ealing comedies that introduced me to actors like Alec Guinness and Terry-Thomas. There were the Shakespeare plays, *Othello, Macbeth,* and the rest. Sometimes there would be a documentary, say about a trip up the Congo River, with the colonial baggage-bearers glistening under the hot sun and an imperturbable English guide trekking into darkest Africa, a sort of Livingston who would dress for dinner, even when no other "civilized Englishmen" were near.

There was also TV, about one hour per week for the older boys. Our favorite was *The Man from U.N.C.L.E.* We were also allowed to sometimes watch *Top of the Pops,* a weekly program with the latest pop and rock hits being lip-synched live. The Kinks, Beatles, Petula Clark, Roy Orbison, and the Rolling Stones became part of my inner vocabulary.

I was overjoyed by the movies and TV. I had been longing to see movies, any movies, not to mention listening to rock music and jazz. I had barely seen a TV set since my memorable polio-operation-summer in America.

Mrs. Parke encouraged everyone to play music. I took lessons and played the piano badly, but that didn't hinder me from joining in our many music evenings where I'd thump out a few minutes of boogie-woogie. We were allowed to carry hatchets into the woods to cut down trees—only birches, though, and brush, never the oaks—to build our camps and rafts. There were three ponds as well as the River Ouse. Sometimes the semiwild pigs from our farm were allowed to root in the forest for acorns and we would make a game out of running past them. And we were allowed to do anything we wanted in the way of climbing the enormous trees, making huts, rafts, and treehouses, digging caves, fishing in the river, bicycling, anything at all as long as we were always back for tea, prep, classes, chapel, and sports.

After sports, we took a muddy, disease-ridden communal "plunge bath" wherein we sat in a big shallow cinderblock-and-stucco wading pool–like tub in the basement of the main house. We got in twenty or so at a time, squatted in three inches of muddy tepid-to-icy water, and scrubbed off the filth and sweat—and caught each other's infections.

At breakfast each day, there was a list of who would be "off sports" or "off plunge bath" read out by Matron. If a boy had particularly contagious boils or verrucae, he might be off plunge bath for the whole term. We got illnesses I'd never heard of, like verrucae—a kind of ingrown boil—and other skin conditions perhaps related to cold, eating our weight in "fried bread" and other saturated fats, and only bathing twice a week.

Of course, no one sued anyone when their child had an accident or sliced open his hand with a penknife. We all carried one. It would have been considered bad form to sue. How could a boy build a fort if he wasn't allowed to climb trees? How could he cut saplings to make bows and arrows if he had no knife? Someone was always getting stitches. We were *boys!*

Freedom from litigiousness meant that we were in young male heaven. Who could have ever learned to *love* life as we did if we had been stuck indoors playing "safely" on video games, plugged in, wired up, and growing obese? Thank God there were no computers! We didn't play games *about* reality, we *were* reality! We built things. We climbed things. We were never indoors if we could help it. There was no tree off limits, no pond too deep, no river too dangerous. Everyone had to learn to swim. And who didn't know how to climb? And everything we did was dangerous, difficult, and challenging; otherwise, what was the point?

It was virtually impossible to be overweight, or restless, let alone suffer from attention deficit disorder in GW. We were just too busy being happy, physically exhausted little boys in a secure and predictable environment.

At night we were asleep in about ten seconds from the time we lay down at eight PM (nine for the older boys). And in class, no matter how grim it seemed during some Latin grammar test, we knew that soon we were all going to spend a great afternoon doing sports, or trekking in the woods. It was all about mud, water, sky, and learning free from psychological or "behavioral" manipulation.

Rules were basic and few, related to how you treated others, not what you did or didn't do with your body. Order was built on respect for authority, which, far from being constraining, allowed us near-total freedom. We were polite, did not bully, and told the truth *or else!* So we were free to pretty much do anything, once we understood the rules about how we were to interact with others. And there were no frightened parents in sight. Who could ever have had Q Day if there had been?

31

Q Day, our version of D-Day, was invented by Bubble in 1946 or thereabouts. Q Day was part military exercise, part rite of passage. The Fifth and Sixth Form boys were divided into sections, F Section, G Section, and so on. Each section had a captain and officers. There were about eight boys in each. There was a cook, first aid officer, Morse code officer, the boy in charge of the building of the hut, a map-reader good with coordinates, a record-keeper/scribe, a boy in charge of defenses, another of intelligence and planning attacks. (I was always the First Aid officer, given that Susan had taught me a certified Red Cross course. I even got the chance to stop a severe hemorrhage after Weeks stepped on a broken bottle while fording the river.)

Each section met through the year for exercises in map-reading, first aid, and various sorts of military-style drill. But the main activity during the summer term was camp-building. We could only use natural materials: logs we cut, ferns, branches leaves, grass, mud, rocks . . . no plastic sheeting.

On the exterior wall of the chapel (yet another converted WWII Quonset-type hut), the Q Day readiness sign was posted. White meant that Q Day was going to happen that term. Yellow, that it was imminent. Red: it had begun!

Once the yellow disk went up, each section assigned a member to visit the sign during the night, because the final signal could be posted at any time. When the red disk went up, it was the job of the boy who first saw it to alert the rest of his section. Once assembled, the section leader would go to Mr. Parke's study to be issued the ammunition, a precious box full of bangers, big firecrackers powerful enough to blow a hole in the bottom of a Wellington boot if you stepped on one. Hence the rule that once the banger landed in your camp, you could not touch it or try to toss it back at the enemy.

The object of the night operation was simple: Explode as many bangers in other section's camps within their perimeter—five yards around the hut—and have as few bangers explode in your camp as possible. Thus the need to choose your camp's location well, one hard to find, especially in the dark.

Until a boy threw a lit banger into your camp (or an unlit one into your campfire), you could do anything short of killing him, to stop him. This included building barriers across forest paths, digging pits, setting all manner of booby traps. The rule was that the master assigned to your section had to be in on these preparations and approve them. So, for instance, if one section decided to place a thirty-pound rock in a tree that would fall on an approaching attacker, the master might nix the idea.

During the night exercise, we'd blacken our faces and hands with charcoal and creep through the woods. If possible, we'd never use our torches (flashlights). However, a campfire was mandatory, so if you could get near enough to an enemy camp, you could see the fire.

When a successful attack was carried out, we would have to declare ourselves—for instance, "Schaeffer and Nichole Two, G

Section!" And the defenders would have to also identify themselves: "Weeks One and Wilmot, F Section!" Then there would be a momentary civilized lull and each side wrote down the agreed amount of bangers that had just been exploded. After that, the attackers would creep back off into the dark, sometimes quietly followed by the recently attacked in the hopes that the attackers would inadvertently lead them to their camp.

Punching was against the rules. So was hitting an opponent with a club. But wrestling was permitted, and huge fights took place involving three or four boys holding down an attacker as he tried to make his way close enough to the fire to throw his bangers. (Montague, our premiere athlete and a giant of a lad, was impossible to stop and once crawled into our camp with everyone in F Section clinging to his back and trying to stop him but to no avail!) We could strip an attacker of bangers, then add his ammunition to ours. So if it seemed all was lost, we would try to dump our ammunition before it could be taken.

There were bloody noses, sprained wrists, scratches, and minor burns. No one got killed. And remarkably, all the scores (of how many bangers each camp had exploded within the perimeter of enemy camps) tallied between the sections correctly. It would have been unheard-of to lie about the results, just "not on at all." Honor was not a word that was met with a derisive snicker. And lying was always punished by a "whacking."

No one but the Headmaster could whack you—in other words hit you with the size-thirteen plimsoll (sneaker) that Mr. Parke kept under the safe in his study, the punishment of last resort when we'd touch our toes and receive from one up to six strokes—"six of the best"—on our bottoms. One stroke with your trousers up was not serious; but six of the best, "trousers down," left welts.

Six of the best, trousers down, was reserved for crimes like lying, stealing, rudeness to Mrs. Parke, and bullying. By the time you had done something requiring six strokes, you would be on the brink of expulsion.

The most I ever got was three, trousers up, for a group cheating effort in Mr. Ward's history class, wherein we took turns learning dates and names for his weekly quiz and everyone else looked at what his neighbor was writing and then passed on the information. We were caught the third time and only saved ourselves from expulsion by instantly owning up. We got a stern lecture and three strokes each. The lining up outside Mr. Parke's study, the trembling as we heard the swish-smack blows fall on others, the shaky handshake with the Head, the exit, the look of anticipation from the others as they asked "Was it bad?" and the satisfaction of pulling a grim face to scare them when you walked past. . . . We didn't ever cheat again. And looking back, it seems that having corporal punishment as a threat—"Would you rowdy Visigoths care to work, or shall I send you all to Mr. Parke's study to explain your miserable selves?"—gave every teacher, no matter how young or inexperienced, a means to keep order. Spanking, when fairly and rarely administered, worked wonders. And it seems to me that it was far less invasive than constant psychological (let alone medical) manipulation.

After two or three years at GW, I was more English than the English. The main lesson of history was that England was in the right. We stood against the Germans. We stopped them from taking over the world, just as we stopped Napoleon at Waterloo. We liberated the Indians and Africans from barbarity, gave them the rule of law, built them railways, and explained that you could not burn your widows along with their dead husbands. We invented the steam engine, and the Spitfire was the best plane ever. We were honest, not like those dreadful "Frogs" across the Channel. Civilization ended at the cliffs of Dover. Wales, Ireland, and Scotland rebelled now and then and had to be subdued to their rightful place. Sherlock Holmes and Watson were the typical Englishmen, resourceful and driven by a desire to do right. We had the Magna Carta and enjoyed the rights of Englishmen while the rest of the world were slaves. The purpose of the Americans was to be there when we needed them. "We can take it," we told the Nazis after they bombed London. "Solid British workmanship" was best; our suits, cut on Savile Row, were what any real gentleman wore. Gilbert and Sullivan wrote opera without "all that Italian nonsense." Elizabeth stood against the marauding Frog and Spaniard and made England safe for a religion as jolly and "free from cant" as cricket, when played by the rules, played honestly, so honestly that the only time I heard a boy dispute the call of the referee was when he told the umpire that he was indeed *out*. He did the right thing, he did what Winston would have done, or at least Dr. Watson. Honor, truth, and openhanded transparency, these were the "attributes of Englishmen." Jesus was a decent chap and more or less English.

It was good to be an Englishman! When we went on vacation, I had a new status. And Mom loved my accent. Now I could tell the whole truth about at least one part of my life to strangers.

Before GW, what was I supposed to say in answer to the usual questions asked a child: "What does your father do?" "Where do you go to school?" The questioner was often an Englishwoman on holiday in Portofino or Zermatt. A truthful answer would have left people staring. "Dad waits for God to send money, and I don't go to school because my parents are too busy serving the Lord to keep track of me."

Boarding school liberated me. I could say, "I go to school in Sussex. I'm on my holls and will go back in two weeks." Boarding school was something everyone understood.

Even life at GW had a dark side that I didn't mention. I didn't know it *was* a dark side. The "dark side" wasn't deliberate. It was just ignorance about my particular problem. The word "dyslexic" had not been heard of yet.

Mr. Parke often called me into his study.

"Do you try, boy?"

"I do, sir."

"But you are not making any improvement."

"No, sir."

"What you write in your essays is rather good, but your spelling . . . *what* spelling? Eh, Schaeffer?"

"Yes, sir."

"When you take that list of words into prep to memorize, doesn't *anything* stick?"

"Not much, sir."

Mr. Parke would sigh and contemplate me for a while.

"Well, you're a good chap, Schaeffer, but we need some real effort. I have no idea how you will ever pass the CE."

"Yes, sir."

"Well, carry on, but *do* try!"

I would. I'd sit and stare at the lists of words. I'd relive the last soccer match I'd played. I'd take imaginary journeys from Ollon up our mountain to Huémoz, wander our village, and look at our mountains one at a time, starting with Les Diablerets, moving to L'Argentine and its sheer smooth cracked-mirror face, to the boxy Grande Muveran, the spiky horn of the Petit Muveran, and the jagged teeth of my beloved Dents du Midi. Or sometimes I'd plunge into the turquoise water off the rocks at the side of the Paraggi Bay, follow a fish to his crevice between the spines of the sea urchins, watch his gills fanning the water, the blood warm water, that dreamy clear water on a perfect late-August afternoon . . . until the list of words would appear and sunny thoughts would evaporate, leaving the deadly list staring at me as if written in invisible ink that would fade as soon as a word was transferred from the sheet of paper into my brain. Another talk with Mr. Parke. "There must be maximum effort now."

"Yes, sir."

"In less than a year, you will be taking the CE."

After I was in boarding school, Dad and I kept up our hiking tradition during the holidays. Dad would use those times to ask about my failed grades. All Dad would say, when I'd bring my report card to him during the holls, was that I'd be in real trouble if I didn't work harder. For whatever reason, Dad never seemed to connect the dots from his own bad spelling to mine. And my parents had no ideas where to send me after GW.

What stands out, though, is not that I failed to learn to spell, but that at GW I actually received an outstanding education in ways that had nothing to do with exams and everything to do with what really counts. And what started there has continued through my life. In that sense, I never left the school.

Sometimes when I read a book and remember to think about the historical context, or when I comprehend a news item because I know my geography, every time I go to a play and think about what a play *is*, what an actor *does*, that drama didn't just *happen*, that the Greeks and Shakespeare came *first*, that cultures have a *shape*, I'll mutter, "Thank you, Mr. Parke."

Great Walstead opened the doors to knowing that doors need to be opened to other doors, to doors beyond those, forever, that learning is freedom, that there are no dull subjects once Mrs. Parke sets your mind on fire with a demonstration of how the rack worked, and then casts you in the role of Figaro in the *Marriage of Figaro* and teaches you to sing, even when you can't.

"Everyone should be in an opera at least *once,* Schaeffer!"

"Yes, Mrs. Parke, but I'm no good at memorizing things."

"How do you know that? Let's try, and then we shall see. It's easier when you put words to music. Mozart won't let you down, and I shan't either."

32

Of course I failed my CE exam. My parents wanted me to keep going in the "English system." After the good experience at Great Walstead, so did I.

St. David's, located in Llandudno, North Wales—founded just four years before I got there—was run by some pacifists. Mom and Dad sent me there without ever visiting the place. (I don't know how they ever found it.) It was a five-hour train ride from London. My parents never visited while I was there either. I might as well have been on the moon—on the dark side, at that.

The first time I saw St. David's was when I walked in at the start of term in the autumn of 1966. I was not nervous or homesick. Boarding school had become routine.

Mr. Ledbetter, the headmaster's frail, cadaverous gray-skinned father-in-law, taught, as did the stocky Head and his guitar-strumming, morbidly cheerful wife. All I remember about Mr. Ledbetter's teaching is a series of lengthy little sermons on why he had been a conscientious objector in the Second World War. I asked him if that meant he was sorry that Hitler lost, and he glared at me but didn't have an answer, except to say "The first casualty of any war is the truth."

Our matron was a bit like a camp guard. She had a bulldog

that she sometimes kicked in the testicles if he humped her leg. Then she would giggle and her triple chins quivered.

The Head used to cane boys quite often. Unlike Mr. Parke, the St. David's Head used an actual cane, not a gym shoe. A beating would draw blood. This seemed to be at odds with the school's pacifism, and the contradiction was never explained, nor was the capriciousness of the application of the cane.

At GW, discipline had been reassuringly predictable and never cruel. At St. David's, it was weirdly disproportionate. One boy was caned for talking after lights out—he came back to our dormitory with six bloody stripes on his pajama bottoms. Yet others were not punished for bullying, stealing, and lying.

The school was new and had no reputation (and so accepted more or less anyone). The teachers were undistinguished and the discipline was a farce. But the buildings were magnificent.

St. David's was housed in a recently defunct girls' school on Lord Mostyn's estate. (The school was leased from the family.) The twelfth-century Great Hall was pristine, the best preserved and most authentically furnished space in the school. The "new" Elizabethan wing was also pristine. Mostyn family portraits hung in the dining hall. There was a priest hole above the Great Hall, left over from the reign of Elizabeth I when the Roman Catholic Mostyns hid their priests from prying Protestant eyes. (The entrance was hidden behind a tapestry and secret door.)

The view of the playing fields and woods as seen from the battlements was lovely. Above the school, a rocky slope led up and over the bare moor to the Great Orm's Head, a huge cliff several miles away against which the Irish Sea pounded; it was full of caves, a place where pirate wreckers had set fires to lure ships onto the rocks.

I was an avid soccer player, and this was a "rugby school."

About every other rugby match, I would be pulverized. My parents had forbidden me to play rugby on the logical grounds that if I broke my bad leg, it might not mend. I disobeyed them. Being the "Yank" was bad enough without drawing more attention to myself. The contemporary Lord Mostyn showed up once a year to shoot pheasants; he kept a gamekeeper in the gatehouse lodge a mile from the school. We boys were allowed to volunteer as beaters, to drive the game from the woods. There would be about twenty guns (tweed-clad hunters) and thirty beaters.

Driving the pheasants was one of the only things we were competent to do. We were a school of failed boys, some thick, others mean, some bitter, others kind but not hard-working, and a few real delinquents. The staff often reminded us that we were "third-raters" and lucky to be in any public school. Mr. Walters, the math and science teacher, told me repeatedly that I'd be a failure.

At GW, we had been taking mock CE exams; at St. David's, we began to take mock O-levels, the mid–high school exams that you had to pass to take A-levels (the exams that got you into university). In GW, I had been one of the only boys failing the mock CE. In St. David's, I had lots of company while failing mock O-levels.

The Head and his wife didn't care about education. What they cared about was that each boy had a personal relationship with Jesus Christ. Their Jesus was a meek and mild savior (at least when he wasn't caning boys!) who, they said, would have refused to fight in both the first and second world wars. Chapel services were no longer low-church Anglican with lots of jolly singing of robust traditional hymns, but long, free-form sessions of guitar-strumming and earnest pleadings to be peace-loving, gentle, mild—just what a room full of sullen dyslexic thirteen-to-nineteen-year-old boys wanted to hear. I gained an abiding loathing of all folk music.

The staff was so ineffectual—a few erratically applied and bloody canings aside—that they more or less let the prefects run the school. (Prefects were senior boys given the responsibility of monitoring the younger students.) To get the job, the prefects had to pretend to be Jesus-hugging milksops, but in fact were mostly vicious bullies who took out their frustrations on the rest of us in quiet corners and leafy glades.

I saw one new boy thrown naked from a second-floor window deep into a bramble-and-nettle patch, where he struggled for over an hour to extricate himself. I was shoved, punched, and slapped until one day I got hold of one prefect after he tripped and kicked me, a tall gangling seventeen-year-old with red hair and pale almost-white eyebrows who always sang loudest in chapel, and I got in close, got him down, and broke his finger. He threw up and fainted.

After that, I had the reputation of being a "nutter," and the bullies kept away. He never told on me, because even in that depraved place, the code of not "sneaking" held sway, and besides, he wasn't about to advertise the fact that a boy a head shorter, with a bad leg, and a bloody Yank to boot, had beaten him.

Even our masturbation sessions were cheerless at St. David's. There was one titled boy at the school. He used to provide us with Danish black-and-white pornographic postcards for a fee. This future member of the House of Lords would rent you a card for five minutes for a shilling.

"And no bloody splatters! If you ruin my card, you'll jolly well owe me a pound!"

On days out, his parents would arrive in a chauffeur-driven

Rolls. He said that it was the family chauffeur who got him the cards.

Our Lord/pornographer would stand outside the "bog" (toilet) timing you.

"You'll owe me another shilling if you don't hurry!" he would bellow.

Somehow, this took the fun out of our sex lives. And he made us use the cards one at a time.

"No group rates, you sods!"

My second winter term, the Head decided we needed "toughening." From then on, there was a window removed in each dorm. After that, we used to sneak empty squash bottles up to the dorms and fill them with hot water and clutch them under our covers. Once in a while, we'd share a bed.

The several boys who were homosexuals sometimes paired off even on warm nights. And we heard a lot of scuffling in the dark. But the line between who was wanking with another boy, merely for good company and warmth, and who liked other boys "that way" was never drawn.

Anyone who went to a boys' school (at least in England) has probably had openly gay friends and has seen boys in bed together. You were "that way" or not. Either way, it was not a big deal. No one seemed to care about what kind of sex stimulated you, if any. I never heard any "faggot jokes," though the term "queer" was sometimes used, as in "sod off, you queer!" But it was applied to everyone.

Since St. David's was new and run by goofs, it didn't attract a good staff. The only good teacher was Mr. Stark. He was also the only teacher who graded our essays based on content, not spelling. He taught history and English and had been a tank commander in the war. Stark was large, wide-shouldered, tweed-clad, had a long sharp hooked nose, and drove an antique Bentley. He could throw a cannonball from below the battlements up to the lawn, about fifteen feet, an impossible thing to do, we boys said, until Stark did it.

Stark was fired after he had one too many run-ins with the Head, and after he hit one of the students—Stapleton. Actually, Stark banged Stapleton's head into his desk, after Stapleton repeatedly flicked ink all over Stark's jacket. Stark also told fabulous war stories, which was what really got him in trouble.

Stark was the only teacher who was honest about the school. A few weeks before he was fired, he gave me a lift into Llandudno to get a haircut.

"Sir?" I asked.

"Hmmm?"

"What do you think of this place?"

"Llandudno is a miserable little pimple."

"I meant the school."

"Is *that* what you call it?" He chuckled. "A bit lacking, wouldn't you say, Schaeffer?"

"I don't like it much."

"Nor do I."

"Why not?" I asked.

"Everything in moderation, eh? They take everything a bit far in the religion department, don't they?"

"Yes, sir."

"Bit less talkie-talk, bit more common sense wouldn't hurt the place, would it?"

"I wish you were the Head, sir."

"As Jeeves would say, 'the contingency is remote,' " Stark said with a laugh.

My grandparents, Jessie and George Seville, Shanghai, China, 1905.

My grandfather, Francis Schaeffer III, in his U.S. Navy uniform, age eighteen.

My father with my sister Priscilla, Germantown, Philadelphia, 1938.

Edith Schaeffer about to leave for Europe, 1948.

My mother with me the week I was born, Champéry Switzerland, August 1952.

Part of the village of Champéry, Switzerland.

My sisters, 1949 (left to right: Debbie, Priscilla, and Susan).

Mom writing her L'Abri Family Letter, 1958.

Dad teaching a Bible class, with my sister Priscilla next to him, Lausanne, Switzerland, 1956.

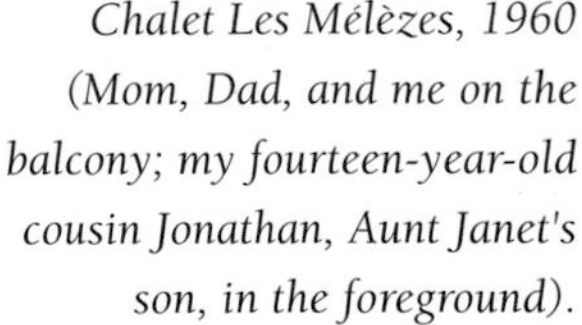

Chalet Les Mélèzes, 1960 (Mom, Dad, and me on the balcony; my fourteen-year-old cousin Jonathan, Aunt Janet's son, in the foreground).

Mom, Debbie, Dad, Mrs. Johnson, with me after my operation, Smithtown, Long Island, 1959–60.

My grandmother, Bessie Schaeffer, 1967.

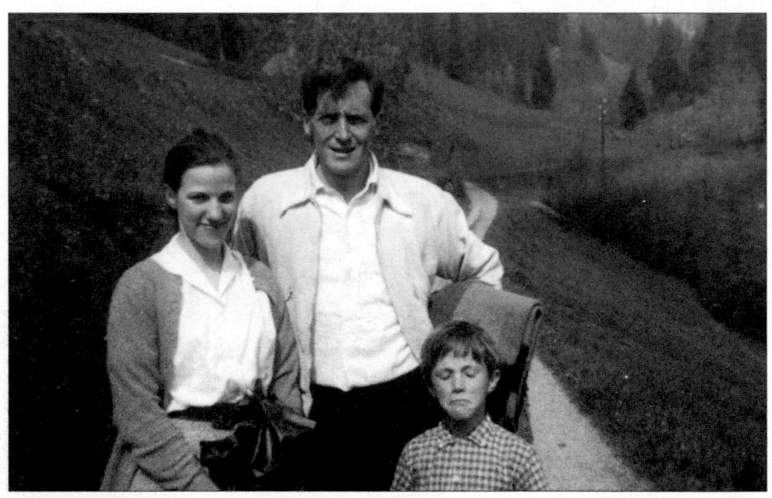

Susan, Ranald Macaulay, and me, Huémoz, Switzerland.

Mr. Gordon Parke, headmaster, Great Walstead School, Sussex, UK (date unknown).

Dad and me. I'm in my Great Walstead uniform, 1963.

At fifteen, I've just run away from school, 1967.

A slide I took during a light show rock "happening" in L'Abri chapel, circa 1967.

Dad leading a discussion at a L'Abri conference, in 1982 (credit: Gary Gnidovic).

Winter 1969 just after Genie arrived at L'Abri (left to right: me, Pam Walsh, and Genie Walsh).

Genie at our New York opening, Frisch Gallery, 1970.

Mom speaking at Wheaton College, Illinois, date unknown (credit: Gary Gnidovic).

Back in my studio painting, 1970.

John Sandri and Gracie Holmes at our wedding reception.

Jessica and baby Francis, Chésières, Switzerland, 1973.

Genie with my paintings at the opening of my first show at the Chante Pierre Gallery, Aubonne, Switzerland, 1972.

Dad, me, and Billy Zeoli (right), 1974.

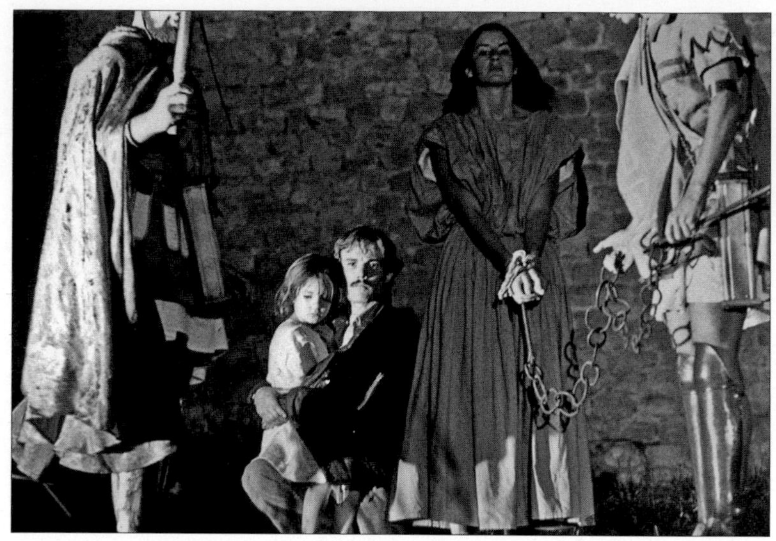

Jessica, Genie, and me on the set of How Should We Then Live? *1974 (Genie and Jessica are "Roman martyrs"; credit: Mus Arshad).*

I'm directing Dad, How Should We Then Live? *1974 (credit: Mus Arshad).*

Dad dusting "David" on the set of How Should We Then Live? *1974 (credit: Mus Arshad).*

Genie and the children return with me to my beloved Portofino, 1976.

One of the seminars for How Should We Then Live? *1976.*

Dr. Koop, Dad, and me on stage at Whatever Happened to the Human Race? *seminar, 1979.*

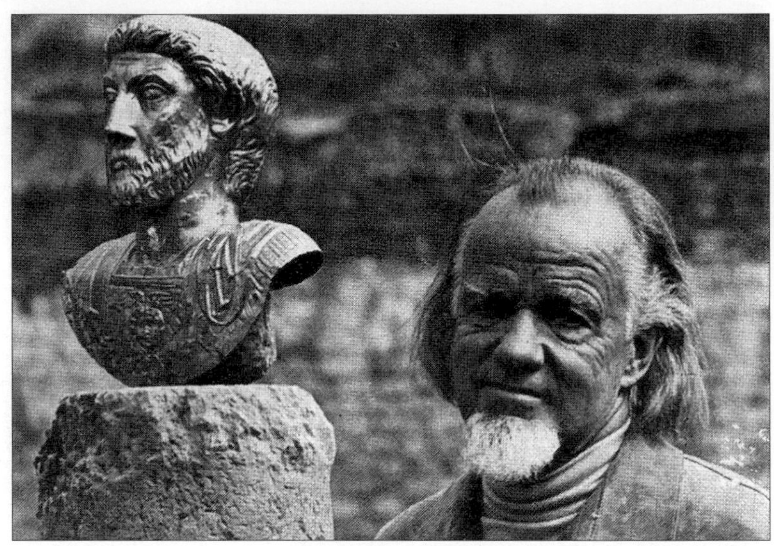

Dad (with the bust of Marcus Aurelius) on the set of How Should We Then Live? *1974.*

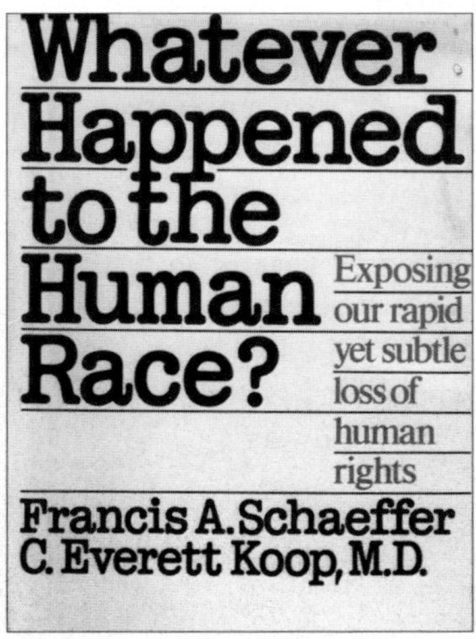

Whatever Happened to the Human Race?
Exposing our rapid yet subtle loss of human rights
Francis A. Schaeffer
C. Everett Koop, M.D.

Book cover of one of our bestsellers.

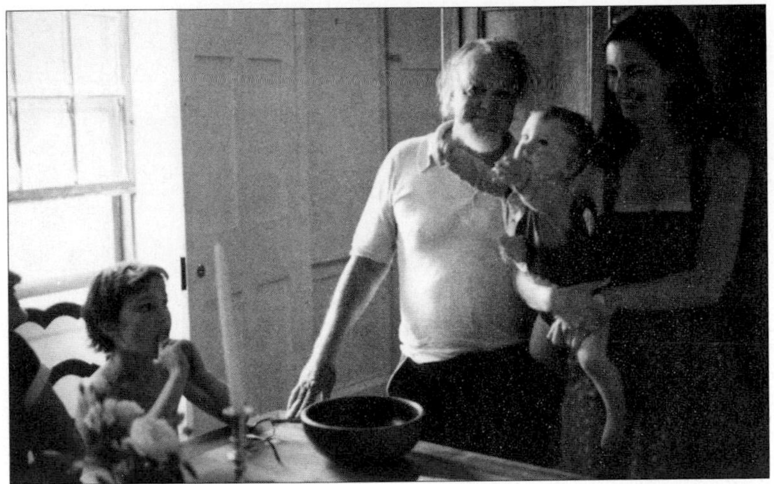

Francis, Dad, John, and Genie gather around the bowl of water in which Dad has just baptized John in our kitchen, 1981.

"The Gang" in my first feature: Wired to Kill, *1985 (Merritt Butrick to the left).*

John in South Africa, 1988.

"Baby," me, and Carol Kane, filming Baby on Board *in Toronto, 1992.*

Wired to Kill *(1986).*

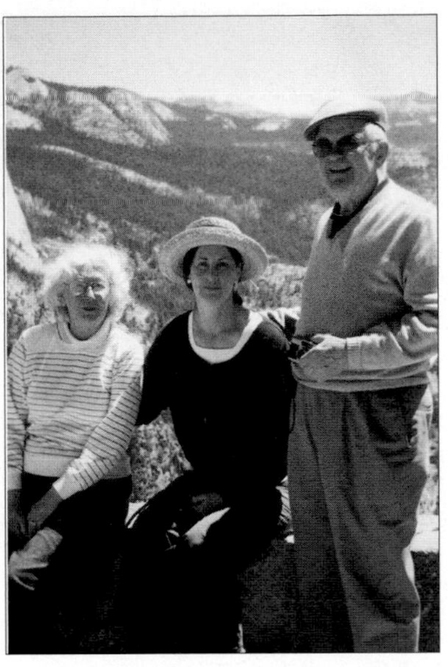

Genie and her parents, Stan and Betty Walsh.

Baby on Board *(1992).*

John, Ted Koppel, and me on the set of Nightline *promoting our book* Keeping Faith.

Francis, Ben, Genie, Jessica, Amanda, and John, Parma, Italy, 2004.

Edith Schaeffer, age ninety-one, at Chalet Tzi-No, Huémoz (2006).

When Stark was gone, there remained nothing but the insipid Head, the feckless masters, and roving gangs of prefects. That was when Stapleton, Carter, and I decided to run away.

The night we ran, I had been at St. David's just under two years and was about to turn fifteen. Our idea was to make it to London and live on the streets until I could look up a young woman who I'd met during the summer holidays at L'Abri. I knew the address of her flat, and I assured my friends that she would be glad to see us.

"Maybe we can live there for a few months," I said, somehow believing this insanity.

We left in the night and walked for two hours to the Llandudno station, where we bought tickets to London. We split up on the train so that if they were looking for three boys—who "they" were was some vague paranoid idea about the police—they would not find us. When we went through stations, we hid in the toilets.

The girl in London was cool about us showing up, although my friends chickened out immediately, called home, and went to their families. They also betrayed our hiding place. Two days later, Ranald came to get me.

Ranald said "You have put a noose around your neck. If you were my son, I would give you a good caning and send you back. Your parents have foolishly said you may go home."

Dad was furious with me. Mom was sad. Dad and I screamed at each other for several hours.

"You never even went there to check it out!" I yelled. "Do you know what it was like?"

"You could have told me!" said Dad.

"I *did* tell you! All you ever said was it might get better!"

Dad was trying to talk me into going back to St. David's. On the other hand, he would not force me. And for several months I just hung around L'Abri. That was when I began to paint and draw almost every day. Then Mom and Dad put me in the Commonwealth-American School in Lausanne, a dumping ground for the usual suspects from the "international community."

I lived in Lausanne (an hour bus and train ride from home) in a rented room five days a week, in the Berthoud family's apartment. (Their son was a L'Abri worker, one of the few Swiss there besides my brother-in-law John Sandri.)

The Berthouds were two middle-aged spinster sisters and their elderly mother. Food was boiled or baked into pale oblivion. I spent my free time roaming Lausanne, looking for girls and sneaking into softcore porn movies presented as heavily subtitled "documentaries" with titles like *Mysteries of Love* or *Women of the Night* with voice-overs by "experts" who sounded like Swedish versions of Dr. Strangelove.

33

After about six months, I quit going to school in Lausanne. One morning sometime in 1967, Dad woke, came to my room, banged on the door, and announced: "I have cheated you! When the girls were your age, I took them to museums. I've been too busy with L'Abri. It is time we did something about this."

I was stunned and nervous. What on earth would it be like to be alone for weeks with Dad? I had been in boarding schools for the better part of six years, and I was starting to see him more as Francis Schaeffer, the leader of L'Abri, than as my father. Our hikes had been getting infrequent during the holidays from school. Recently they had stopped. Dad was just too busy.

When my father and I took our father-son trip, it was an art pilgrimage. I never saw Dad so happy as when he was looking at and discussing art. His face literally changed. He looked younger. At night when we ate in restaurants, Dad never said grace over meals. It was as if Dad and I had a secret agreement that away from L'Abri, we would pretend we were secular people. Anyone overhearing our conversations would have assumed that Dad was an art historian. If God got mentioned, it was as a subject of art. Dad left his Bible at home.

We'd check into a small, inexpensive hotel. Dad would sort

out his tattered pile of city maps and dog-eared art books and plot a course. We would always comment on the pitifully tiny bars of soap, the strange little dishtowel-like "bath towels," the low wattage of the bedside reading lamp, the precariousness of the small, slow, dimly lit elevators, and the joy of being in Italy, anywhere in Italy. The next morning, we'd set out on a pilgrimage to places like the Carmine Chapel to see Masaccio's *Eve*.

Dad was a great art history teacher. We looked at the art in Florence, Rome, and Venice in chronological order. Dad would insist that I tell him what I liked and why, before talking about a piece. (My sister Susan told me that she remembers how grateful she was that when she was a child visiting museums, Dad always let her pick out something she liked to look at, before he told her what she should pay attention to.) Dad would gently guide me to the best works from some period, explaining the evolution of style, of subject, something about the period the art came from. We would start with Etruscan and Roman art, look briefly at the Byzantine and pre-Renaissance works in churches and museums, and then take the Renaissance painters in order, beginning with Giotto. We might as well have been on a tour arranged by Vasari, as we followed the Renaissance from its beginnings all the way up to Leonardo, and beyond to the baroque, to "crazy old El Greco" and the mannerists.

What is interesting is to note that, in theory, Dad was opposed to the "humanism of the Renaissance" and was a champion of "Northern European Reformation art," the works of the good Protestants. But in practice, it was the art of the Italian Renaissance that we spent much more time soaking up. We stood in front of pictures like the *Birth of Venus* and the *Primavera* as if before altars. And we looked, really *looked*, having waited to reward ourselves with these ultimate Renaissance visions of loveliness, order, and idealism as we plodded through countless pre- and early Renaissance Virgin and Childs in lovely dark old churches where we'd insert fifty-lira coins in a slot to turn on the lights that would illuminate faded frescos. Dad would build up a verbal picture of the rediscovery of perspective, of the lost methods of the Romans, point out at what moment Renaissance painting surpassed Roman and Greek inspiration.

In his L'Abri lectures, and later in his books, Dad would explain and even lament all this "humanistic art" that placed "man, not God, at the center of the universe." But when he was looking at the art with me, all we talked about was how beautiful it was, how remarkable it was that competitions were held to design Florence's baptistery doors, how stunning the achievements were: Brunelleschi's dome for the cathedral, Giotto's bell tower, the Della Robbia family and their blue and white glazed terra-cottas, not to mention our favorite, the choir stall carved by Della Robbia and preserved in the Museo dell'Opera del Duomo.

I saw Dad as he might have been, free of the crushing belief that God had "called" him to save the world. And my father became my biggest fan when I began to paint more and more seriously. Along with Mom, he backed me to the hilt after I began to show and sell paintings.

On our Italian trips, I always had a sketchpad along, and sometimes I painted small oils, as I always had done while we vacationed in Portofino. Dad would sit, reading, next to me while I drew or painted, and he traipsed around with me looking for locations to shoot my 8-millimeter movies. When I wanted to make a film of some of the statues in the Loggia in

Florence and said I would like some young pretty girl to walk through the shots as part of my movie, Dad hired a beautiful young Dutch girl we met in San Marco's and paid her for several hours of work so I could get my shots.

Many years later, in 1983, the year before Dad died and when he was already very ill—he was in St. Mary's Hospital at the Mayo Clinic in Rochester, Minnesota—I went out, found an art-supply store, and then sat down next to Dad and painted and drew for two days. I worked from memory, producing drawings of favorite places, the Dents du Midi at night, views of Portofino, Florence, a mother and child, and several paintings of my heavily outlined, oversized apples and leaves. (I hadn't painted for over ten years.)

I pinned and propped up the art all around my father, turning his hospital room into an impromptu gallery. The warm friendly scent of the linseed oil overwhelmed that hospital smell. I held Dad, and we cried together. And Dad answered my thoughts when he said, right out of the blue, "We had fun in Florence, didn't we, boy?"

34

L'Abri was at its zenith in 1968. Hippies and other assorted "seekers" were thronging the community. Dad was traveling to lecture more and more. Mom was giving many talks at L'Abri and all over Europe and America. In imitation of some of our wilder students, I was wearing knee-high motorcycle boots in which I carried a dagger. I was painting up a storm in my attic studio. I smoked and drank wine and shandies (a mix of lemonade and beer). L'Abri was filled with backpacking young men and women not too much older than me. We all knew every word of Sergeant Pepper's.

I wanted to be an artist, wanted to write plays, and was taking hundreds of photographs. My parents had lost control of me, yet were proud of my accomplishments as a painter when they (very occasionally) noticed I was alive. It seemed that they just thought of me as one more L'Abri guest. I certainly looked the part. But my parents did keep paying for art supplies and also set me up with Donald Drew, one of the L'Abri workers, who had been a literature teacher before he retired and took up full-time ministry.

Donald was dapper, a lifelong bachelor, white-haired and distinguished-looking, and a classical music record collector whose one possession was a monster sound system. We studied

Shakespeare, Chaucer, and the Brontë sisters. I would write essays for Donald once a week. He was a good teacher, and over the course of about eighteen months I more or less received a "great books" British university-level literature course.

Dad was wearing his hair longer and longer, and he grew a goatee. He took to wearing beige Nehru jackets, odd linen shirts, and mountain-climber's knickers (a Swiss alpine version of old-fashioned golfing plus-fours). Dad had evolved into a hip guru preaching Jesus to hippies, a precursor to, and the spiritual father of, the Jesus Movement that some of Dad's disciples like Jack Sparks—who a few years later, was featured on the cover of *Life* baptizing hippies in a San Francisco swimming pool—founded after they studied at L'Abri.

The last vestiges of my family's fundamentalist taboos were forgotten. The constant stream of students and their questions and interests had changed my parents radically. The L'Abri I left to go to GW at eleven and the L'Abri I came back to at fifteen (almost sixteen) were completely different places. I could listen to any music I wanted.

On any given evening, several of the L'Abri guests were out in the fields smoking pot. By the time I was barely sixteen, I was hanging around with twenty-year-olds, mostly the bell-bottom-clad, long-haired "English crowd" that were then regulars at L'Abri.

Dad was about to become one of the most famous and influential evangelical leaders of his time, after his first book, *Escape from Reason,* was published. He was preaching against "middle-class Christianity" and used the word "bourgeois" when he talked about "plastic Christians" and the "generation gap."

The ethos of the sixties suited my parents perfectly. Dad had dropped out of the mainstream evangelical missionary movement in the late 1940s and then discovered the world of art. In the 1960s, he was swept up in a subculture of rebellion when he began to listen to artists like Bob Dylan. The times mirrored Dad's individualism. He was "into" big ideas; and, suddenly, so was everyone else. Dad knew how to "speak to young people so they understand," and suddenly other evangelicals wanted to know how to do that, too. Born-again Christians were confronted by a rebellious youth culture. Suddenly they needed Dad's pop-culture expertise.

Dad said that middle-class values, bereft of their Christian foundation, were empty. He sided with "the kids" against their "uptight parents." Dad warned that once the memory of the truths upon which "middle-class Western norms" were built—in other words, biblical Christianity—had been forgotten, that within a generation those values would be swept away. "Then people will want order at any price."

L'Abri was now on the radar screen of a whole generation of backpacking bohemian travelers, on their way to or from ashrams in India, London's trendy Carnaby Street, or San Francisco's Haight-Ashbury. Dad's answer to the rebellion of the "happening generation" was that the hippie analysis of our plastic culture was correct but that their solution—free love and drugs—would not work. Mankind had a God-given moral character. If you did not obey God's law, you were flying in the face of reality because "The universe is what it is, no matter what we say it is."

Dad's answer was not to return to middle-class ways but to accept the truth of the Bible and then encourage the artists, poets, and rebels to rebel with a purpose: to restore truth to its rightful place, and to redeem all of creation through putting Christ back at the center of our lives. While they did this, there was no need to conform to "petty bourgeois rules." You could keep your hair long and your music hip, and smoking a little pot was no better or worse than that martini your uptight parents drank every night. Rock and roll was fine. It often told the truth about the human condition far, far better than all those American "plastic preachers" did.

On a speaking trip sometime in 1967 or early 1968, Dad took me along. (I forget if this was during a holiday before I ran from St. David's, or just after.) We were in California, where Dad was speaking at Westmont College in Santa Barbara. I hooked up with the daughter of a L'Abri worker who happened to be a freshman at the school. I spent a pleasant evening necking with her on a bench overlooking the sports facility while she steered my hands away from her crotch.

In one lecture I did attend, Dad berated the administration for not acquiescing to the demands of a local environmental group. The school had refused to spare some trees that some local hippies were trying to save when the school built a new wing. Dad had found out about this while walking around the neighborhood. The school revisited the issue and, because of Dad, a stand of trees was saved. (Not too long after that incident, Dad wrote a pro-environmentalist book that went more or less unnoticed in the evangelical market, at least compared to some of his best-selling works.)

One night in San Francisco, Dad and I went to the Fillmore West and heard Jefferson Airplane. Dad loved the concert and stayed the whole night. When the hippies packed around us passed a joint our way, Dad smiled and mouthed the words "No, thank you" but cheerfully handed it on down the line. The next day, Dad bought several Airplane albums. After that, once in a while he played them at top volume in his bedroom.

He was the coolest dad anyone I knew had, and the only one who knew the words to "White Rabbit."

Bob Dylan scheduled a visit to L'Abri, then at the last minute didn't come. Mick Jagger also failed to show up at the last minute. (He and Keith Richards had a chalet in Villars and called to say they were on their way down to us several times.) My cousin Jonathan (his mother was Aunt Janet, of the Communist Party and later of the Closed Brethren) was hanging around London with Paul McCartney. Dad was carrying on a long handwritten correspondence with Leopold Senhor, President of Senegal (a famous African poet in his own right). When I met Jimmy Page, lead guitarist for Led Zeppelin (in 1969 or thereabouts), he had a paperback copy of *Escape from Reason* in his back pocket and pronounced it "very cool." Eric Clapton had given him Dad's book, Page told me. One of Joan Baez's best friends was at L'Abri.

Of course, we were all hoping Joan Baez *would* come to L'Abri and get saved, because that would be a "great way to reach so many young people for Christ." The more famous, the more hip the convert, the more "the Lord could use that person." There was a type of unofficial aristocracy. A born-again Wheaton College student (Wheaton is a major evangelical school in Illinois), who showed up just to do Bible studies and to "deepen her walk with the Lord," was low on the totem pole compared to, say, a British heroin addict-artist who was hanging out with Keith Richards.

When former Harvard professor and LSD drug guru Timothy Leary came to Villars and stayed in a hotel for several days to meet with Dad, we canceled everything and had a special day of fasting and prayer. "Just *think* of what it will mean if *he* gets saved!" Mom exalted. When Bob Dylan *didn't* show up, "the Devil won a victory."

According to Dad, Samuel Becket, Jean Genet, The Beatles, Bob Dylan, et al., were doing God's work. They were preparing men's hearts, in "pre-evangelism," and "tearing down the wall of middle-class empty bourgeois apathy." Jimi Hendrix was *right* to scorn that plastic business, man! All we needed to do was provide the answer after the counterculture rebels opened the door by showing people that life without Jesus was empty.

The great thing was that since Jimi Hendrix saw the problem—"the problem" was materialistic middle-class life without eternal values—listening to Jimi became essential to "understanding our generation" and "reaching them." As Dad said, "We have to speak their language."

Since that language was rock and roll, art and movies, it suited me perfectly. Not only had the fundamentalist taboos of my childhood lapsed; they were reversed. In fact, during our many arts weekends I was encouraged to play the latest records, and then we would have discussions on what it all meant. Dropping out and turning on was cool now, so I was going with the flow, no longer an oddity.

The twenty-year-olds I was hanging out with were not interested in necking, but in having sex. They weren't smoking a little dope; those on drugs were addicts or had hitchhiked through India and arrived at L'Abri like backpacking private pharmacies. There were some who had attempted suicide, girls who talked about the multiple abortions they had had. Everyone wore clothes like a badge. How long your hair was defined who you were.

I grew my hair past my shoulders and organized shows of my art and photography in the L'Abri chapel from time to time, as did other artists visiting L'Abri, as did the poets who read at poetry evenings, as did the composers and musicians who performed at the many concerts, from Jane Stuart Smith's classical recitals to protest songs. The art was not some Christianized pablum; it had an edge. Poems were often pornographic, my paintings were sometimes of nudes, and the music was loud.

It was imperative that we "go into the world" and paint, compose, write, and direct movies. I was not only *allowed* to go to movies but organizing film festivals for L'Abri, including Fellini and Bergman. And there were a host of Schaeffer clones who were starting to get into the be-cool-for-Jesus business, too. Oz Guinness, Dick Keyes, and many others who were at one time or another L'Abri workers, learned their I-can-explain-everything-to-modern-people strategies for evangelical intellectual renewal while sitting at Dad's feet.

The dorms were full. Discussions in the chapel were packed. At two AM on any given day, we were up discussing the world and everything in it. And my studio was a great place to chat up a bird.

Mom and Dad had completely abandoned even a pretense of parental guidance. They were now so busy writing books, getting famous, and working night and day in L'Abri, or on the road speaking, that had I died they might have gone a week or two without noticing. (As a parent, I look back at this time with stunned wonderment.)

I found stability in my friendships within the ever-changing kaleidoscope of guests, helpers, and workers. One sweet young woman provided my transition from childhood crushes to almost-grown-up love. (Years later, when I saw the movie *Rushmore,* I completely understood and identified with the protagonist and his hilariously humiliating quest to be taken seriously by a woman ten years older than him.)

Kathy was a student at L'Abri, then became a worker. I think she got to L'Abri when I was about thirteen, and left when I was almost sixteen. For a year or so, I was wildly, madly in love with her. She was about twenty-five, had a rounded kindly face, bright blue eyes that glittered when she laughed, dimples to die for, and frosty gold-blonde hair. And Kathy was kind, and yet frighteningly virtuous.

She let me tag around after her, but she kept a very appropriate physical distance from this lusting man-boy. Kathy kept me so busy with unrequited longing that she prevented me from chasing many more available but—in retrospect—much less wholesome young women. (I probably *didn't* contract syphilis, herpes, or gonorrhea from the hitchhiking crowd that year because of Kathy.)

I have a "snapshot" of Kathy pleasantly fixed in my brain: the-endlessly-frustratingly-wholesome-pietistic-super-evangelical-female in our vegetable garden, brushing a strand of golden hair out of her face with the back of her hand as she picked peas, while looking as if she was in some scene cut from *The Sound of Music,* my very own Julie Andrews.

I recently tracked Kathy down via e-mail (we had been out of contact for forty years) and asked her how she remembered my parents. Her reply is a good representation of the absolute devotion that so many evangelicals have to them even today, and also of their disapproval of me, or anyone, that might do anything to diminish their worshipful regard for my parents.

> February 17, 2007
>
> Dear Franky, (Sorry, I just can't bring myself to call you Frank, unless you insist, that is). . . . What I can tell you is that I absolutely adore and admire your parents. Of course, I was the closest to your mother. She taught

> me how to cook and how to pray. I was inspired by her creativity and energy and strong faith. After I left L'Abri I couldn't wait until the "Family Letters" arrived and I read each one the moment I received it, hanging on to every word. There isn't a book that she wrote that I did not read enthusiastically, once again treasuring all her details and gleaning from her words of wisdom. . . . I also have to be honest and tell you that I heard about a book you wrote [*Portofino*] that was very hurtful to your parents.
>
> Your friend from almost 40 years ago (Yikes!!!), Kathy

Kathy left L'Abri, and just before she did I lost my virginity to Mandy, a beautiful twenty-year-old, all because Dad took me along on a speaking trip to Covenant College, an evangelical school located on Lookout Mountain, Tennessee. Actually, I lost it back in L'Abri with Mandy a few weeks later; but I met her at Covenant, where I kissed her in the library and, while Dad was lecturing to the whole student body, got my hands down her panties while on the bed of Dr. Barnes, the college president. (Mom, Dad, and I were staying in his home.) When Mandy traveled to L'Abri, I met her at Geneva Airport and we necked for an hour, all the way from Geneva to Aigle station. We had cheerless intercourse in my attic studio a few days later. I ejaculated after about three seconds and two thrusts. Within a few weeks, I was able to manage five or six thrusts. Why she was interested in sex with a young bad lover, a horny dolt, remains a mystery. Maybe it had something to do with me being the guru-of-the-moment's son.

I played sex like I played soccer: no hands and go straight

for the goal. She had had six other boyfriends and an abortion, she said. Our "relationship" lasted for about three months. Kathy-the-virtuous used to pound on my bedroom door when she knew we were having sex, trying to make me behave according to the principles L'Abri officially stood for. My parents, as usual, were nowhere in sight, either to reprimand me or to tell me to use condoms. How their failure to be effective parents squares with Kathy's worship of my mother and father as people oh-so wise, I don't know.

The odd thing was how the line between whom we were trying to reach for Jesus, and those doing the reaching—in other words, my parents—was blurring. American pastors would sometimes visit and compliment my parents on being able to "reach," and put up with, "all these hippies." What they didn't realize was that we Schaeffers had *become* these hippies.

Mandy modeled for me, and most of the modeling sessions ended in my lickety-split version of in-out bad sex. My nude paintings from that period seem rather hurried.

During the period Kathy remembers so fondly, Dad was at his angriest. And my sister Priscilla was about to have her first complete nervous breakdown. A fight was brewing between my brothers-in-law that would eventually split L'Abri. On some days, Mom was hiding bruises on her arms; on other days, she was flirting shamelessly with Roger, a handsome "sensitive poet" from San Francisco, twenty years younger than her. This was the source of my parents' biggest fights.

Mom would take Roger to pray with her in the woods, to her prayer trees—a great and unique honor!—where he would collect moss, twigs, and flowers and make lovely Japanese-style arrangements. Dad was reduced to glaring fury by these activities. He never so much as picked a bunch of flowers, and now here was this Roger, writing poems, empathizing with Mom's "if-only" wistful remembrances of opportunities lost, and endlessly seeking her spiritual advice.

In other words, my parents were no better or worse than most people and went though a few really bad patches. But groupies have to believe in something or someone.

35

I had become an art- and sex-driven wraith haunting L'Abri and our mountainside. I was in The Work, but not of it. The intrusion of the students, the hurly-burly of the comings and goings, the growing crowds of people who came on Sunday to church in the summer, the constant noise around the house, everything made me hate where I lived—and love it.

The chalet contained all the swirl of activity any teen could want, but none of the privacy. It was all action all the time. I would retreat to my bedroom or to my studio; do everything I could to carve a little privacy out of the groupings and re-groupings of the students.

I went on raiding parties, cutting through the new students like a particularly hungry tuna through a school of sardines. First and foremost, my target was girls. If one was pretty, I would plot to be near her, see what I could get going. Sometimes I'd find a temporary patron, someone to buy a painting or to introduce me to a gallery owner, or read some of the play I was writing or watch one of my Super-8 movies on the little editing console I set up in my studio.

Lady Edward Montague was one visitor who became a patron. A year or two later, she introduced me to the Frisch Gallery in New York. Later still, Audrey Jadden, who lived down by Lake Geneva with her husband Bill, two of the best and kindest people I have ever known, introduced me to Mr. Chante Pierre of the Chante Pierre Gallery in Aubonne, outside Geneva. Another set of lifelong and lovely L'Abri friends, John and Sandra Bazlinton, organized a show in London for me.

Of all my shows, the one at the Chante Pierre Gallery was best. It was a serious gallery, and my work was shown alongside paintings by Miro and Picasso. At the well-attended opening, I almost threw up with nervousness and was also thrilled. It was a wonderful and terrible thing to see my paintings hanging in a real gallery.

At the opening, Chante Pierre introduced me as a young, new, and talented painter, and I watched as "real" (non-L'Abri people), actual art collectors looked at my work. As if by some miracle, several little red dots appeared on the catalogue price list, indicating sales. The feeling I got was like looking over a precipice, thrilled and frightened. And somewhere in my brain, a little explosion went off. It was if I had just heard a whispered message: "You can escape the madness!"

It was the first time that I felt I might have a future, with or without any college degree, with or without a normal childhood. I was going to soon forget that hopeful moment and plunge into my dad's ministry with a vengeance. But the message of freedom-through-art stuck in my brain someplace. And years later, when I hit rock bottom, that voice reminded me that there are possibilities beyond one's background. When I would feel most trapped, it would "speak" of freedom.

Some of the workers became my friends, at least for a while. Thirty-year-old English L'Abri worker Oz Guinness, for instance, compared notes with me on which girls we thought were the prettiest, which ones I was going to "have a go at," and which ones he "fancied." If he spoke up for one, I'd honor our friendship by not flirting with her, and vice versa. I always envied him. He seemed to get so much further with the girls most of the time, which, given that he was a thirty-year-old eligible bachelor, makes sense now, but didn't then.

Sometimes I'd mine the students to find companions for little adventures, like sledding. Every year there was a night when the snow was perfect, packed, icy, and smooth—this was before the days of sand and salt on the road—and I'd take my group with me to Chésières using someone's car, usually one of the workers, to ferry us back and forth with our old-fashioned wood sleds with steel runners. (We Schaeffers still didn't have a car, but many of the workers did by this time.)

I'd been sledding since I was barely a toddler, and many of the students had never even seen snow. We would head down the road on some night filled with starlight that made the snow shine. The sleds were designed for one to sit on and steer with your heels. But I lay head-first and steered by leaning this way and that and touching the ground with my hands as rudders. You had to judge the corners right, fly through at the right speed, or pay the price.

We'd have a few girls in the sledding party, and none of the young men wanted to appear slow or inept. So every year there was usually somebody from someplace without mountains who would be showing off, hitting the corners too fast, and we'd have accidents. On three occasions, these were serious. The fact that it was dangerous made the adventure all the more wonderful; not to mention the clear air, the velvet blanket of snow so thick that all the contours of the mountainside, trees, even the thickly covered chalet roofs looked soft and rounded.

The mountains across the valley would be bright, snow

clinging and making everything look huge and close in the starlight, even lovelier if there was a moon. There were so many stars visible and the air was clear, light pollution so low, that even without a moon the snow was bright. When you looked up, it seemed as if there were more sharp glittering stars than gaps between them. The universe seemed friendly and near. Girls looked wonderful, their frosty breaths blooming from red lips, frost-touched cheeks, and wisps of hair peeking from under wool caps, eyes reflecting sparks of starlight.

I'd always be way ahead of the pack and head off with a "Follow me!" that I knew was an idle challenge since no one could. I never crashed, never fell, hardly slowed down for the curves, could hit the curve inside and feel myself slashing over the ice as I slid across the road to the outside while cutting the straightest line through the bend. There were straight sections where I would be going so fast that the snowbank and trees seemed to turn into one long white flickering ribbon streaking past in my peripheral vision while the road flew under me like a rushing river. The least touch of one hand to the ground was enough to turn. And my "brakes" were my toes, hanging over the end of the sled, providing drag when the corners were sharp but held off the road the rest of the time so nothing would slow my headlong careening race to the valley.

You could smell the snow. The cold pinched your nose and had a whiff of fresh-picked cucumber, maybe a touch of frosty lemon, distant, hard to pin down, but cold and clean as if it came from inside a crystal. If it was snowing, we'd sled while squinting through eyelashes crusted with flakes, and seeing the road was impossible. You steered by looking for the faint outline of the hillside rising on one side and falling away to dark nothingness on the other.

Jan Van Loon, a hulking Dutchman, all 230 pounds or so of him practically crushing the little wood sled he was hanging over at both ends like a big hot dog laid over an undersized bun, shot down the road at breakneck speed. We were on the Panex road to Ollon, a road that led to the valley from the little village of Panex a couple of miles from ours; unlike our road that cut mainly through fields, the Panex road went down through forest the whole way. Even in winter, when the leaves were off the beech trees, the pines were as dark as ever and covered up the stars or cast patchwork shadows, turning the moonlight into a confusing crisscross pattern of light and dark. But because it was so steep, steep enough that cars had to stay in low gear when driving up it even in summer, the ride was fantastic . . . if you could steer.

Jan Van Loon hadn't ever been on a sled before, but he was a showoff. He was a loud bearded artist who chain-smoked, drank in the village pub, and always had the more arty girls clinging to him. At the start of the run, he talked about it as if it was a race that he planned to win. On the first long straight section of road, Jan passed me. He hadn't had to negotiate a corner yet. The first hairpin bend doubled back on itself as tightly as a corkscrew. Below it, the forest clung to a mountain-side so steep that you looked out through treetops growing below the road. Jan hit the first corner, crashed through the hedge, and left no tracks.

We only noticed he was missing about eight minutes later when we got to Ollon. It took us half an hour to get Claire Olson, a single worker with a VW bug, rousted out of bed, and another half hour before she got to Ollon and we drove slowly back up the road, with chains on her tires, looking for our missing Dutchman. We stopped at the corners and called. At last we got to the place Jan had gone off the road and saw the gap in the hedge where he'd smashed through. His sled's tracks ended abruptly.

The moon was out, so we could see the mountainside below between the stripes of shadow, but there was no sign of him, just sled tracks and then unbroken snow. Then we heard singing. Jan's sled lay smashed at the foot of the trunk of an enormous beech tree fifty feet below the road. From there, footprints led a little way to where Jan sat, head bleeding and face steaming, singing in a slurred voice. He had hit the tree about fifteen or so feet above the ground, having flown from the edge of the road through the air and smashed into the trunk high above the mountain's side, which fell away beneath him almost vertically.

Jan was heavy. He laughed, raved, and sang like some cartoon caricature of a drunken pirate. It took five of us to hoist, pull, push, and drag Jan back up to the road, using the undergrowth poking through the snow for handholds. He was cheerfully out of his mind, had no idea he was hurt, let alone that his beard was crusted with blood. It took us the better part of an hour to rescue him. He was in the Aigle hospital for a month.

36

I got to know Priscilla well only after she moved back to L'Abri when I was ten. She came home with John and their firstborn, Elizabeth. Priscilla became my best friend and was soon mother to three remarkable children, Elizabeth, Rebecca, and Giandy. All of them remain close friends of mine to this day.

By the time Priscilla moved back, she had analyzed a lot of what her own childhood had been about. She had become this sweet libertarian, someone who still was a believing evangelical but who was also literally allergic to the strict pietism of her childhood, as well as to theology in general. And she hated the fact that Mom and Dad were more or less worshipped by some people.

Priscilla became this wonderful bohemian, full of ineffable kindness, as well as a refreshing nonconformist. She was an anti-Christian Christian. And the students, like everyone, adored her and of course loved her husband John Sandri, too.

Even before L'Abri's evolution in the late sixties, Priscilla and John's little home, Chalet Tzi-No, was the place I could go to hear rock music, listen to the BBC, hear about the profane modern novels Priscilla was reading, hear stories about the bad old days and just how lucky I was to be raised by Mom and Dad now, not then.

Priscilla rebelled against my mother's excruciatingly fancy ways. Where Mom had a closet full of fabulous clothes, Priscilla prided herself on never dressing up and on always wearing the same clothes until they fell off her. And she refused to alter anything in her tiny chalet. It had only cold water in the kitchen. There was no living room, just the little kitchen, red checked curtains, a few antique kitchen implements hanging on the walls, a simple wood-burning stove, and no central heat. Priscilla and John's chalet became my favorite destination. It became everyone's favorite destination.

All the little children at L'Abri, including my children after I got married and was still living in Huémoz and then nearby in Chésières, went to Priscilla's play school. They grew up loving her passionately. My sister was like some good witch down a mysterious forest path, a woman who provided endless sympathy and, like her husband John, never judged you, had a house so simple that you could not do anything to hurt it and could be utterly free therein.

It was a land of finger paints, cheerful music, stories read out loud as beautifully as they would have been read by Meryl Streep. It was also a place that became off-limits when my sister had her big breakdowns, a virtual hermit's cell where John sat with her for months at a time protecting her from the fear, anxiety, and depression that left my sister numb, unable to cope with even the simplest daily routines. John nursed Priscilla as she'd crawl back from the brink of mental collapse, thoughts of suicide, and being unable to see even her closest family members, let alone L'Abri students. John helped her adjust to a regime of antidepressant medications that could keep the demons at bay. Whatever else the reasons were for my sister's problems, she was paying a heavy price for simply being a Schaeffer daughter, for having lived in a fishbowl, having a mother who let everyone know that she could outwork, outpray, and spiritually outshine everyone else, including her daughters.

When Debby moved back, I'd visit her, too. She and I also became best friends. My sisters, perhaps remembering how trapped they had felt in our home before there were other chalets and families in the work to escape to, kept an open door to their wayward little brother. I spent hours sitting in Debby's kitchen in Chalet Les Sapins. Her husband Udo was a lot more serious than John but was also extremely kind and welcoming. And given that I was a demanding, attention-grabbing pain in the ass, often pretending to be a lot older and more sophisticated than I was, I must have been insufferable. But Udo treated me with dignity and respect and would discuss seriously when we argued about philosophical ideas or art, as if I actually was saying something worth listening to, which I am sure I wasn't!

I could tell Debby anything. When I started having sex, it was Debby I told, and she asked me if I had intercourse or was "just fooling around." I wasn't embarrassed to tell her the truth. I knew that no matter what she thought of my actions, Debby wouldn't tell on me. I also had always known that she loved me, and that she was on my side come hell or high water, a certain knowledge that persisted through life, even when Debby, some years later, was upset after my novel *Portofino* was published. I knew it was temporary and that we would soon be friends again.

37

Time stumps me. When I begin a sentence "I always used to go up to Villars any way I could, hitchhike, walk, catch the bus, all for the purpose of being at the Grenier Discothèque. . . ," it sounds as if I'm describing something I did every day for years. But it was most likely for a summer.

In any case, by the summer of 1968 I was "always" going up to Villars to the Grenier. I'd dress carefully. Should it be the turquoise scarf tied like a cravat, the tight T-shirt, the velvet jeans, the leather jacket, or the smelly Afghan coat? Should I wear my blue sunglasses?

Many fashion decisions were inspired by album covers. Hendrix was wearing tight white pants on one. Of course, the Beatles had set a high standard with the jacket photo of "Sgt. Pepper." I'd go for the cobalt blue shirt, pink waistcoat, white suede shoes, the long scarf, the bell-bottom green pants, and the three-inch-wide belt. Once "dressed," I'd have to figure out how lazy I was feeling. Walk to Villars about three miles up the mountain, or hitchhike? That was the question. Then I got a moped.

I had wheels, albeit slow wheels: max speed thirty kilometers per hour on the flat, sixty to eighty kilometers per hour when freewheeling down the mountainside. (I learned the hard way to always ride with my leather jacket on and to watch out for huge wet cow pies on sharp corners! I also learned, as I slid across the road, to try to distribute my weight evenly between my elbows and chest so that the gravel would be more evenly distributed under my skin, rather than allowing all the pressure and sanding-off, gravel-embedding effect to concentrate in one place—say, the palm of one hand—while thumb-sized chunks of flesh got torn off.)

I would order a coke or beer, and pay my three francs (a hefty price). I'd hope that Mickey Barilon, the son of the Hotel Curling owner, would be there. Usually he was. Mickey's mother was English. We were best friends, both displaced foreigners who could talk about "the Swiss" and their narrow foolish ways and feel superior to them, yet fit in when we had to. There were other international kids at the Grenier Discothèque, too, mostly older boys at the private high schools of Aiglon and Beau Soleil. We'd sit, nursing our drinks, never buying more than one (the three francs had to be stretched), and waiting for other kids to show up, hoping that they would include unaccompanied girls. The big problem was my age. Mickey and I were fifteen. The girls were looking for twenty-year-olds.

How could I convince the girls that I was old enough to pay any attention to? The key was to not get greedy and go for the prettiest girl in the knot of sweet-smelling females that might walk in, but to ask the slightly more homely girl to dance, once some twenty-year-old Italian from Aiglon had grabbed the one everyone was really looking at. If you were lucky, one of the lesser girls would dance with you. By then, the rich-looking Italian from Aiglon (who really was twenty, having been kicked out of several other private Swiss high schools and who was repeating twelfth grade for the third time) was already in a dark corner necking. He would be with the really stunning girl from

Paris in the miniskirt, while I would sit awkwardly at a table with the two remaining girls and Mickey, and we'd begin to chat them up while jealously eyeing the Italian Don Juan.

Of course our "conversations" were really nothing more than perfunctory questions shouted over the blasting sound system. Where did they live? What were they doing in Villars? What music did they like?

I'd shout that I was in school in England, or that I was going to Portofino the next week, or that I thought I'd seen the girl I was trying to hold hands with under the table in London once, anything to make it seem as if I was older, more worldly than they thought I was. Then if the actual question came up, I'd push my luck and say "seventeen" when asked the inevitable "how old are you?" Sometimes they believed me or pretended to.

At a certain point I'd try a kiss. Sometimes they would go for it. Sometimes we'd neck between sets, or at least I would get to slow dance with one of the girls. I was a horrible dancer, but so were they; in fact, horrible writhing, and/or bouncing, was all "dancing" was, post-Twist.

Anyway, dancing was beside the point. The agenda was the most coveted of coveted destinations so maddeningly just out of sight under the hem of her excruciatingly minuscule miniskirt that would—please God—show everything if she so much as bent to itch her knee. And then there were the black lights that made bras show up under blouses and our flesh look roasted.

The best way to break the ice was to ask for, or offer, a cigarette. Everyone smoked. I chose my brands carefully. American cigarettes were cool; so were the English luxury brands like Rothmans Gold. We avoided Gauloises or the bitter and even stronger crap-tasting Gitanes.

By midnight, the place was so thick with smoke, I'd feel sick. Between the smoke, bopping up and down, the intense longing for what was only inches above that hemline but a million miles away, or folded into a neat little V under skintight jeans, on most nights when, at last, they played the last song at about three AM and kicked us out, I'd step into the crisp mountain air gasping and nauseated.

I wasted many a hard-won three francs. After all that effort, I never once managed to do what so many other boys I met at the Grenier casually bragged (lied?) about, take a girl someplace and have sex with her after meeting her on the dance floor. All my successful conquests were in L'Abri, not out in the worldly "scene." It was a bit ironic. I got laid in the Lord's work; but in the immoral secular world, the girls weren't so easy.

I was fifteen or sixteen when I also started going to the Strobe Club in Montreux. This was a huge disco right in front of the Montreux Palace Hotel. It took me two hours to get there on my moped. It was in the lavish Victorian pavilion across the street from the huge hotel. It had a gigantic light show, a huge sound system, and drug-taking French hippies who lived in the basement running the place. Pot was smoked openly, and the average age of the clients was probably thirty. There were plenty of middle-aged men cruising for the young baby dolls.

I'd park my moped on the main street. It kept company with Ferraris, Alfas, and Maseratis. Nabokov was living in the Montreux Palace. Sometimes I'd see him or Mick Jagger, Keith Richards, or other gods at the Strobe. And when the Montreux Jazz Festival was in full swing, B. B. King might come in for a drink after playing at the Montreux casino, where the festival took place.

The girls were way too old, rich, and sophisticated. The drinks were five francs, too expensive. But after the French guys got to know me, I'd head right for the booth and climb into the trailer-sized enclosure (raised about five feet off the dance floor).

I soon became part of the crew. The guys that ran the show and spun the records let me hang around in the booth. We projected bits of Super-8 film, including several of my shorts, and used three overhead projectors to concoct the light-show effects. These effects were created by placing large glass salad bowls one inside another on the overhead projectors. We'd mix oil and colored water in the bowls, then press down and turn them, creating streams of colored bubbles out of the oil, water, and air trapped between the bowls. The overhead projectors bathed the dancers in our light show and made them appear as if they were deep under water thrashing around in some multicolored foaming sea. Cartoons, softcore porn, and pictures of rock stars were also projected. The strobes and black lights were on all the time. The sound system was so loud, it seemed to bypass my ears altogether and throb in my lungs, knocking the air out of me.

The Strobe connection led to my first paying job. I was part of the crew when we were hired to do some lighting at the Montreux Festival for Led Zeppelin. I got to "hang out" with the band.

My big moment came when Robert Plant (Zeppelin's lead singer) called out to me from across the bar in the casino, "Frankie boy!" For a golden moment I was mistaken for "someone" by several beautiful women. They *actually looked in my direction.*

I also got invited along to several after-disco parties in villas in Montreux and Clarens and other wealthy enclaves where English, sometimes titled, young men and women, French hippies, Swiss businessmen, minor royalty from Monaco, and lots of overdressed beautiful women hung out. This was much the same world that I got to know, or at least got to envy, in Portofino. Conversation was about movies, where everyone was going to spend the summer, travel, sex, music, where one lived, and who one knew.

I met Claude Nobs at one after-disco party. We were eating French onion soup at five in the morning, following a night of drinking. Claude was the founder and producer of the Montreux Jazz Festival and knew all about my family. For several years, he had been on a spiritual search and had attended several Bible classes Dad taught in Montreux. I was shocked. To be hanging around in this worldly company and to have to answer questions about my parents was unsettling.

The idea that these worlds could mix seemed crazy. I wanted to be cool; and now the most cool person I met at the most cool club in the world, a place that made the poor little old Grenier look like a peasant's kitchen, well later that night, *this* person was shouting over the music in the luxurious living room of a huge villa and asking me how my father was and if he was still teaching Bible classes in Mr. Halbritter's house above Montreux! And there I was trying to send signals that Dad was nothing to do with me, that I was *not* part of some ministry, a Peter denying Christ before the cock crowed three times if there ever was one.

I was propositioned by some smooth old homosexuals several times, not verbally but with hands laid in a friendly casual manner on my thigh or crotch, that I would brush away. They never persisted. That had happened when I was twelve and in

Portofino with my painter friend Lino, or rather a friend of his. Late one afternoon, I'd been walking around the cobblestone piazza watching fishermen repair their nets, when Lino waved his languid manicured hand in my direction and called me over to join them.

I found myself sitting next to Lino at one of the little tables covered with a ubiquitous pink linen tablecloth. Lino's friend was quite frank and polite as he asked "Do you like this?" while he stroked my thigh. I said no, and he took his hand away and we resumed discussing a painting of mine I had brought them the day before. Later Lino's friend said "I hope you don't mind, but some boys like this, and if you were that kind it would be a pity to waste the opportunity." He added "Please do not tell your father, I do not think he would understand."

I took that as a compliment. I knew they knew that my parents were in religious work. But they always treated me as if I wasn't, as if I was an artist, and that the brotherhood of art transcended whatever circumstances I might be in now. How I knew this, I don't know, but I did.

38

In October 1969, I met Regina Ann Walsh, Genie, object of thirty-seven years of passion and devotion, daughter of a self-made Irish lawyer, granddaughter of an Irish blacksmith, daughter of a mother whose ancestor was a signatory to the United States Constitution, hippie princess, the most beautiful girl I have ever seen, my final and best defense against meaninglessness, my other eyes, this woman, this girl, this goddess, ineffably patient, screaming warrior who won't-take-shit-past-a-certain-point, absolute center of the universe, oasis of calm, final arbiter, she who does the taxes.

Strange to think that Genie carried in her the potential that was Jessica, Francis, and John before she was born, before we met, before we became a country of two. Did I exist before we met? Did she?

Genie says she did. She says she played and flirted on Half Moon Bay near her home in San Mateo, California. She necked in cars, smoked pot, went to Catholic school, lost her faith and insisted on transferring to public school, watched her upstanding kindly father grill London Broil and drink scotch, grew up in a home right out of a 1950s TV show: her sweet mom played bridge; her parents mixed cocktails; both had served in World War II; Betty, Genie's mom, in the FBI; Stan, her father, in the Coast Guard.

Genie was a middle child, dropped acid, saw the Beatles and the Rolling Stones in concert—*twice*! hung out with the drummer from Jeff Beck's band—and all along was carrying our future within her.

When Genie first walked into Chalet Les Mélèzes with her sister Pam, she wore impossibly tight dark brown wool pin-striped slacks and an olive green shawl and a white blouse. They were traveling around Europe—as Pam's graduation present from Berkeley, and Genie's graduation present from high school. Genie was *supposed* to start college that fall. Their trip was *supposed* to be for a few weeks, not months, not a year, not a lifetime.

Genie didn't come to L'Abri on purpose and wasn't looking for God—just for Pam's best friend. By that time, I never ate in the Chalet Les Mélèzes dining room. I'd grab food from the kitchen and head for my studio, not willing to sit through more discussion with Dad holding forth answering the same questions again, as we sat jammed, back-to-back, shoulder-to-shoulder eating meatloaf—again—with stewed tomatoes—again—while Dad talked—again—about why Camus couldn't live logically by his philosophical presuppositions.

But that night, by God's grace, I was there, sitting by the door to the front hall. So when I heard the door open and poked my head around the corner, there she was, standing under the old, spiky, Venetian wrought-iron-and-glass lantern, eyes literally sparkling, long auburn hair down to her waist, points of pelvic bone defining her hips, belly tight under those second-skin slacks, high glossy boots up to her knees, full breasts, and that *face!* High cheekbones, lips so red and full I wanted to bite them, hazel eyes, almost Asian, slightly slanted at the corners, almond-shaped. A glittering white smile, tall, absolutely carefree, straightforward . . . and wanting to hear *Abbey Road,* the new Beatles album that I just happened to have downstairs in my studio.

My life began from the moment Genie walked downstairs after dinner to listen to *Abbey Road.* I was in love from that moment, was from the minute she opened the door, really, really in love or in something, in delirious, in a state where my brain stopped working and some prophetic instinct took over, my future as yet unwritten reaching back to make that stupid boy take steps to seize a life he could know nothing about. And all the other girls, those shadow women, those posers, pretenders, just faded away and my life became about Genie, and only one question remained: How do I keep her here?

I enlisted Mom.

It would be necessary to get Genie saved. I wanted to marry her. She would have to accept Jesus. I wanted Genie for a life mate, and how could you marry someone who wasn't saved? I also wanted to have sex with her, and so I didn't want her *too* saved, just saved enough.

I explained to Mom that I was *in love!* And Mom, a firm believer in St. Paul's admonition that it is "better to marry than to burn" with lust or in hell, whichever he meant, didn't laugh and say I was nuts and barely seventeen; she said "maybe Genie *is* the one God has chosen for you."

At first, Genie said she would stay a week. Then she decided to stay another week. I kept proposing marriage, and Genie kept laughing. But she let me kiss her the second day, and after we started having sex, the second week, each day had a shape.

There were two parts of the day; before we had sex and after—like flight: takeoff and landing.

Mom broke all the rules and got Genie into L'Abri, even though there was no room, and Genie didn't even want to be there, and only stuck around to be with me. This caused problems with some of the workers, many of whom were sick of my shenanigans and figured this was just one more "Frankie episode." But Mom and Dad liked Genie.

Soon after Genie showed up, I started to work harder at my painting and my literature tutorials with Donald Drew. In fact (sex aside), I more or less shaped up. I quit smoking cigarettes and pot. I quit going to the Strobe Club. Why bother? I'd only gone there to meet girls, and now I had met *the* girl! I even attended a few L'Abri lectures and discussions with Genie. The matter of getting her saved had to be attended to.

Mom declared that Genie was having a good effect on me. Dad was charmed and, after several talks with Genie, declared: "She has really good questions!"

Genie's "work," once Mom made her a L'Abri helper (so Genie could stay longer than the three-month maximum imposed on the students), was hanging out with me. While some other young man or woman got to peel carrots and potatoes in her place, Genie and I took walks, talked, made love, and acted as if we were in some alternative universe.

Mom and Dad *knew*! How could they *not* have known? Dad even walked in on us once. We were on my couch in my studio, naked. I pulled a cover over us. Dad asked me some mundane question and left and never said a word about it.

After Genie and I were married, I asked Mom why she let us be, even aided and abetted us. "I *loved* her, that's why," Mom answered. And on a recent visit back to Switzerland to visit

Mom (age ninety-two), she clasped Genie to her and loudly exclaimed, right out of the blue, "*Thank you for marrying him*!"—which made us all laugh. The implication was that Mom was grateful that *anyone* would have bothered, let alone stuck with me.

Only a few weeks after Genie got to L'Abri, we were practically living together. Since all the dorms were full, Genie was staying in a rented room down in the village. Every morning, she walked up the back road to Chalet Les Mélèzes, cooked bacon and eggs in our kitchen (yet another rule was thus broken), then climbed the stairs to our family apartment, woke me, and we'd have breakfast together.

When Genie walked to our chalet, if it had been snowing in the night, she sometimes passed the words "I LOVE GENIE" stamped out in giant letters on the fresh snow on the steep hillside above the path. I made those signs by moonlight during my walks home (at two or three in the morning), having spent the better part of the night in Genie's room.

Madame Ruchet (the farmer's wife L'Abri rented Genie's room from) slept across the hall from Genie, so I couldn't use the stairs during my visits. Fortunately, Genie's second-floor window opened over the farm's backyard. I'd place one of the long pieces of wood the farmer kept there against the wall and climb up.

After breakfast, we'd hang around my bedroom. Then I'd go to my tutorial with Donald, and Genie went to the L'Abri study center at Farel House, to listen to taped lectures. In the afternoons we hung out in my studio. Sometimes Genie modeled for me while I drew or painted her.

All those talks about ovaries and missed periods, and the seed and the egg, did no good, because I *did* get Genie pregnant—but not for a while, not until we were in New York City a year after Genie stumbled onto L'Abri. Genie had been home to California for a short ten days after she had been away at L'Abri for so much longer than planned. Then she disobeyed her parents and came back to me.

I was in New York City having my first American art show (at the Frisch Gallery). Genie came to the opening in a short white dress. She told me that she had found nothing to keep her at home. That she didn't feel close to her old friends and wanted to be with me and to return to L'Abri. With Genie beside me, I barely noticed anyone else, though the opening was rather successful. Mrs. David Rockefeller bought a painting.

Genie called her friend Denise and asked her to sneak into her bedroom and get her passport and send it to New York. And ten days later, and against her parents' wishes (they wanted her to come home and start school), Genie, aided and abetted by my parents—GOD BLESS THEM!—got on the SS *Leonardo da Vinci* of the Italia Line. We sailed out of New York after my show's opening and headed back to Europe.

During the seven-day voyage, Genie discovered that her period was late. So actually I must have gotten her pregnant before she left Europe, about a month before, and she went home, then came back to me unknowingly carrying our child.

A day later, I told Mom and she told Dad. He was furious, but only for a day. Years later, Mom said she had told Dad "It could have been me!" then added, "And *that* shut Fran up, because *he* hadn't waited either!"

When we disembarked at Genoa, we found that there was an Italian train workers' strike. Mom decided that given "the situation"—as she summed up Genie's pregnancy, Dad's grim Mood, and the lack of transport—we needed an impromptu vacation to "use this time." Mom booked us all into the Hotel Nazionale in Portofino. (Portofino is an hour's bus ride from Genoa.)

Dad relaxed. Mom prayed. And Genie and I took a long walk down the familiar path to Paraggi.

I showed Genie my old childhood haunts, the spectacular cove, the turquoise water, the beach where my happiest childhood memories are locked. And on the walk back to Portofino, we stopped to sit on a sun-warmed wall overlooking the bay.

I asked Genie—for the hundredth time—to marry me. She said yes.

That morning, Mom took off her mother's engagement ring and gave it to me, the one my grandfather Seville had given his future wife when they were missionaries in China. I had told my mother that I intended to ask Genie to marry me that day. Genie slipped on the ring.

I don't know if Genie said yes because she was pregnant or because she loved me. My mind was blank, as if the circuits had overloaded. What I felt was apprehension. Genie cried for a moment. I stared at the bay and the anchored yachts. We held each other for a long time and said nothing.

Three days later Genie called her parents from Switzerland, and they said that she certainly didn't have to marry me but could come home and have the baby and have it adopted, or keep it, either way getting on with her life. But Genie told them she loved me.

Genie still loves me, even though she knows me now. And thirty-seven years later, we have no idea what those children had in mind or who they were. And when Genie takes a trip alone, say to visit her mom, or the time she went with my mother to China for five weeks, to take Mom back to where she was born, my life stops. When Genie comes home, life starts again. I cook for Genie. We drink wine every day at five. And standing in the kitchen together is the best part of any day. And it is hard to believe that someday one of us will die and leave the other alone.

39

I hover over mother and child. Genie's eyes are exhausted, dazed. Genie's face is puffy. My neck is scarlet, chafed from wearing the surgical mask too tight. I'm afraid to ask the Swiss nurse how to adjust it. I see her looks, know the nurses and doctors think I'm just a child, pathetic, stupid, only "the boy that got this poor girl pregnant."

Jessica stayed in the hospital in Vevey, Switzerland, for a month after she was born. She wasn't gaining weight. The Swiss wanted to add something to her milk, thicken it, keep her sitting up while the sphincter of her esophagus finished forming, or something like that. It did, and she came home. But those first days were all about worry, sadness she wasn't with us, a young couple at the mercy of doctors who didn't take them seriously.

Genie pumped milk. So much for glamour and teen sex! We carried the little refrigerated bottles to the hospital each day, taking the bus to Aigle, then the train to Vevey. Some days, we stayed down in the valley at my parents' hideaway apartment. (They had recently rented it, to get away from L'Abri once in a while.)

The universe bent, then changed form as everything centered on that child eating, gaining weight, what a doctor said, if another doctor said something else, if Jessica would be home soon. No one said she would die. They all said she would be fine sooner or later, maybe with surgery, maybe without it. But from that moment at age eighteen, I learned that this force, this love, was going to override every other emotion, every other fact. In that moment, I had the first taste of days and nights thirty-two years later when another child, my son John, would be in Afghanistan, a young Marine on back-to-back combat tours in a war that started on 9/11, but never seemed to end.

With Jessica not keeping her food down, I learned the prayer that has no words, the one I'd be praying forever after I became a father, whatever I called myself, or converted to, or abandoned, when the feeling of dread *is* prayer—prayer and longing for what I could never give a child in danger, or myself: the guarantee of joy.

When Genie and I had gotten back to L'Abri (and the gossip spread about the fact that she was pregnant), several of the more Calvinistic, pietistic workers told Dad that they thought he should denounce Genie's and my sin. They wanted him to state publicly that what we had done was wrong and that we repented and were getting married, but that Dad (and L'Abri) in no way condoned such behavior. They thought that as a pastor and L'Abri's leader, Dad had to "make an example."

Dad threw a fit. From then on, it was as if Dad was Genie's and my second in a fight. He was in our "corner" and ready to literally tear off the head of anyone who so much as looked at us funny.

When Dad preached at our wedding (in the medieval Ollon church where my sisters also got married), he delivered his normal wedding sermon with no mention that Genie and I were so very young or that she was pregnant. The church was packed with everyone from L'Abri, as well as many of the villagers from Huémoz who I had known all my life.

My heart leapt when I saw Genie coming down the aisle. She had a crown of daisies in her hair and was wearing the simple white eyelet cotton dress I had designed for her and that Mom sewed. But other than that momentary spark of joy, I was out of it.

I spent our wedding feeling overwhelmed, cold, nervous, numb. I don't know how Genie felt. All she says is that it was "a blur."

Jane Stuart Smith sang "Ruth" at our wedding. I insisted that wine be served at the reception. And as Priscilla toasted us with a glass of good Swiss white Aigle, in a quiet and rueful aside she whispered that wine would never have been served in her day.

There was fog blanketing the mountains across from where we held the reception above Montreux. It matched my mood: everything-is-happening-too-fast. This mood of confusion continued through our honeymoon in Venice. That was where Genie's morning sickness really kicked in.

Living in a community with two sisters on the same mountainside, a father and mother upstairs, and (mostly) friendly L'Abri workers around us was a perfect place to be a young foolish couple in. Everything that had previously driven me crazy about community life became the lifeline that was the difference between Genie and me surviving as a young penniless, immature couple and splitting apart.

We lived on the bottom floor of Chalet Les Mélèzes. The year before I met Genie, I had commandeered the living room as my studio; now Genie and I were given the whole floor as our rent-free apartment. One end of the living room remained my studio, the other end was our bedroom. My mother's old office down the hall became Jessica's room. We had a little kitchen across from our studio bedroom.

I was painting; and since there was no other way for me to earn a living, Genie and I became L'Abri workers for a few months. Our "job" was to serve some students a meal several times a week in our apartment. During those meals, we, like the other workers, were supposed to have a discussion that consisted of students asking questions and of me holding forth, honing my bullshit skills and trying to articulate all those things I'd grown up hearing my parents hold forth on. It was pretty silly. The students must have been biting their tongues. I was insecure and loud; and being sent to my table for dinner, when a student could have been with Dad, Udo, or John, must have been like winning a milkshake while the guy next to you won the lottery.

Genie and I spent lots of time with my sisters. Debby and Priscilla were incredibly kind. Each week, we'd go to dinner with Debby and Udo on the evening when they read out loud to their students from all sorts of wonderful books like John Updike's *Turkey Feathers*. We would bring Jessica, and she slept upstairs while we sat downstairs with Debby in the kitchen, as she prepared the meal for twenty or thirty students. After dinner, Debby and Udo would wait for the students to drift off, then sit with Genie and me and talk for hours.

We also hung around Priscilla and John's chalet. No matter how many times we'd show up, Priscilla would welcome us. We'd sit in her kitchen and drink tea. And as the shadows grew long over the mountains, Priscilla would inevitably ask us if we wanted to stay for dinner. We always did.

Debby and Udo, and Priscilla and John exuded a sunny pro-marriage-in-spite-of-everything optimism that was infectious. They were rooting for us, and at the same time treating us as grownups, on a good path where the expectation was that we'd succeed.

My daughter got the benefit of being raised where her aunts could keep an eye on her. They also helped and advised Genie and me. They encouraged Genie in her new-mother role, answered my questions about married life, helped us heal wounds after our many tempestuous fights, and told us that they had "been through all this, too."

My mother turned out to be the kindest and best mother-in-law. She never interfered, only came downstairs to our apartment when Genie asked her to, took Jessica any time Genie asked her to watch the baby, provided endless gifts for us. And any time we didn't feel like cooking, we could go upstairs at mealtimes, help ourselves, and take the food back down to our apartment.

With my mother and dad upstairs and my sisters down the road, not to mention health insurance from L'Abri, our "worker's" hundred-franc-a-month stipend, and a rent-free apartment, Genie and I were living in our own little paradise. It was like a miniature Scandinavian socialist state, with layers of safety net providing a sense of balmy security.

Genie's parents also began to help. They sent a monthly check for several hundred dollars. And when we went to visit Susan and Ranald in England, we got a lovely welcome. However harsh Ranald had seemed when I ran away from school, he made sure I knew that he was completely on our side now. Susan and Ranald were also very encouraging of my painting. They purchased some work and were enthusiastic about the work itself.

If every couple received such love and care, the world would be filled with a lot more happy young families. In that sense, my parents' idea that Christianity, or at least their version of it, could be proved is true. When it counted most, my parents stepped up for Genie, Jessica, and me. Mercy, grace, generosity, love, unconditional support were given us "pressed down and running over."

Nevertheless, I was an immature asshole. I'd nitpick Genie and then we'd argue. We fought in our galley-sized kitchen in the Chalet Les Mélèzes basement. I took a swing at Genie, she saw it coming and picked up a magnum of red wine to deck me with. I grabbed a soup ladle. Ladle and bottle crashed over our heads, drenching us in red wine and splinters of glass. We slipped on the wine and slammed, clawing and screaming, onto the slippery floor.

I was violent in other ways, too. Jessica intruded immediately into our lives, arrived when we were so young, almost literally crashed our honeymoon. While she was growing up, I pulled her hair sometimes and slapped her, not every day, not every week, not every month, but enough times so that when I see a parent lose control with a child, I want to tell them not to do anything that, years later, they will feel sick about, so *very* sick.

I lavished Jessica with love, too. I got up in the night with her, held to my shoulder for hours, her cheek plastered to mine, almost drunk with glee at the fact that I had this daughter, this child, something real that did not depend on anyone's ideas about me, just was.

Sometimes it was hell, a hell of my making. In thirty-seven years, Genie has never started a fight. But she has certainly won most of them. And our children always know whose side they are on. "Mom is right!" has been the family motto. I'm glad.

In any place but our tight-knit community, we would have divorced fifty times over. But within L'Abri, divorce was not an option. The only option was to talk to Mom, Dad, Debby, Priscilla, and a few of our friends among the other L'Abri couples, to hear how they had survived their worst fights, to repent, learn, and move on.

I remember some good advice I got from gospel singer

Gloria Gaither, of the Bill and Gloria Gaither Gospel Trio. "We didn't have good sex for the first ten years of our marriage. You have to work at it," said Gloria.

I have no idea why she told me this. We were standing in her kitchen in Texas or Indianapolis, wherever, somewhere in the vast nondescript middle, while I was touring with Dad several years after Genie and I got married. Gloria was advising me after we got talking and I told her how bad some days were, what a lousy father I was, how much I loved Genie, but how things didn't seem so good a lot of the time. And that was what she blurted out.

Gloria was smart. The idea of working at a marriage was something that, for some reason, stuck after what she told me, although of course I'd heard the marriage-is-work advice many times before.

Stan and Betty Walsh, Genie's parents, had asked us if we would rather that they come to the wedding, or for a longer visit later. We chose the longer visit. I was immensely relieved to not have to meet them right away!

A few months after Jessica was born, they came to Switzerland, along with Genie's little brother and sister, Jim and Molly. I was incredibly nervous. I had stolen their daughter away. I had gotten her pregnant. I had "ruined her life." Anyway, that was how I was sure they saw the matter. Meeting my father-in-law seemed about the worst nightmare I could imagine. But I needn't have worried.

Whatever they were really thinking, Stan and Betty Walsh could not have acted more loving. Genie's mom was a trim, handsome, down-to-earth woman who never mentioned her distinguished blueblood family history. She was the opposite of my mother in almost every way. Betty wanted to avoid fuss, and the last person she ever wanted to talk about was herself. (One of Betty's ancestors, as I said before, had been a signatory to the United States Constitution, another was the first marshal of Arkansas. Betty steadfastly refused to join groups like the Daughters of the American Revolution. It was years before I could pry any family history out of her.) Stan Walsh was a tall, strong, second-generation Irish-American, self-made rags-to-riches lawyer.

Genie's parents exuded down-to-earth common sense and calm. I was accepted into their family and began a friendship with Genie's brothers Tom and Jim, and with Pam (who was already a friend ever since she had walked into the chalet with Genie). And, on that first visit, I met Molly, who was then twelve, and I became close with her even though she was forlorn because her big sister had suddenly disappeared. Remembering how sad I had been when my big sisters got married and were whisked away, I felt a stab of guilty empathy.

A year or two after we were married, my parents moved out of Chalet Les Mélèzes and we all decamped to Chésières, two miles up the road. Mom and Dad had bought Chalet Chardonnet, a big old rambling four-story chalet that had been the home and office of a doctor. (My parents didn't own Chalet Les Mélèzes, L'Abri did, so Chalet Chardonnet was the first house they ever owned.)

There was plenty of room for them on the top three floors and a big apartment for Genie, Jessica, soon-to-be Francis, and me on the basement floor that had been the doctor's offices. At about that time, L'Abri also bought the chalet next door to my parent's new home, and Debby and Udo moved in with about twenty students.

Soon after that, Genie and I borrowed money from my father and bought a barn that sat between his chalet and the new L'Abri house. Over the next few years, Genie and I fixed it up into a wonderful little gem— "Chalet Regina." We moved in after we had been married for about six years.

L'Abri was growing. And I was more and more aware that my life was being defined by my parents' choices. I was very grateful for their kindness to Genie and me, but also conscious that I was like some asteroid caught in the orbit of a giant planet. I had several fights with my mother, accusing her of folding her children into her ministry by using us as an illustration in her talks and books and by "volunteering" us to be raised in a small weird community after inviting a horde to invade our home.

"Did you ever *ask* us if we wanted to be part of this?" I said more than once.

Mom never had an answer, other than to claim that the Lord had led Dad and her. That always seemed to excuse everything.

Genie and I took several trips to see her parents. It was such a relief to visit the Walsh family. They were blessedly ordinary, liberal-leaning Democrat-voting Roman Catholics.

Unlike my family, the Walsh children seemed to have lives independent of their father and mother. Genie's mother seemed pleased when her children made their own ways. The frantic talk about the Lord's leading, or the "direction of the work," and the constant wrangling and positioning between family members over what amounted to the family business—L'Abri—was absent. And my admiration for Genie's sensible family was one of the reasons that I began wondering if the ideas I'd grown up with were really the only good ideas to live by. The Walsh clan didn't believe what we believed, and yet they seemed to be doing just fine.

PART III

TURMOIL

40

When Billy Zeoli, the president of Gospel Films, came to L'Abri in 1972 (or thereabouts), L'Abri was known for its defense of the "inerrancy of scripture" in a minor way, its appreciation of art in a major way, its ability to give answers to Big Questions, its penchant for connecting the dots of popular culture and explaining the failures of modernism and the triumph of the gospel. Dad was holding forth on issues such as the hippie movement's inability to realize its promise or to provide an alternative social and moral model because "While their analysis of the problem of our plastic society was right, they had no answer." Dad also spoke prophetically: "You wait," he said; "the hippies are going to wind up more middle-class, bourgeois, and materialistic than their parents."

Dad would often say "The next generation will follow anyone who will promise personal peace and affluence. If they are asked to make a choice between freedom and security they'll choose security. It will be the new fascism."

Billy Zeoli was a heavyset, swarthy, handsome fast-talking man with a strong chin. He was charming and generous in a godfather-wanna-be way. And Billy paid top dollar (actually top franc) and didn't seem to care what he bought, just as long as I noticed how fat the wad of cash was that he pulled out when he came to my studio to buy a painting.

Billy and I got to talking. In a series of conversations over the next few weeks, we cooked up the idea that Dad should take his lectures about art and philosophy and make a documentary series to answer the BBC-produced series by Lord Kenneth Clark—*Civilization*—and another called *The Ascent of Man* narrated by Jacob Bronowski.

Lord Clark's "secular humanist" series portrayed the Renaissance as a triumph of Reason over Christian medieval superstition. Bronowski's was about evolution. Both were smooth, well made BBC productions. From Dad's point of view, they were belittling evangelical faith.

In a series of lectures, Dad strapped on his armor and defended Christ against the BBC and Christendom against modernism. Dad's argument was something like this: The art of the Renaissance was beautiful, but gradually religious meaning had been stripped away. All that was left was the hubris of humanism shaking its fist in the face of God. Conversely, the golden age of Dutch seventeenth-century painting proved that you could produce a brilliantly lovely Protestant Reformed alternative to proud Renaissance humanism. Great art could be created but be about a Christ-centered worldview, where the simple and beautiful was exalted as a way of pointing back to the Creator who gave everything, even the smallest daily chores and activities—say, in a Dutch household as portrayed by Vermeer—transcendent meaning.

Dad said there was a "line of despair" that separated modern secular man from all who came before. Moreover, the fruits of Christianity created the rule of law and human rights as we now understood them. For all the talk about the so-called

Dark Ages and the evils of Christendom, from the Spanish Inquisition to the burning of witches in Salem, to the slave trade, the twentieth century—a virtual textbook experiment in godlessness—was the most inhuman and bloody of all centuries. So, Dad argued, before secularists glibly critiqued religious and especially Christian culture, perhaps they should take time to explain Marx, Lenin, Hitler, Stalin, and Mao, not to mention the Gulag and Auschwitz.

On a good day, the social and political results of secularism made the horrors of Christendom look like a Sunday-school picnic, Dad said. And, unlike secularism, Christian culture had a self-correcting impulse. For instance, it was Wilberforce (and other evangelicals like him) who had fought to free the slaves. And it was the Common Law of Christian England that was the basis of our Western, especially our American, freedoms we now took for granted.

My father taught that if the idea of biblical God-given absolutes was abandoned, there would be a real question as to where a new morality would come from. Since humankind did not like chaos, Dad warned, either we would turn to authoritarian systems (some sort of technocratic elite), or we would be ruled by the "tyranny of the majority, with no way to challenge the popular will, nothing higher to appeal to."

Billy Zeoli heard Dad's lectures. And like many evangelicals who visited, he loved the fact that my father was arguing intelligently for biblical Christianity and pushing back against what seemed like an unstoppable secular tide. The evangelicals also loved the fact that Dad, somewhat like author C. S. Lewis, was a kind of proof that we evangelicals weren't as dumb as the secularists said we were. (The irony was that Lewis and my father were not "evangelicals" in the American sense of the word.

Lewis was an Anglo-Catholic; and Dad liked art better than theology and people better than rules and was most comfortable in a room full of hippies.)

"Others must hear this message!" said Billy. "We're losing our young people!" Nice kids from good Christian homes would go to college and pretty soon they were questioning everything. All their born-again parents could do was wring their hands and quote Bible verses at kids who came home from school no longer believing in the concept of absolute truth, let alone that the Bible was literally "the answer" and accurate in every detail.

Confused evangelical parents confronted by this "generation gap" had no answers for the art student seduced by Pop Art or the philosophy student reading Camus. And what could be done for the biology student studying evolution, or, worse, the student of English literature whose politics was moving to the left as she marched in anti-Vietnam War demonstrations? Christ was being driven out of our young people's lives by clever intellectuals bent on stripping faith away and replacing it with nothing at all!

One man had the answers. And while American evangelical parents didn't care to visit Florence, let alone listen to the music of Bob Dylan or subscribe to *The BBC Listener,* Francis Schaeffer did. And he was so sincere and so good at answering "the kids," especially those who had been "turned off" by their bourgeois middle-class parents.

Evangelical leaders came to L'Abri so Dad could teach them how to inoculate Johnny and Susie born-again against the hedonistic out-of-control culture that had Johnny's older brother on drugs and Susie's older sister marching on the Capital. The evangelical elite didn't stay in the dorms but rented big chalets, as did Billy Zeoli and many others, including Lane Dennis. Lane was the publisher and editor at Crossway Books. In the case of Lane Dennis, he also came to woo two of the hottest evangelical authors, and to inspire a third to begin to write: me.

Lane was a kind and honest man. We all liked him, and soon Mom and Dad gave Lane their new books to publish. Actually, I did. I was acting as their agent. (Several years later, on the strength of the Schaeffer books sales, Crossway went from being an obscure mom-and-pop tract-printing company to one of the major evangelical publishers.)

L'Abri had prided itself on doing the Lord's work in the Lord's way. Dad and Mom were very critical of the fund-raising methods of the Billy Grahams, Billy Zeolis, and other high-powered evangelicals who didn't really "live by faith" but who used "slick worldly methods." How could "these people" prove the existence of God when clearly their ministries were the product of clever fund-raising? "Those American Christians" were all just too commercial, too worldly.

Until Billy Zeoli showed up, Dad, with his preference for the small-is-beautiful hippie ethos, with its love of all things organic and natural as opposed to planned and businesslike, had avoided the temptation to capitalize on his growing fame. He was to the evangelicals of the late sixties and early seventies what the Grateful Dead were to Deadheads, an eccentric all the more attractive because he was on the cusp of going big-time but refused to take that last step. His work, Dad felt, would lose its meaning if he "sold out."

But Dad and Billy Zeoli had a special bond that helped overcome Dad's resistance to Billy's idea that he take his message to a wider audience: Billy was the son of Anthony Zeoli, a first-generation Italian-American old-time evangelist who had happened to be holding a tent revival in Philadelphia half a century before Billy came to L'Abri. Dad had walked into Zeoli senior's tent revival when he was seventeen. He heard Anthony Zeoli preach and discovered that there were other people out there also convinced that the Bible was the answer.

So there was an unlikely yet special connection between Dad, the self-effacing hippie guru, and Billy Zeoli, the leisure-suited, luxury-car-renting big spender from Gospel Films. There was something else, too: Billy offered to help me.

Billy saw me as a lost shadow on the edges of L'Abri, a drop-out child who'd gotten some hippie princess from San Francisco pregnant—and who did "nothing more" than paint. After spotting several 16-mm and Super-8 cameras in my studio, Billy discovered that I wanted to realize a star-struck dream of making movies. And Dad wanted to help his son. And I was ambitious. I wanted to make films, real movies, movies like my idol Fellini was making. But how could I get from here to there? Billy offered me what seemed like a way.

What is sad to me now (in a maudlin, self-pitying way) is that some of my paintings were good. And they were getting better. If I'd had the discipline to concentrate on my art and had found a way of distancing myself from the evangelical community (and the easy money it soon offered), I might have gotten somewhere. In fact, I *was* getting somewhere in New York, Geneva (Aubonne), and London.

But I was also broke. And Genie was pregnant with our second child. I also happened to sincerely believe in my father's message, though "believe" is perhaps the wrong word. Rather, I had not yet begun to question my indoctrination.

But once we all swallowed hard and decided to work with

Billy Zeoli, it was "clear" that with all those people being deluded by The World into falling away from Christ, that the "L'Abri way," the small-is-beautiful way, had to be replaced so we could "reach out to this lost generation" before it was "too late." And Billy with his multimillion dollar backing from the Amway Corporation and its far-right founder-capitalist-guru, Rich DeVos, was about as slick and worldly and far away from the L'Abri way as anyone could get.

I didn't know it then, but my life as an artist had just ended. As months turned into years, I never got back into my studio. I was sucked into a whirlpool of activity by making evangelical documentaries and, eventually, into becoming my father's sidekick.

The paint on my huge old palette dried hard as a rock. The smell of linseed oil was replaced by the hot-paper smell of the photocopy machine.

After I quit painting, looking at my paintings depressed me. It was something like running into an old childhood friend I had abandoned for sexier better-connected new acquaintances, pretend "new old friends" of convenience. I knew I had betrayed something important.

Dad seems to have been saddened by my choice to quit painting, too, even though I helped take his message to a vast audience because I did quit. He dedicated his book *How Should We Then Live?* to me. In the dedication, my father expressed deep regret that the book and film project took me away from my art.

41

Within six months of Billy Zeoli's coming to L'Abri, Dad was writing and researching *How Should We Then Live?* At age twenty (or was it nineteen?), I had an office, three secretaries, two assistants, and a budget of a million and a half dollars. And this was back in the days when that was real money, especially for a thirteen-episode documentary on history, art, culture, and theology.

How Should We Then Live? and the second series Dad and I made, *Whatever Happened to the Human Race?* are still standard works today in thousands of evangelical high schools, colleges, and seminaries around the world. For many evangelicals, Francis Schaeffer is their first, and perhaps only, introduction to what "we" think about art, history and culture, and politics—not to mention the "life issues." More than thirty years after working on those films, I still get several thousand dollars a year in royalties, from the tiny percentage I'm due as the writer/director and producer. And the book companions to the films are in print, a mainstay of every evangelical library, having sold several million copies.

In *How Should We Then Live?* (film series and book), the thesis was that the best of Western culture, art, freedom, and democracy could be traced to a Christian foundation. And that foundation was under attack from humanist and secular ideas and elites. In consequence, we were losing our freedoms because there were no longer absolutes that we could all agree on to guarantee them.

The last two episodes of *How Should We Then Live?* concentrated on the legalization of abortion through the 1973 *Roe v. Wade* Supreme Court decision. This was presented as the prime example of the erosion of the values that had once made the West great.

Once the production got under way, we were no longer just praying that the Lord would meet our needs. I was running all over America talking to people like Mary C. Crowley (founder of Home Interiors and Gifts), Bunker Hunt (of the notorious Hunt brothers in Dallas, who were busy with their oil empire while trying to corner the world silver market), Amway's founder and president Rich DeVos (based in Grand Rapids), Mrs. Nancy DeMoss (of the Arthur S. DeMoss Foundation), and every other evangelical philanthropist Billy had on his list, or we had on ours, or who had ever visited L'Abri. (We even got the Pew Charitable Trust and Kresgey Foundation to kick in.) And later, for other related film/book endeavors, we pitched young Howard Ahmanson (heir of the Home Savings bank fortune).

Mom and Dad relied on Billy and me to do most of the fund-raising legwork, though they would sometimes get on the phone to "soften up" the prospective donor. Billy's method was to send me.

"They love young people," Billy said. "The way you come off works better. You can speak for your parents, and you come off as really sincere."

At first I was nervous. But I soon got used to telling wealthy evangelicals that it was time to "take our country back," to "answer the humanists," to "defend our young people." I was also watching Billy Zeoli operate and learning how to imitate him. He was the master of asking without asking.

I would fly from Switzerland to Chicago, then to Muskegon. (I took so many trips, it seemed as if I was on a first-name basis with half the Swissair crew members.) I'd check into the local Holiday Inn (where I ate my weight in steaks, still a big treat given my meat-deprived L'Abri background). For a week or so, I'd go to the office of Gospel Films for meetings on the scripts and fundraising. Then I'd hit the road and crisscross the country, asking for money.

Billy bought me a garish herringbone wide-lapelled seventies-style three-piece suit and an equally dreadful plaid overcoat and sent me out on a series of trips to see "the money." (I had cut my hair and thought that my new clothes made me look very important!) Billy never seemed all that interested in the scripts. "Do whatever you all want. Just do it on budget!" was his usual reply to any question. But we would have long, intricate, and seemingly endless strategy sessions about how to approach donors.

"Mary Crowley doesn't like to be asked," Billy would say. "You have to get her to take you to her private chapel and pray about the project with her. Make *sure* you kneel down next to her *and hold her hand*! Then let *her* ask you how to help."

With Rich DeVos, the tactic was different. "Talk to Rich about saving capitalism!" Billy would say. "Tell him your Dad is standing up to the socialists! Do *not* talk about art!"

With the "Hunt boys," as Billy called them, he advised "Don't talk too fast! Do *not* mention the word 'intellectual.' Stick to the simple Gospel. We're doing this for Jesus! Got it?"

We would approach Nancy DeMoss as if she was a skittish runaway colt, sidle up with many friendly calls, never really ask, just tell her about the project. "Get Edith to call her again! Nancy needs to feel excited, and she loves your mother's books! Let *Edith* do the talking on this one!"

Billy knew what he was doing. We were raising money by the fistful. I was learning how to suck up to, stroke, and "handle" the super-rich. Approaching one was like trying to gain favor with the Queen of Hearts in *Alice in Wonderland.* Do it wrong, and it was off with your head! Stroke the target correctly and, for a few minutes, you might become a coddled favorite. Above all, as Billy said again and again, you had to pretend to be interested in them "as people."

My English boarding-school days paid off. I was polite, knew how to relate to grownups respectfully, stood when anyone entered a room, held out chairs for women, called men "sir," and never talked about myself. Having been trained by my mother paid off, too. I had an inexhaustible reserve of useful spiritual platitudes at my fingertips, a databank of God-talk implanted through years of being around my mother. And my enthusiasm for our project was genuine. When it came to making the films and taking Dad's message to the world, I was excited and sincere. I was also being taught by the best evangelical fund-raiser in America.

"Look," Billy would say, "They know you're there for the money. That's the only kind of person they ever meet. But you have to *play the game* that you're there for *them*! Be *interested* in their ideas! Take Mary flowers! Ask the Hunt boys about their family. Remember, they know more than you do about money, so no bullshit, tell the truth if they ask for budget details!"

I was starting to see that it paid handsomely to babble loudly about Christ and saving America and to present myself—and Mom and Dad and our new "ministry through film"—as the last best defense of truth against the enemies of the Lord. I also learned that I could turn my fund-raising "spirituality" on and off at will, something like a Swissair flight attendant's smile.

42

The democratic Dutch apportioned their state TV budget between various production entities based on demographics, so much for the Roman Catholics, so much for the liberal Protestants, so much for the communists, so much for the evangelicals, and so on. We hooked up with EO, the evangelical state-funded Dutch TV producers. They supplied the logistics that a state TV entity has and got us permission to film in museums all over the world, where Dad would stand in front of great artworks, from Michelangelo's *David* to Marcel Duchamp's *Bride Descending a Staircase,* and proclaim our answers to modern culture.

When we started making *How Should We Then Live?* Dad had not wanted to even mention abortion in the series. We were already in production when the Supreme Court handed down the *Roe v. Wade* decision legalizing abortion.

If it hadn't been for me, Dad's reputation as an evangelical scholar—a somewhat marginal but interesting intellectual figure—would have remained intact. As it was, my absolutist youthful commitment to the pro-life cause goaded my father into taking political positions far more extreme than came naturally to him.

There was nothing intellectual, let alone religious, about my visceral opposition to abortion. My antiabortion fervor was strictly personal. It had a name, Jessica, my little girl, proof that conception is good, even an unexpected teen conception. I knew that "unwanted" can become very wanted indeed. I also think that my gut reaction against abortion originated back when I was a child pressing my ear against a series of fat lovely bellies of my sisters, various unwed mothers (who were guests), and several L'Abri workers and listening to all those unborn babies' hearts beating. There was also another very personal motive: all the CP kids at Chalet Bellevue I had played with, and, in the case of Jean Pierre, merrily jacked off with. I didn't want people just like my spastic friends to be eliminated. And perhaps my polio, being the only "Yank" in an English school, my dyslexia, and a weird childhood, all also gave me a natural empathy for outsiders, and the unwanted.

I barged into Dad's bedroom while he was eating his daily breakfast of two soft-boiled eggs with toast, and tea. I had just come home from yet another successful fundraising tour in the States. Dad and I had been arguing for several weeks before my trip. We picked up where we left off.

"They're Catholics!" Dad said, before I even opened my mouth.

We instantly got into a screaming match.

"How can you say you believe in the uniqueness of every human being if you won't stand up on this?" I yelled.

"I don't want to be identified with some Catholic issue. I'm not putting my reputation on the line for them!" Dad shouted back.

"So you won't speak out because it's a 'Catholic issue?' "

"What does abortion have to do with art and culture? I'm known as an intellectual, not for this sort of *political thing*!" shouted Dad.

"That's what you always say about the Lutherans in

Germany!" I yelled. "You say they're responsible for the Holocaust because they wouldn't speak up, and now you're doing the same thing! *Fucking coward!* You're always talking about the 'dehumanization of man'; now, here is your best example!"

"It isn't in the script!"

"*We're* writing the script! We can change the fucking script!"

"Don't you dare say 'fuck' to me again!"

"I didn't say 'fuck' to you, I said '*fucking script*!' "

Mom walked in as I yelled "fucking script." She stood frozen by the door. Dad reclined on his mound of pillows, his spoon poised above the soft-boiled eggs. He glared at me. Then he glanced at Mom's shocked face.

Dad laughed. Then I laughed.

No one has more power over a loving father (especially if that father feels a bit guilty for neglecting his children) than a beloved son. I would know! Years later, I practically followed my youngest son John into the Marine Corps and dedicated almost seven years to writing about military service out of solidarity with his choice to volunteer.

My son had stood up for something. I wanted to back him. And when I issued my father a moral challenge, he didn't want me thinking he was ducking the issue. Anyway, Dad agreed with me about abortion in principle. He had already noted in several lectures that *Roe v. Wade* was a "horrible decision." We had only been arguing about how much of a public stand he wanted to take.

Dad and Mom prayed over the matter. My father came to me a few days after our screaming match and said he had decided that, "rude and abrasive" as I had been, my call to him was nevertheless "prophetic." We would change the last two episodes of *How Should We Then Live?* and talk about abortion.

43

The production of *How Should We Then Live?* was intense. Over the two years it took to make, the crew paid for my inexperience, not least because I hired a middle-aged Swiss-American former L'Abri student to direct the series. (He had once been a commercial director in New York.) It was a decision we all soon bitterly regretted.

I should have been fired for hiring him. I did so because I was insecure and wanted "my" director to be someone I could control. And of course, being an overconfident smartass, I also thought I knew it all, and that this man was a "real artist," unlike "some American evangelical that Billy Zeoli might foist on us," as I told Dad.

The only thing our director was really good at was stroking my young ego. Ironically, when at last he was fired by Billy Zeoli, for not shooting the script on time and on budget—the episodes wouldn't cut, there were huge gaps, and he was refusing to show us his dailies, so no one knew how much of a mess we were in—*I* took over as director! It was a very undeserved promotion, no doubt all the more galling to our crew of professionals because of the naked nepotism involved.

When *How Should We Then Live?* was complete, we launched it with a massive and well promoted seminar tour sponsored by Gospel Films. We projected our movies from a giant arc projector that we trucked all over America. My parents and I flew from city to city on the private plane Billy Zeoli hired. The events were mainly held in civic arenas.

We were in fifteen cities, including a gig in Madison Square Garden. We talked to a total of over forty thousand people. They would show up for a whole day and watch each half-hour episode in order, and we had discussions led by my father and, later in the tour, sometimes by me.

Our seminars were unique. Crowds of this size would have been nothing unusual for evangelistic crusades or Pentecostal "charismatic" shindigs. But evangelicals were coming to us to watch movies about art history and to hear Dad talk about philosophy! Each event got bigger as the word of mouth spread. By the end of the tour, Dad was one of the most sought-after and best-known evangelical leaders in the United States.

There were memorable moments during the production and the seminars: Dad standing on a scaffolding, next to the shoulder of Michelangelo's *David* while dusting the statue's head for the close-up . . . Dad and me alone in the Sistine Chapel at night, waiting for the crew . . . eating a tray of delicious lasagna at midnight in the Uffizi, with the run of the whole place . . . realizing that the lights were too close to Van Eyck's *Marriage Supper of the Lamb* in St. Bavo's Cathedral in Ghent, Belgium, and that we were about to strip the paint . . . wondering again and again how so much art in Italy, Belgium, and other European countries had survived for so long, given the complete indifference of so many museum guards and curators, who literally turned over some of the world's greatest treasures to my crew, then disappeared for a coffee . . . stepping out alone on the platform at our Dallas seminar to launch *How Should We*

Then Live? and looking at a crowd of six thousand, and realizing that we were on the road to a monster success, then being introduced to Roger Staubach (the Dallas Cowboys' quarterback), who showed up with half his team—and not knowing who he was, being that I was some Swiss, movie, art nerd. . . .

One event stands out as foreshadowing one of the many reasons I would later flee the evangelical world: The best material we shot for *How Should We Then Live?*—genuinely historic and unique footage—was filmed in the Accademia that houses Michelangelo's *David.* Dad was on a scaffolding that we built right up next to the statue, so people would get the sense of scale. (That was when I handed him a featherduster to clean off David's head! We noticed it was dusty!)

We filmed a magnificent dolly shot past Michelangelo's *Captives* (or "unfinished works") that line the hall up to the *David.* Then the shot continued all the way around *David* and ended on Dad.

Gospel Films insisted that I cut the scene and replace the shot with stock footage bought from an old NBC show because our shots revealed—oh, horror!—David's genitals. The old NBC footage conveniently blacked them out.

"We can't have this for a Christian audience," said Billy Zeoli. "Churches won't rent it."

"But we have other nudes and you never said anything. What about Mary's breast in that Virgin and Child?"

"That's bad enough! One holy tit is okay, as long as you don't leave it on screen too long. But churches don't do cock!" said Billy with an uproarious laugh.

I fought and lost. When I told Dad, he muttered, "We're working with fools."

44

I may have lost the cock argument over *David*, but, undeterred—and thoroughly bitten by the movie bug, not to mention the ambition bug—I went right on to make our second series for the evangelical market. At the same time, I was already starting to plan my long-term exit strategy from the evangelical subculture. I figured I could kill two birds with one stone: make another series on a subject I believed in, and also create more footage for my show reel, so I could get a "real job" making movies.

Whatever Happened to the Human Race? was the brainchild of Dr. C. Everett Koop and myself. He had seen our first series and wanted to team up to expand on the last episodes of *How Should We Then Live?* where Dad had denounced the "imperial court" for stripping the unborn of their right to life.

Dr. Koop was an old family friend. He was also a leading pediatric surgeon and surgeon-in-chief of the Philadelphia Children's Hospital. He was an ardent pro-lifer and Calvinist evangelical. His pro-life passion was based on having spent a lifetime saving the lives of babies that were sometimes the same age as those killed in late-term abortions.

Koop was delighted with the abortion episode of *How Should We Then Live?* In the mid-1970s he traveled to Switzerland to talk to Dad and me about it. Dad had known Koop for years, but I first met him at our Philadelphia seminar. We had talked and discovered we shared deep antiabortion convictions.

After having dinner with my parents, Koop came down to the apartment where Genie and I lived. We talked for three or four hours and mapped out the idea for a new series and book.

Koop's parting shot was: "This needs to be done! You're the one who really understands this issue. It's up to *you!* Talk your father into it!"

When I asked Dad to collaborate with Dr. Koop, he went along. There was no more talk about avoiding becoming too political. Through the *How Should We Then Live?* film series, book, and seminars, my father had been able to reach more people (directly and through the general "buzz") in a few months than in his whole previous lifetime. And Dad had enjoyed the attention.

I wrote the screenplay and directed *Whatever Happened to the Human Race?* Jim Buchfuehrer produced it. The series dealt with the issues of abortion, infanticide, and euthanasia. Jim and I raised all the money and Gospel Films merely signed on as the distributor. Jim and I formed a new 501(c)(3) (not for prophet company) to make the movies: Schaeffer V Productions.

We didn't use dead-fetus pictures but stuck to allegory and visual metaphors to make our points. I illustrated Koop's and Dad's arguments with actors playing caged slaves, elderly people disappearing into a whiteout, thousands of plastic dolls on the salt flats of the Dead Sea, as well as a lot of footage (and interviews) shot in the Philadelphia Children's Hospital. The musical soundtrack was recorded by the London Symphony Orchestra. The budget was again one and a half million dollars. And those dollars were well spent and were, as they say, "on the screen."

The impact of our two film series, as well as their companion books, was to give the evangelical community a frame of reference through which to understand the secularization of American culture, and to point to the "human life issue" as the watershed between a "Christian society" and a utilitarian relativistic "post-Christian" future stripped of compassion and beauty.

The title sequence of *Whatever Happened to the Human Race?* involved Genie, my seven-year-old daughter Jessica, and my four-year-old son Francis, painting the main title on a huge sheet of glass that was then shattered. My wife and kids popped up all through my documentaries. (I had also included them in the sections I directed for the first series after we fired the director.)

I asked my daughter Jessica what she remembers:

> Where other directors left noisy young children behind, Dad brought us along. We knew why; his parents had often left him, and he wasn't going to do the same to us. Anyway, he said, we humanized the set. During *How Should We Then Live?* my brother Francis and I not only visited Roman ruins we *climbed* them. We would clamber up and scamper off along the crumbling walls.
>
> I remember my first little movie part when I was about three or four. My job was to be a Roman Christian child running away from a guard. I remember the night air coming through my thin white nightgown and the prickly grass under my feet. I was to run toward a distant light. The "Roman Guard," a sweet gentle L'Abri student, would run out and catch me, then push me down. (Mom also had a white nightgown, they caught her first.)
>
> For *Whatever Happened to the Human Race?* we traveled

to Israel. On the salt shores of the Dead Sea, I fell and scraped my elbow so later I had to float like a little buoy with my arm stuck up above my head so it wouldn't sting in the concentrated salt water.

I remember looking down from the helicopter as we flew over the desert to film Av on Mount Sinai. ("Av" was what all the Schaeffer grandchildren called our grandfather.) They shot a pull-back from that mountain: Av is standing on the top, the wind from the helicopter blowing his hair in every direction, as he squints up looking at the copter flying away from him. He is on a large rock alone in the desert but he is talking and talking, telling everyone the things they should know. I miss him. My brother Francis and I were in a scene filmed in Mom and Dad's bedroom where we played dress-up and then had to sit very still for the closeup. Dad told us not to move but to look straight ahead. Francis's nose itched and a tear of frustration came down his cheek right when the voice-over was talking about the killing of the unborn. Dad was nice to Francis but he was also pleased. The tears fit perfectly.

Av was quite grim during these shoots. He would pace back and forth learning pages of narration. I wonder how he did it. Eventually Dad started to cut away so that Av didn't have to know everything at once but could say less at a time.

Dad reveled in the love and war of getting the films "in the can"; capturing light and shadow and space, the immense struggle against time, exhaustion, and human error. He also believed in what he was doing.

45

To try to get a bit of perspective on the "Schaeffer juggernaut," I asked two old friends, Jim Buchfuehrer and Ray Cioni, to write a short summary of events related to the film series' making and the rise of the "Schaeffer phenomenon." Jim was my best friend, more like a brother. (He still is, though we rarely see each other these days.) Jim's story represents the many hundreds of people who were inexorably drawn into the Schaeffer firmament and who offered their services. Jim was also typical of many other evangelicals, because his encounter with my father's ideas changed his life.

Jim wrote:

> February 9, 2007
> After going to college and getting married I worked for an evangelical organization for 10 years. I became cynical about the Christian [evangelical] world until I came across the writings of Dr. Francis Schaeffer. . . . I wanted to go deeper into his thinking, so I went to L'Abri for 3 months of study.
>
> It was there that I met Frank Schaeffer, then known as "Franky." The first time I met him he was standing on the road through Huémoz where a bike race was coming

through town. He seemed friendly enough, although I had heard a number of negative things about him. He was known in some circles as the "Little Shit from Switzerland."

My next encounter with him was a dinner discussion, which took place at the various Chalets at L'Abri, where he argued and tried to dominate the discussion. He could not quite accomplish the domination part. His sister Debby, whose place we were having dinner at, held her own with Frank. Later he would tell me that his sister was the only one that he could not "out-argue."

Dr. Schaeffer said I should see Frank's paintings and I did go down to his apartment and meet his wife Genie, who was terrific and a real beauty. Frank told me he was selling his paintings. I didn't buy one.

I left L'Abri with a rather negative view of Frank, although I really liked the rest of his family including Frank's young wife who was nothing like him. We all wondered why in the world she would marry a guy like him.

I came back to the evangelical organization that I had worked with leading a staff of about 35, and started to teach things and concepts that Dr. Schaeffer had taught me and this led me to resign my position, since I could longer justify the philosophy of that organization based on the new insights I'd gotten from Dr. Schaeffer.

I resigned not knowing what I was going to do.

I got a call from my mentor and brother-in-law, Wendell Collins, who was vice president of Gospel Films. He knew I was unemployed and that maybe I would like to work on this new project they were producing, *How Should We Then Live?* with Dr. Schaeffer.

He thought I would be a good fit since I knew Schaeffer's material well. The President of Gospel Films was a man named Billy Zeoli. I knew all about "Z" and had met him from time to time, and did not like this guy. If you saw the *Godfather* films, he *was* the Godfather. (I later learned to like Z and found him to be one of the most trustworthy men I ever worked with. If Z gave you his word you did not need it in writing.)

The bad part of the job is that Franky was "producer." This guy was a 19-year-old kid who hung out in his basement painting and knew nothing about organization, working with people and his film experience totaled doing a few 8-mm movies, running around the mountains of Switzerland like a crazy person, and he was made producer!

Z must have given Frank the job to get the deal done with Dr. Schaeffer. I figured that Dr. S would have done anything to get the Little Shit out of his ass.

The Swiss-American director who Frank insisted on hiring was a madman. He was the worst person that any of us ever had the "pleasure" of working with. I had a run-in with this director in a hotel lobby. He was making some outrageous demands and I came up to him and got in his face. The demands went away, and I think that from that point on Frank and I did a little better together. Not friends, or anything, but better.

When the state-side shooting was done, Gospel Films planned a 3-month seminar tour with the 5-part film series and Dr. Schaeffer in person. GF (Gospel Films) hired me to work with Wendell ("Wendy") Collins to set these up all over the country.

We were still in production on the series. And this crazy Swiss-American director was finally fired, before the project was over. . . .

Then Z did something that I thought was even crazier than making Frank producer, he gave him a budget and said you finish this thing, you direct the remaining scenes.

Short story: Frank pulled it all together and put together a superb final product. I thought, maybe he has more talent than I'd credited him with. But I still didn't like him.

The seminars were a great success. Two things happened that changed my relationship with Frank.

First, Frank, who may have been 21 years old by then, and with no college, was going to fill in for Dr. Schaeffer one evening in Oakland, Calif. What a disappointment since Dr. Schaeffer was a master at question-and-answer sessions! But he had lost his voice after the flu. "Frank, you've got to do this," said Z. "We have three thousand people waiting to see your dad."

I was really blown away by how well Frank took over for his father and in some ways was even better. Afterward I paid him a compliment. He said, "I sat at my father's feet and listened all those years."

Second, Frank said, "let's go to lunch," and over a sandwich he said, "I know you think I'm a prick" (or something like that), "and I know that I got the producer's job because of my father, and if I was producer I would be able to talk my dad into making this series. I'm a terrible producer, and I don't want to produce. I want to direct and write. You are a producer and I want us to be partners."

I was blown away, again. Here was a young kid with not much life experience outside this film series, who knew who he was, and wasn't afraid to tell you the good and the bad.

With the huge success of this project Frank was in a position to do whatever he wanted to do. Z tried to hire him and give him a budget to do what he wanted to do. Frank had other ideas.

We formed a nonprofit 501(c)(3) and raised $20,000 to start. We called it "Schaeffer V Productions."

Frank was in Switzerland when a old friend of the family stopped by, Dr. C. Everett Koop, surgeon-in-chief of Philadelphia Children's Hospital. Frank called me and we discussed a new project, which would team Dr. S. and Dr. Koop. It sounded good to me and we were off and running. Another film series and a second seminar tour.

The problem was the budget, 1 million or more for the film and another million for the tour. So Frank and Koop started working on the script for the first 3 hours of the series, and Frank and his dad worked on the last 2 hours. I started to figure out how we were going to get the money and organize this whole thing.

Ray Cioni had the best animation studio in Chicago (until computers swept away the old cel-painting, art-based business, and Ray's studio with it). Ray is still an evangelical and looks back with fondness at that period of our lives.

After not seeing Ray for more than twenty years, I met him in Chicago in February 2007, at the opening of a play at the Chicago Cultural Center produced by the Griffin Theatre—*Letters Home*—based on several of my books, principally *Voices from the Front—Letters Home from America's Military Family* and *Faith of Our Sons—A Father's Wartime Diary.* I asked Ray to try to remember what we were up to thirty years ago:

> February 8, 2007
> Having become a born-again believer during freshman year of college, I was directed by Inter-Varsity leaders to read the works of C. S. Lewis and Francis Schaeffer. [Inter-Varsity was a leading college ministry.] These two writers shaped my emerging faith and changed the direction of my vocation and guided my career path.
>
> After opening my own animation studio in Chicago, I divided the focus of my workload between advertising agencies and Christian film distributors. I felt I could use my passion for animation to communicate Christian truths to children.
>
> I first heard the call of Frank's message to creative Christians on the West Coast on a vacation drive with my in-laws to San Diego. They had a tape from the recent *How Should We Then Live?* seminar. It was a speech by Frank Schaeffer (then known as "Franky"), challenging Christians to use their talents to make a difference in the arts. My in-laws advised that "You've got to meet this guy!" "Yeah, right," I thought.
>
> After offering my animations and design services to several Midwest-based Christian film distribution companies, I soon found each had severe quirks and major limitations in creativity and a general "tackiness." Then, I remember getting a call from a film editor I'd met through my Christian contacts. He said he'd helped assemble the first Schaeffer series, saying that a second

series was in preproduction. Due to the nature of the subject matter, he said that the director felt the series needed some animation, and that my name had been discussed. The director was Frank Schaeffer.

I sent my show reel. A few weeks later I got a call from another associate of the Schaeffer series who said that Frank was coming to Chicago and that he wanted to meet me.

The day I met Frank was full of anxious anticipation. I wanted so badly to impress him and his partner Jim Buchfuehrer. Though Frank's stature was short like mine, the intensity of his gaze meant all business. He was prone to express strong opinions on any of a variety of subjects; music, movies, art, but when he locked onto a serious topic there was no stopping him.

I spent that first day with Frank, listening to him describe the new project [*Whatever Happened to the Human Race?*] and experiencing Frank's intensity and odd lapses of un-preacher-son behavior (including an affinity for premium pipe tobacco and a "lively" vocabulary).

At the end of the day, I sat exhausted in the lobby of the Holiday Inn lobby. Frank had gone off to the washroom and I asked Jim, "Is Frank for real?" He told me that Frank was the most intense person he'd ever met; that his standards of excellence were unparalleled and that so far as Christian filmmakers go, there was no one else in the business with a greater sense of purpose, vision, or talent.

This was an adventure I wanted to be part of!

A few weeks later, I was in Frank's chalet at L'Abri in Switzerland working on the script to *Whatever Happened to the Human Race?* I met Francis Schaeffer at a classy restaurant in Lausanne. After introductions he leaned over to me and softly asked, "How many of my books have you read?"

Judging from the quantity of ideas I contributed that ended up in the final script, I knew how much my contribution was appreciated. I came to feel like a member of the Schaeffer family. I used to kid that I was Edith's "other" son.

Every time we met for creative brainstorming, I felt as if we had worked together all our lives. Frank's wife Genie was always a gracious host, joining discussions and offering candid opinions. In the setting of their lovely home I felt gratified that our creative sessions yielded the best ideas on any given day.

For the next seven years I devoted my best efforts and directed the talents of my studio to every project Frank Schaeffer drew me into. In addition to the film projects, this included promotional materials, a newsletter [*The Christian Activist*], as well as [covers for] a shelf-load of books by Schaeffer family members, as well as works of other authors supplemental to Frank's "work."

46

After Bishop Fulton J. Sheen saw the abortion-related episode of *How Should We Then Live?* and then heard from Dr. Koop that we were working on a pro-life series, he invited Jim Buchfuehrer and me to meet with him in his Park Avenue apartment. Sheen wanted to strategize on ways to advance the pro-life cause. The bishop was kind, tall, pale, gaunt, and quiet. His apartment smelled faintly of lavender with a touch of vegetable soup.

"The problem is," Sheen said, "that abortion is perceived as a Catholic issue. I want you to help me change that. The unborn need more friends."

After talking for about an hour, Sheen invited us into his private red-velvet-draped chapel across from his bedroom. It felt strange to be kneeling in front of a big "very Catholic" crucifix, as Mom would have called it.

I didn't mention to the bishop that as a three-year-old I had been kicked out of our village (along with my family) by his brother bishops because we were Protestants having a "religious influence" on his co-religionists. Nor did I mention that for years, Dad had been denouncing Billy Graham for compromising by inviting a Roman Catholic bishop to join him on the platform of his 1957 New York crusade, nor that I grew up on

Dad's stories about the extreme cruelty of the Spanish Roman Catholic Church and how the bishops were in league with Franco and the fascists.

Before I left, Sheen blessed me by making the sign of the cross over me. From that time on, we had the full cooperation of the Roman Catholic Church in America. The Knights of Columbus helped raise money for the making of *Whatever Happened to the Human Race?* And when we wanted to shoot a scene in the huge Catholic cemetery in Brooklyn and were denied permission (because Francis Ford Coppola had shot a scene there for *The Godfather* of the funeral of Don Corleone, and people had complained), we called Sheen. We got permission ten minutes later.

About two years after I first met Sheen, and after *Whatever Happened to the Human Race?* was out, I was being interviewed by *Newsweek* religion editor Kenneth Woodward at his offices for an article he wrote on Dad. Ken was one of the few reporters who seemed to "get" what was happening with the emergence of the evangelical pro-life movement, Dad's leadership of that movement, and the scale it was happening on.

He was lamenting the fact that *Newsweek* had just dropped its religion section as "irrelevant." Ken spoke ruefully about the fact that religion stories were getting rare and that all he could do was "Pick up the scraps once in a while, get a papal cover every few years or something."A few months before I talked to Ken, I had met with Jack and Joanne Kemp. Jack was a congressman and would soon be the Secretary at HUD under Reagan, and later a vice presidential candidate with Bob Dole. I had been introduced to the Kemps several years before, after Joanne Kemp started a book club called the "Schaeffer Group," made up of about twenty born-again senators' and congressmen's wives who came together weekly to study my parents' books. Mom and Dad had been guests in the Kemps' home.

Jack and Joanne were very attractive people and their house was lovely, crammed with silver-framed family pictures of their handsome family. I was nervous. I was also very impressed with myself. I had "arrived." The Little Shit from Switzerland was showing his movie series to a leading congressman!

Jim Buchfuehrer and I set up the 16-mm projector in Jack's living room, and we gave Jack and Joanne a private five-hour screening of *Whatever Happened to the Human Race?* Jack liked the movies and was, I think, genuinely moved. He also immediately saw the possibilities for the Republican Party. By the end of that evening (actually, it was nearer dawn), the pro-life cause had a new champion. From then on, Jack would give Koop, Dad, and myself access to everyone in the Republican Party.

For the next several years, I often saw Jack. And whenever Dad wanted something done in Washington, he would say "Call Jack!"

As the years passed, Dad used to be somewhat dismissive of Jack in private. "I like Jack, but he has a bee in his bonnet," Dad said. This was what Dad called Jack's supply-side economic theories. "It's hard to get Jack to concentrate on the important issues," Dad would grumble.

Jack would tell me: "I like talking to you better than your father. You seem to understand the real political picture. There are other things besides all his 'biblical absolutes theology' talk. He's too narrowly focused."

Soon after we showed the film series in his home, Jack hosted a meeting at the Republican Club in Washington, DC. We screened three episodes cut into a ninety-minute special.

(It had also just been shown on Dutch National TV.) There were more than fifty congressmen and about twenty senators there, from Henry Hyde to Bob Dole. Dad and I spoke to those assembled and took questions. We were there for over four hours, and no one left early. Media were invited but didn't choose to cover this unimportant "Christian event."

The National Right To Life Committee purchased time to show the ninety-minute special cut from our series on ABC's Channel 7 in Washington, DC. Judy Mann of the *Washington Post* took notice. The headline of her article was "No Matter How Moving, Show Is Still Propaganda" (January 2, 1981). Her article basically repeated word for word a press release that had been sent out by Planned Parenthood denouncing our series. The article began: "Score a resounding 10 points on the emotional Richter scale for the antiabortion forces that have produced a film, *Whatever Happened to the Human Race?*"

The *Post*'s coverage was unusual. In the 1970s and early '80s, what we did was largely ignored by the cultural gatekeepers. This only added to our martyr luster within the evangelical ghetto. We thrived on the perception of persecution. "Never reviewed by the *New York Times*" was a proud banner for us.

When, several years earlier, in connection with the book sales of *How Should We Then Live?* I had run a full-page ad in the *Times*, about the paper's ignoring Dad's huge book sales, the headline was: "This Story Should Have Been on Page One." Actually, it should have been.

The *Times* "best-seller" list was misleading. Evangelical books were often outselling the *Times*' best-sellers. But the paper did not bother to count sales in religious bookstores. The people hurt most weren't evangelical authors (our books sold anyway); rather, the losers were Democratic Party leaders and other liberal readers of the "paper of record" who were blindsided by subsequent events. The *Times'* readers were not given a heads-up about what was going on "out there."

The media generally ignored our seminars and the political impact they were having. If some major paper or network had sent a reporter to follow Dad, Dr. Koop, and myself on our coast-to-coast seminar tours, he or she would have seen a cross section of Americans of all races, denominations, and economic backgrounds at our events. And had the Democratic Party leaders read about or watched reports on these events—often filled with people *who still identified themselves as Democrats in those days*—they might not have been so sanguine about allowing their party to become so exclusionary on the abortion issue.

The reality of who was at our meetings—thousands of working-class and middle-class churchgoing women and the men they dragged with them—was very different than the image of loony "misogynistic" pro-lifers propagated by Planned Parenthood and parroted by the media. We didn't fit that image and so were ignored.

In 1982, Koop was nominated as Surgeon General by Reagan. Both the pro-life and pro-choice camps interpreted this as Reagan giving the pro-life community a reward for our support. During Koop's confirmation hearings, I went on the *700 Club,* twice, to raise support for Koop while he was being attacked in a pre-Bork "Borking" by the Democrats, led by Edward Kennedy. Koop would call me every day and beg me to redouble my efforts and to "Get the calls pouring in to the Senate!"

My last conversation with Jack Kemp was in 2000. We hadn't been in touch for about twenty years (other than his yearly Christmas card), and I called him to ask why the Republican Party establishment wasn't backing Senator McCain, and why the Bush people were spreading lies about McCain. I told Jack that I thought that Bush Jr. was obviously terribly wrong for the job.

Jack got angry with me after I said I was planning to "use the Schaeffer name again" (for the first time in twenty years) to do a series of radio interviews on conservative stations endorsing McCain. Jack snapped: "McCain is a warmonger! Bush is a peacemaker, just as I am!" When I kept arguing, he hung up.

47

Americans have experienced many cycles of religiously inspired political fervor, from the Bay State Puritans' mix of religion and law, to the various so-called Great Awakenings, to the evangelical-inspired and led antislavery movement, to Prohibition and the church-based antiwar movements advocating isolationism in the 1930s and early '40s, to the religiously motivated parts of the anti-Vietnam War movement. But in terms of the political involvement of evangelicals, as it has carried forward into the twenty-first century, it was my father and I who were amongst the first to start telling American evangelicals that God wanted them involved in the political process. And it was the *Roe v. Wade* decision that gave Dad, Koop, and me our platform.

Abortion became *the* evangelical issue. Everything else in our "culture wars" pales by comparison. The anger we stirred up at the grass roots was not feigned but heartfelt. And at first it was not about partisan politics. It had everything to do with genuine horror at the procedure of abortion. The reaction was emotional, humane, and sincere. It also was deliberately coopted by the Republican Party and, at first, ignored by the Democratic Party.

Our *Whatever Happened to the Human Race?* seminars

helped launch the crisis pregnancy-center movement (directly and indirectly). The centers offered a practical alternative to abortion. They also became bastions of pro-life political protest and activism.

The centers became places where ordinary Americans reached out with compassionate care to literally millions of women and babies of all races and economic conditions. (As of 2007, there were more than three thousand centers across America.) They also brought a growing number of Hispanic Pentecostals and former Democratic Party Roman Catholics into the Republican Party. And the crisis centers galvanized hitherto apolitical evangelicals into political action. The centers also brought black churches (which were often liberal on other issues) into close contact with culturally conservative white evangelicals and became places where local Republican action committees informally organized.

If things had fallen out slightly differently, the crisis centers just as easily could have been bastions of the Democratic Party, or at least nonpolitical. Abortion had been mostly a "Catholic issue," just as Bishop Sheen had said. And at first, most evangelical leaders, following Billy Graham's lead, weren't interested in "going political." When Dad asked Billy why he wasn't taking a stand on abortion, Billy answered that he had been burned by getting too close to Nixon and was never going to poke his head over the ramparts of the "I-only-preach-the-gospel" trench again. He said he didn't want to be "political."

Other evangelical leaders were similarly nervous when our films first came out, just as Dad had been nervous when I fought with him while urging him to add an anti-Supreme Court pro-life message to the end of our first film series.

Our second seminar tour to launch *Whatever Happened to*

the Human Race? lost almost one million dollars. (The first tour had made twice that on book sales, tapes, and film rentals.) We had raised around one and a half million to make *Whatever Happened to the Human Race?* and another million to promote it through the tour. We lost the money because we had moved from the comfortable subjects of art, culture, and theology (with abortion only tacked on in the last episodes of *How Should We Then Live?*) to the uncomfortable "life issues."

At first the evangelical media leaders, like the editors of *Christianity Today*, met *Whatever Happened to the Human Race?* with stony silence. And where, several years before, we had looked out over crowds of thousands, early on in the second tour we could barely fill the first row of seats in the same venues. Then things began to change.

They changed for two reasons. First, we raised grassroots consciousness in evangelical circles. Second, the pro-choice forces were so hubristically aggressive when belittling their opponents that they alienated everyone who even mildly questioned their position. They drove people to us.

If Planned Parenthood, NOW, and NARAL had sat down to figure out the best way to energize the evangelical subculture, they couldn't have done a better job. With their absolutist stand, they might as well have been working to help the Republicans take Congress and the White House. They branded all who even questioned *Roe* as backward women-hating rubes. *Roe* was the law! There was no need for further debate! There could be no compromise! Shut up! Go away! All that was at stake was "fetal tissue"! People who didn't agree could just be ignored, mocked, or sued into silence. Besides, the "progressives" had history on their side. We were entering a new secular and enlightened age!

This dismissive attitude backfired. For instance, after Planned Parenthood and NOW sent people to a few of our seminar venues to challenge us, the latter part of the tour began to pull a bigger evangelical crowd in an "us against them" spirit. Our small audiences listened to Dad, Koop, and myself try to debate in-your-face (and often off-the-wall) NOW and Planned Parenthood plants sent by those pro-choice organizations to protest the fact that we even wanted to discuss "their" issue. And our audiences were also sometimes treated to an exhibition of pro-choice self-righteousness that made our fundamentalism seem nuanced. We could not have scripted it better. A screamed chant of "*My body! My choice!*" isn't much of an argument.

Sometimes our events were picketed. Our rather quiet and timid evangelical audiences had to run a gauntlet of angry "Keep Your Hands Off My Body!" sign-waving pro-choice protesters.

Leading up to *Roe*, abortion had been pitched as a sad but inevitable solution to rare and agonizing dilemmas, like pregnancy resulting from rape and incest. But in the context of the post-*Roe* firestorm, pro-choice people seemed to also be defending abortion not only as a way to end a pregnancy but as an in-your-face triumphant political statement. They even seemed to be goading anyone who had doubts about *Roe v. Wade*. For instance, in the mid-1970s, the Washington, DC chapter of the ACLU auctioned off free abortions at a fundraising raffle held at a dance, and they made sure their action was publicized.

Even some people on the pro-choice side were shocked by the callousness of pro-choice supporters. For instance, in an article in the *Village Voice,* "Abortion Chic—The Attraction of

Wanted-Unwanted Pregnancies" (February 4, 1981), Leslie Savan, a self-described pro-choice advocate, discussed how abortion had become "subliminally chic." She quoted women who deliberately became pregnant, without any intention of carrying their babies to term. Some of the reasons Savan listed that the women had given her for getting pregnant, then aborting, were: "A desire to know if they were fertile, especially if they had postponed pregnancy until later life. . . . To test the commitment of the man. . . . Abortion as a rite of passage."

The debate became vicious. And Dad and I went from merely talking about providing compassionate alternatives to abortion, to actively working to drag evangelicals, often kicking and screaming, into politics. By the end of the *Whatever Happened to the Human Race?* tour, we were calling for civil disobedience, the takeover of the Republican Party, and even hinting at overthrowing our "unjust pro-abortion government."

48

I began to write. My evangelical books—for instance, my hastily dictated *A Time for Anger*—became best sellers. Like Dad's books, my evangelical screeds were ignored by the media. Although several decades later, author and comparative-religion historian Karen Armstrong, in *The Battle for God: Fundamentalism in Judaism, Christianity and Islam*, quoted a passage from *A Time for Anger* as an example of the paranoid anti-status-quo spirit animating American fundamentalism.

Dr. Dobson, founder of the *Focus on the Family* radio program, gave away tens of thousands of copies of *A Time for Anger* as a fund-raising fulfillment. And he interviewed me twice on his (then relatively new) show.

Inspired by my father's call for civil disobedience in his best-selling *A Christian Manifesto* (and also urged to action by *A Time for Anger*), the picketing of abortion clinics by evangelicals started on a large scale. Formerly passive evangelicals began talking about shutting the abortion clinics with a wall of protesters.

The "other side" reacted to the picketing of clinics with sledgehammer tactics, invoking so-called RICO (Racketeer Influenced and Corrupt Organization Act) laws, originally enacted to shut down organized crime. Pro-choice organizations used RICO to intimidate what, until then, was a peaceful grass-roots movement. And groups like the ACLU began to work to stifle the type of free-speech and civil-disobedience activities that in any other context they would have defended.

Dad's and my books were doing the advance work for people like Ronald Reagan and helping to craft Republican victories out of our fellow travelers' resentments. Dad and I were also beginning to advise friendly political leaders specifically on how best to woo the evangelical vote. For instance, encouraged by Dad and others, President Reagan contributed an article to a leading pro-life journal, the *Human Life Review.*

The *Human Life Review* routinely included articles by Clare Boothe Luce, Prof. James Hitchcock, Dr. Jerome Lejeune, Ellen Wilson, William P. Murchison, Malcolm Muggeridge, Harold O. J. Brown, George Gilder, Nat Hentoff, and dozens of other American and European pro-life writers and intellectuals. The authors included evangelicals, Republicans and Democrats, as well as liberals, an editor at the *Village Voice,* a professor of educational psychology at Boston College, a professor of humanities at the City University of New York, the former editor of Britain's *Punch* magazine, and a winner of the Medal of Freedom, as well as the chairman of the Department of Fundamental Genetics at the University of Paris.

The Spring 1983 issue of the *Human Life Review* carried President Reagan's article, "Abortion and the Conscience of the Nation." I pitched a slightly expanded version of it to Thomas Nelson publishers as a book.

We cranked the book out. The *Times* never reviewed it, of course, but it put a whole generation of pro-life evangelicals on notice that the Republican Party was "our" party.

When Mom and Dad talked to Presidents Ford, Reagan, or

Bush Sr., they would reiterate the pro-life position. Unlike Billy Graham, who made sure everyone knew he was the "chaplain to presidents," Dad made sure his conversations were private. He used to often say "You can be seen to do something, or actually do it."

Dad's strategy seemed to work. When I wanted to turn Reagan's article into a book, I only had to call the White House once.

49

Dad and I were mixing with a new set of people who had not known much, if anything, about my father. If they had even heard of Dad before he came on the pro-life scene in the mid-to-late seventies, they probably hadn't liked the sound of him. These people included Jerry Falwell, Pat Robertson, James Dobson, James Kennedy, and all the rest of the televangelists, radio hosts, and other self-appointed "Christian leaders" who were bursting on the scene in the 1970s and early '80s.

Compared to Dad, these slick media figures were upstarts. They were "not our sort of people," Dad often said. What people like Robertson and Falwell got from Dad was some respectability.

Dad had a unique reputation for an intellectual approach to faith. And his well-deserved reputation for frugal ethical living, for not financially profiting from his ministry, for compassion, openness, and intellectual integrity, was the opposite of the reputations of the new breed of evangelical leadership, with their perks, planes, and corner offices in gleaming new buildings and superficial glib messages. Empire builders like Robertson, Dobson, and Falwell liked rubbing up against (or quoting) my father, for the same reason that popes liked to have photos taken with Mother Teresa.

What I slowly realized was that the religious-right leaders we were helping to gain power were not "conservatives" at all, in the old sense of the word. They were anti-American religious revolutionaries.

The secular pre-*Roe v. Wade* right had been led by people like James Buckley and the old-fashioned Republican anti-socialist conservatives left over from the Hoover era, or people like Senator Barry Goldwater who stood for the separation of church and state. The "lunatic fringe" old right was represented by groups like the John Birch Society. But even their sometimes paranoid activism had been directed at secular issues such as stopping communism.

The new religious right was all about religiously motivated "morality," which it used for nakedly political purposes. This was a throwback to an earlier and uglier time, for instance to the 1930s pro-fascist "Catholic" xenophobic hatemongers like Father Charles Coughlin and his vicious anti-Roosevelt radio programs.

Father Coughlin would have understood Dobson, Falwell, and Robertson perfectly: Begin a radio ministry, move steadily to the populist right, then identify the "enemy"—in Coughlin's case, socialism and Roosevelt; in the new religious right's case, the secular humanists and the Democrats. Then rip off your priest's collar—something Coughlin literally did—and talk about politics pure and simple, maybe even form an independent party if you can't sufficiently manipulate the levers of established power.

The leaders of the new religious right were different from the older secular right in another way. They were gleefully betting on American failure. If secular, democratic, diverse, and pluralistic America survived, then wouldn't that prove that we evangelicals were wrong about God only wanting to bless a

"Christian America?" If, for instance, crime went down dramatically in New York City, for any other reason than a reformation and revival, wouldn't that make the prophets of doom look silly when they said that only Jesus was the answer to all our social problems? And likewise, if the economy was booming without anyone repenting, what did *that* mean?

Falwell, Robertson, Dobson, and others would later use their power in ways that would have made my father throw up. Dad could hardly have imagined how they would help facilitate the instantly corrupted power-crazy new generation of evangelical public figures like Ralph Reed, who took money from the casino industry while allegedly playing both sides against the middle in events related to the Abramoff Washington lobbyist scandal. And after 9/11, the public got a glimpse of the anti-American self-righteous venom that was always just under the surface of the evangelical right. Pat Robertson, Jerry Falwell, and others declared that the attack on America was a punishment from God. And after the war in Iraq began, some loony group of fundamentalists started picketing the funerals of killed soldiers and screaming at bereaved fathers and mothers that God was punishing "faggot America." What they shouted openly was what the leaders of the religious right were usually too smart to state so bluntly, but it is what they had often said in private.

What began to bother me was that so many of our new "friends" on the religious right seemed to be rooting for one form of apocalypse or another. In the crudest form, this was part of the evangelical fascination with the so-called end times. The worse things got, the sooner Jesus would come back. But there was another component: the worse everything got, the more it proved that America needed saving, by *us*!

Long before Ralph Reed and his ilk came on the scene, Dad got sick of "these idiots," as he often called people like Dobson in private. They were "plastic," Dad said, and "power-hungry." They were "Way too right-wing, really nuts!" and "They're using our issue to build their empires."

To our lasting discredit, Dad and I didn't go public with our real opinions of the religious-right leaders we were in bed with. We believed there was too much at stake, both personally, as we caught the power-trip disease, and politically, as we got carried away by the needs of the pro-life movement. And however conflicted Dad and I were, like the other religious-right leaders, we were on an ego-stroking roll. We kept our mouths shut.

50

Genie and I lived in Switzerland throughout the productions of *How Should We Then Live? and Whatever Happened to the Human Race?* We had traveled together with the children on the shoots and seminar tours. Then I became a sought-after speaker on the evangelical circuit. This put me on the road when the children could not travel: They were in school. I missed Jessica and Francis's growing up in horrible chunks of time that left me feeling as if I was being hollowed out.

Genie and I wanted to be together. The only way we could was for me to quit what I was doing or to move to America.

The year before we moved, I was on the road for six months. By then, I was capitalizing on my connections by representing other evangelical authors as well as my parents. I had twenty or so authors I was representing, including John Whitehead (founder of the Rutherford Institute), Dr. Koop, Mary Pride (who more or less became the leading guru of the evangelical homeschool movement), and my sister Susan, who by then was writing books on education. And, of course, I was always meeting with Gospel Films and my partner Jim Buchfuehrer and our donors.

There were other reasons for our wanting to leave Switzerland and the L'Abri community. Genie and I were no longer

L'Abri workers, but we were very much still in the center of things. We lived only a mile away from L'Abri, and all my family was in the work. (We also had one L'Abri chalet next door, where Debby and Udo were.)

My sisters and brothers-in-law were dividing into enemy camps. John Sandri and Priscilla were easy-going libertarians with a more liberal view. Udo and Debby were stricter when it came to maintaining the traditions of L'Abri as established by my parents. Ranald was our hard-line Calvinist.

My sisters and brothers-in-law were lovely taken individually; but when the families mixed, they were increasingly toxic to each other. Ranald used to make remarks about Udo and his "Germanic attitude." Udo would talk about Ranald's "rigid sense of British superiority." Ranald felt that the secular books and movies Debby and Udo loved, read, watched, and talked about were "dangerous." To Udo and Debby, Susan and Ranald were "unbearably pietistic." Everyone found Ranald's Calvinism harsh. John Sandri never said much unpleasant about anyone, but he was not about to give up his biblical literary studies to suit the more conservative theology of his brothers-in-law.

"They just don't like each other," Genie would say. "Why *do* they have to drag God into it?"

At first, Genie and I talked about moving to California (in view of my movie ambitions), but Genie had had enough of that life, at least as she remembered it, and told me that she didn't want to raise her family "in all the craziness and materialism."

At our family reunion in 1979, and after a particularly bitter fight between Udo and Ranald, Genie and I happened to be reading the *International Herald Tribune* and saw an ad for a seven-acre farm in Plaistow, New Hampshire, about an hour from Boston. (We had liked the Boston area when we visited during several of our seminars and during the movie shoot at the Museum of Fine Arts for *How Should We Then Live?*)

We had twelve family reunions before my dad died in 1984. The clan always checked into the Hotel Bonivard in Montreux, where Ranald, Sue, Priscilla, John, Debby, Udo, Mom, Dad, Genie, I, and all our children gathered for three days of walks, meals, train and boat rides, and loud discussions that turned into fights. The L'Abri workers and members resented these reunions, since it was clear that it was our family, not the other L'Abri workers and members, who were really calling the shots in L'Abri. The workers suspected (rightly) that they got talked about in our closed and exclusive get-together.

Mom paid for the reunions from her book royalties. At our reunions, we supposedly gathered to experience the family "togetherness" Mom wrote about in her best-selling books like *What Is a Family?* where she held up the Schaeffer clan as an example to evangelical mothers everywhere. She even used group pictures of our reunion on several book covers. (Anyone looking closely would have seen a lot of clenched jaws!)

By the second day of the reunion, my brothers-in-law would barely be speaking to each other. But the little cousins had a great time. Mom would buy the girls matching outfits, and we all got a T-shirt she designed each year with the date and family reunion number on it.

On the next trip to the States, I asked Jim Buchfuehrer to pick me up in a rental car in Boston. (We were on a fund-raising tour.) We drove up to Plaistow. The farmhouse was too close to the road, and there were problems with the building. But as we were driving south, we happened on Newburyport, Massachusetts. On the way through town, we stopped at a realtor's office. The realtor talked Jim and me into staying at a local bed-and-breakfast for the night. Then she drove us out to the Plum Island nature reserve the next morning.

We walked on the little winding boardwalks over the rolling dunes and watched the waves crashing on the long wide empty beach. Later we strolled around the newly renovated eighteenth-century center of Newburyport. (It reminded me of Lindfield, the village near Great Walstead.) I felt at home. And Genie liked the pictures of a certain old house I brought back. . . .

In July 1980, when Genie, the children, and I moved, it was a shock. We left our perfectly renovated beautiful little "Chalet Regina" for a big old tumbledown brick house on the banks of the Merrimack River. We had left L'Abri; but now that we were actually on our own, we missed the family. And I felt very shaky. My self-confidence seemed to evaporate. Could I really make it on my own? We left cool summer nights for the heat of an East Coast summer, the freedom to lie in a hayfield looking at the moon rising over the Dents Du Midi for mosquitoes that had us running from the house to the car, from walk-anywhere-woods to a poison ivy-bordered marsh. I spent a lot of time muttering "What the fuck have I done?"

Genie grew up in San Mateo, but I'd never lived in America, applied for a driver's license, shopped in a supermarket, gotten a building permit, or stopped for a school bus. (I had always been a privileged visitor, whisked by taxi or limo, planes, production managers, and hosts to one place after another. Hotels were "home" when in America.)

In Europe, children are expected to look both ways all by themselves before crossing a street. The first time I saw a school bus stopped, lights flashing, I just zoomed past, nearly ran down several children, and heard the driver honk furiously and the shouts of the angry children: "You're supposed to stop!" I asked Genie what the hell all that was about, and she explained that in America when a child gets off a bus, the world stops.

I liked being in a country where if you ordered a phone it was installed a day later, not three months after your name was put on the state-run phone company waiting list. But when we started renovating our 1835 home, began to turn it into a single-family house from one divided into two seedy apartments, I discovered that there is an advantage to having some things bureaucratically regulated.

In Switzerland a carpenter, electrician, mason, or plumber is actually a carpenter, electrician, mason, or plumber. They can't work unless they have passed the *maîtrise fédérale* exam, following a lengthy apprenticeship. Carpenters in Switzerland were as skilled as the best American cabinetmakers. They used no prefabricated doors, windows, or kitchen cabinets. Everything was built to order. And the work was done perfectly. The building codes were enforced by the builders themselves. All the bids for a job were made by local men who had spent their youth training for that work and rightly regarded their trades as a high professions, right up there in respectability with being a lawyer or doctor.

Our first American "contractor" went bankrupt in the middle of renovating our attic into a new bedroom and bathroom. He failed to pay his subcontractors, who then came after me. I was running around showing them canceled checks to prove that I'd been paying all along. That was after the contractor got in his pickup and headed for Florida.

Genie was pregnant with John when we moved. We thought electric fans would be enough to keep us cool in one of the hottest, most humid summers on record. We went looking for a pro-life doctor to take care of Genie and deliver the baby. We couldn't find food we liked in the supermarket, and the bread was horrible. Humidity-sodden hunks of plaster were falling from the old cracked ceilings in the heat. There was no screen porch—we added one later—and we huddled inside around the fans. Jessica, age ten, Francis, seven, and I worked outside slathered in Off, clearing sumac and poison ivy from enough of the front yard so we could start to get the garden back to where it had been in 1960, when the owners had moved out and began renting the property.

John was born. Gradually our new house became home. We learned that if we cut the grass short, cleaned up our yard, and avoided being outside at dawn and dusk, the garden was lovely. We discovered that if you looked around, there were very good builders and tradesmen in our area, like Gerry the plumber; Rick, our carpenter; and Don, our electrician, who were skilled and conscientious and became our friends. Then, much to our joy, Bill and Jane opened Annarosa's Bakery in Newburyport, the best bakery in America, maybe in the world. And we bought air conditioners. And the tours that used to take me away from Switzerland for weeks could be broken down into mostly overnight trips now.

The children had a hard time adjusting from the excellent Swiss school system to the small inept private school we put them in. And a year later, when we enrolled Jessica in a swanky local private middle school, she still had a tough time. The Swiss children were just that, children, unconcerned by fashion. Jessica didn't have the "right" shoes; she had the "wrong" slacks and tops.

We still traveled back to Switzerland once a year for our

ritualistic family reunions. The fights got worse each year. At the last reunion, Dad yelled at Mom because it was our twelfth reunion and her T-shirt design that year was a clock with the hands pointing to two minutes to midnight. Dad was dying of cancer and hated that image.

"Why did you make this fool thing?" he yelled. "That's nice, two minutes to midnight! *Just* what I want, some omen that I'm dying and won't make next year's reunion!"

Dad didn't make it.

51

The influence of the right-wing fundamentalist we were working with rubbed off on us. I wrote several more liberal-bashing books about American "decline." Dad also moved to the right, or should I say back to his fundamentalist roots. His new, harsher persona even bled back into L'Abri and the heart of our family.

From the mid-1970s until he died, Dad was drafted (from time to time) by the Missouri Synod Lutherans, Southern Baptists, and other conservative denominations as a kind of intellectual heavy gun-for-hire. They were fighting their own updated versions of the 1920s antimodernist battles. The fight was against a new crop of "liberal" theologians who were "infiltrating" heretofore solidly conservative denominations and seminaries. These theologians were not fundamentalist enough. They were not strong enough on the issue of the inerrancy of the Bible or were "weak" on our social issues, like abortion—or, even worse, were prepared to *compromise* with people even more liberal than themselves. ("Inerrancy" was the belief that the Bible is literally true with no errors of fact in it, even when it seems to be contradicted by science or history or within the text itself.)

Dad, like some old warhorse long absent from battle, jumped into the fight over the inerrancy of scripture. He spent the last years of his life intermittently shuttling between secret and public meetings where he was used by hard-liners to stiffen the spines of various seminary and denominational boards so they would make the necessary break with their own people and fire "untrustworthy" professors. Dad was telling people to "take back" their denominations before it was "too late."

Priscilla was aghast that Dad was turning back to his former passion for doctrinal purity and away from his more enlightened views. She told me that the denominational fights that Dad got involved in in the late 1970s reminded her of her traumatic youth in the 1940s and early '50s, when our family was deeply embroiled in the bitter splits between various fundamentalist groups. Priscilla mourned this return to the "ugly days." She was very upset and accused me of being "part of this," because it was my movies and book deals that "got Daddy back into this mess."

John Sandri, Priscilla's husband, paid a heavy price for Dad's rekindled fundamentalist enthusiasms. John had been giving well attended Bible studies in L'Abri that some of the more strictly Calvinistic L'Abri workers (including Ranald and Udo, who for once agreed on something) said were bordering on "heresy." John was reading the Bible as a literary work, and not giving it the "correct" theological spin. John was a liberal! The sky was falling! John had compromised!

John's "crime" was his interest in how the Bible states things and how you draw meaning from the biblical text. John knew that if you push the so-called Sola Scriptura Calvinist approach and the "inerrancy" ideas to their absurd limit, all real study of the Bible stops. It becomes a magical text. It is no longer open to interpretation. Dogma replaces study, because scholarship can only be meaningful when you are allowed to ask real questions and let the chips fall where they may.

It was decided that John should no longer teach in L'Abri. Dad instigated this anti-John, purity-of-the-visible-church purge. In the case of John—who was *by far* all of our family's favorite person and the picture of kindness and Christian love, as well as common sense—the absurdity of trying to demand one-note theological purity became clear.

If L'Abri produced one true saint, one self-effacing gentleman willing to help everyone do everything from clip their hedges to solve marital problems, to do their taxes, one real biblical scholar, it was John Sandri. If John—who spent a good part of his life selflessly nursing my sister Priscilla after her three massive nervous breakdowns—was no longer good enough for L'Abri, then who was?

But how could Dad be running all over America giving fiery speeches on the inerrancy of the Bible and the "purity of the visible church," when his *own* son-in-law had quietly evolved into the type of Bible scholar that Dad was insisting the Southern Baptists, Lutherans, and others fire from their seminaries? So Dad did to John what he had refused to do to me when I got Genie pregnant: he made a public example of him.

Dad went so far as to come up with a statement that everyone in L'Abri had to sign if they wanted to remain in the work. It was a McCarthy-type loyalty oath to the "inerrancy of scripture" concept. And of course John, to his credit, didn't sign. Everyone else, to their discredit, did.

The updated fundamentalism-versus-modernism battle that Dad let tear his family apart seemed to bow him down. He kept telling me how sorry he was about John. He also kept saying "But what choice do I have? I can't take the public stand I take on the scriptures and not do anything about John!" And Dad unwittingly set the stage for the power struggle in L'Abri that happened after he died. Once fundamentalists start to sniff out "impurities," they don't stop.

John was Dad's favorite son-in-law. He had always told me that. How could Dad have been so cruel? Maybe there were just too many people treating Dad like a prophet. Maybe he had just gotten too used to always being in the spotlight, a hush falling on any gathering when he spoke.

When L'Abri banned John Sandri from teaching, they asked if he would stay on nevertheless and help run the work! The smallness of our village, with John living a few hundred yards from the other L'Abri chalets, made his banning doubly absurd. Since John had the best (in fact the only) day-to-day knowledge of everything from residency permits to taxes, from the tricky water heater in some chalet to who in the village could fix a rotting roof, and since he did *all* L'Abri's complex international financial, tax, and insurance work, he was irreplaceable. And since John, unlike Dad at that point, didn't take himself too seriously, he volunteered to help out, rather than let The Work collapse under the weight of an absurd theological fight.

It was a lesson I never forgot. To me, John's selfless actions came to represent what faith looks like when lived, as opposed to what theological "purity" looks like. And one reason I still bother to struggle to have faith is because of John Sandri's example. He truly returned good for evil.

My sister Priscilla remembers her husband's mistreatment in a kinder, gentler light. I don't think she can bear having to choose between her husband and our father's memory, so she puts the rosiest spin on these events possible. And in a way, her lack of bitterness—even perhaps her state of denial—is as inspiring as John's forgiveness of those who wronged him.

Priscilla writes:

Dad did change his emphasis in his later years. His books had been published and he spent more and more time in the United States lecturing and going back into the U.S. "church world." His burden became caring for where the evangelical churches were heading. It was at this time that he got cancer, meaning even more absences from Huémoz. What I missed was the one-to-one involvement with our students, his discussions with nonreligious language. I was sad but it didn't affect me personally, as working in Swiss L'Abri the workers here were going on in the old involvement of one-to-one discussions with the students, as we still do today. Of course when he would return for short stays in Huémoz, Dad would carry on Saturday night discussions in the chapel and preach on Sunday mornings, but it couldn't be the same as before.

My husband John and Dad did have some theological differences about the wording of Christ's place in the Trinity. They discussed for hours. Dad was distressed since he was so fond of John. But finally after tears over the situation, Dad realized that although John wasn't heretical, the way he expressed himself was misleading. Actually, it took me longer to understand John's position but over the years, as I've listened to John's New Testament teaching I've become more and more excited by it and do understand what he is really saying.

52

I was not getting rich off the film productions, let alone the seminars. I never paid myself more than $39,000 a year from my Gospel Films budget or, later, from Schaeffer V Productions and, for most of the time, earned less than that. (Even back then, that wasn't much.) And I didn't milk the "perks." But soon I was earning a lot more, when I started to get book royalties from my evangelical books, several hundreds of thousands of dollars a year for a few years, that I invested very badly and more or less threw away. (My father and mother gave half their royalties to L'Abri and then gave away an additional ten percent of what they kept on top of that. Even so, they suddenly had plenty of money.)

But besides the pro-life cause—in which I sincerely believed—it was never about the money anyway. It was about self-righteousness, adrenaline, and power. Nevertheless, I was starting to get tired of the whole thing.

Jim Buchfuehrer writes:

> Frank had become a name in the evangelical world equal to his father. He was a much better communicator and learned much from his father. Frank had spoken at all the big events in the evangelical American world

> such as the Southern Baptist Convention. Whatever the venue Frank always stole the show.
>
> Everybody was calling. I was fielding all the calls; serve on this board, consult here, all the top evangelical leaders were calling saying, we want Frank to be on this board, speak at this conference. We were in the driver's seat so to speak. But that was the last thing Frank wanted. It was time to move on. . . .

The Francis Schaeffer of the Uffizi, who hiked with me and told me that he had doubts about many things, even God, gradually disappeared, and the absolutist defender-of-the-Bible and father-of-the-religious-right took his place. The young painter I had been was gone, too. And even the young idealistic pro-life activist was fading away, to be replaced by a pain-in-the-ass upstart earning great book royalties and speaking fees from hanging onto his father's coattails and shrilly denouncing "secular America" and the evils of liberals.

I was turning our cause into a solid profession. *Roe v. Wade* turned out to be my personal lucky break.

Most absurd of all, I really knew *nothing* about the real America. I might as well have been raised on Mars. My ignorance went far beyond not knowing to stop for school buses! Once I moved to the States, I gradually came to realize that my version of "America" had come from others: first, from my parents' jaundiced view of the country they left in 1947 (it was being "taken over by theological liberalism"); second, from the political battles we were plunged into. I had no context, no sense of proportion, no hands-on experience.

As I became a more and more successful "professional Christian," I began to sense the depth of my ignorance about the country I was talking about. On the road, I'd be parroting the party line, saying that America was godless and doomed. But the America I was *actually experiencing* (for the first time as a resident) was not doomed. It was more complicated and wonderful than I had ever imagined. I began to get the feeling that maybe I was on the wrong side.

The public image of the leaders of the religious right I met with so many times also contrasted with who they really were. In public, they maintained an image that was usually quite smooth. In private, they ranged from unreconstructed bigot reactionaries like Jerry Falwell, to Dr. Dobson, the most power-hungry and ambitious person I have ever met, to Billy Graham, a very weird man indeed who lived an oddly sheltered life in a celebrity/ministry cocoon, to Pat Robertson, who would have a hard time finding work in any job where hearing voices is not a requirement.

Dad and I were sitting in Falwell's study just after Dad spoke at Jerry's church. (Later I preached there, too, endorsed Falwell, and also gave a talk to the whole student body at Falwell's college.) Out of the blue, Jerry brought up the gay issue. Dad said something about it being complicated, and Jerry replied: "If I had a dog that did what they do, I'd shoot him!"

The offhand remark came from nowhere. Jerry wasn't smiling. He was serious and just tossed his hatred out there the way gang members throw down hand signals. Dad looked nonplussed but didn't say anything, though later he growled, "That man is really disgusting." Later still, Dad commented: "You can be cobelligerents, but you don't have to be allies."

Dad, Jim Buchfuehrer, and I were with Pat Robertson in a secret meeting Pat called to help John Whitehead, Jim, and me set up the Rutherford Institute, a (then new) group that was going to be the "Christian answer to the ACLU." I was a founding board member, along with John Whitehead and Jim Buchfuehrer. It was a measure of our absurd paranoia that the meeting was "secret." (John Whitehead was a lawyer who had the idea to start the new ministry, and he would lead it.)

While the ACLU was suing to keep Christians out of public life, the Rutherford Institute would sue to protect Christians' rights, or at least the "last vestiges of rights that have not already been stripped away by the secular humanists in the courts." And the ACLU made our lives easy. We thanked God every time the ACLU sued municipal governments to get crèche scenes off public property, or stopped some school district from allowing prayer before football games, or sued to take some dusty plaque with the Ten Commandments off some obscure statehouse or court building. Our fund-raising (and often the Republicans winning the next election in some locality) depended on the ACLU "outrage" of the day.

Since the ACLU was the Rutherford Institute's mirror image, depending on us stupid fundamentalists doing stupid things, just as we depended on the stupid actions taken by the sort of lefties who lie awake at night worrying about the "In God We Trust" inscription on coins, life was good for all concerned.

"Standing up to the ACLU" was so popular that several dozen other Christian civil liberties groups were springing up at the same time as Rutherford was founded by John Whitehead, Jim, and myself. America-the-hysterical is a profitable place for shrill activists of all persuasions. In some back room, away from the TV cameras, the busybody do-gooders who ran the ACLU and like-minded organizations, and the busybody do-gooders who I was working with on the religious right, would have understood each other perfectly. We all claimed that the *only thing* that could stop the loss of "all our rights" was *us*! Just send in your donation today! "*Urgent!* Open this time-sensitive material *right away!*" The sky always had to be falling, otherwise we all—of the paranoid left and delusional religious right—would have been out of a job.

While we were with Pat at those meetings, Dad and I were also going to be on the *700 Club*—again. So after the closed-door meeting ended, Dad, Jim, and I were standing in the green room before the show in a circle of prayer—in other words, squeezing some stranger's sweaty hands with our heads bowed.

Dad looked about as comfortable as a cat being held over water. The man to my left, a preacher from Kansas City with bad dandruff who claimed that his church had just been "closed down by the IRS for preaching the Word," called out "Thus sayeth the Lord! We must repent!" And Pat's producer bellowed, "Yes, Jesus and Amen! And *Aaaamen!*"

The preacher from Kansas City had just "interpreted" someone's "tongues" utterance that had been shouted moments before, something like "*Nagaz, shagaz, spiffy-biffy blabooo*!" In other words, he translated the godly gibberish of the "heavenly language" into English.

We all held hands while people shouted out this and that to God, or whispered heartfelt prayers, until a very cute girl in a tight pink dress opened the door, quiet and prayerful and oozy as Liquid Plumber, and the producer murmured a last "Amen *and Aaaamen*!" and the oozy cute girl whispered, "Pat's ready, praise the Lord!"

Then we started to shuffle for the door. But we tried to act polite because even though we all wanted to get down the hall first to see Pat, so we could get a couple of seconds of his undivided attention and make sure he put in a good plug for whatever we were hawking that day—the point is, you want Pat to tell the director to cut to a close-up of your book when he holds it up—we didn't want to look like we were *too* pushy, because of all that stuff in scripture about being meek that we were still supposed to believe.

Pat had a private makeup suite that he shared with the *700 Club*'s other star, old Ben Kinchlow, the friendly sidekick. They liked frozen air. You could see your breath in Pat and Ben's makeup suite. Pat was sitting in a big old-fashioned barber chair with his makeup and hair girls fussing around him, doing last-minute touch-ups.

Pat still had the paper makeup ruffle tucked around his neck. It made him look like a stripped-down Dutch seventeenth-century pastor in a Rembrandt, only under Pat's neck ruffle he had on a cashmere tan jacket rather than black robes. And any sober Dutch Reformed pastor would have had Pat burned at the stake as soon as he heard him speaking in tongues, let alone the stream of gibberish he was about to unleash on us.

Pat's makeup was more or less done. He was ready to share from his heart and dedicate that day's show to the Lord. Ben was ready, too. His job, on and off the air, was to do his part for Jesus by hanging around and laughing at Pat's jokes and saying "Yes, Lord" every time Pat said something wise and heartwarming, or even looked like he might.

The first wise and heartwarming thing Pat said to us—with plenty of his trademark goofy giggles and laughs, and his voice going up an octave for emphasis—was "Today the Lord showed me a special sign concerning the spirit of the age!"

"Yes, Jesus!" shouted Ben.

The rest of us nodded and thanked Jesus, too.

Then Pat said, "I went out to my garage this morning, and a

snake was curled up right next to the passenger-side door of my car. So I got a shovel and killed it. Then I go outside to throw its body into the woods, and there's *another* snake sitting on the path! [Long goofy chuckle.] Well, folks, you need to know that I've lived in that house *ten years* and never seen a snake before! I knew the Lord was trying to tell me something!"

Pat chuckled and Ben laughed and we all chuckled, too, and said yes, Jesus. And I tried not to catch Dad's eye.

Then Pat said, "Would you believe it, but *everywhere* I turned there were more and more snakes! My arms got tired smiting them! Finally God spoke to my heart and said 'Pat, no matter *how* many serpents you smite, I'll send more; so trust in me, Pat, not in your own strength!' Then I fell down and wept before the Lord, and when I looked up all the snakes were gone, *even the bodies of the dozens I had killed*! I can't tell if I was in my body or caught up in the Spirit."

Ben: "Lord, You are so great, we just worship you."

"Oh, *Jesus,* we just thank you for Pat!" whispered a makeup girl.

Pat cut her ass-kissing short. "You want to know what [long goofy chuckle] the serpents signify?" he asked.

We all said yes, yes we did. Ben moaned and shivered, as if what Pat might say next was probably more than regular folks could bear. Meanwhile, the makeup girl dabbed at Pat's face with a foam wedge, smoothing out the makeup where she'd missed a spot. This was all business as usual to her. Pat could have claimed that Jesus was sitting on his knee eating an ice cream cone, and she would have just kept dabbing away.

"I'll tell you what, ladies and gentlemen," said Pat, swiveling the makeup chair to survey us all: "The snakes are the sins contaminating the Body of Christ! The Secular World's not our only problem, ladies and gentlemen; it's *our own sin* that's grieving the Lord's heart and delaying His return!"

Ben: "That's right!"

Now Dad was shifting his weight uncertainly back and forth from one foot to the other.

"The other day," said Pat, "I was invited to speak to the Orlando chapter of the Full Gospel Business Men's Association. At the end of my talk on how God will bless us if we plant a seed of faith and give richly to His work, by supporting the *700 Club*'s special fund, I said 'Now bow your heads, open your hearts, and close your eyes so no one but God and me can see you. Now each one of you men'—they were all successful, *married* Christian men in their midforties to fifties—'raise your hands if you still masturbate.' And do you know, over half raised their hands!"

"O Lord, just forgive us!" Ben wailed.

On the *Club* that day there was an interesting moment. The floor director was doing what floor directors do everywhere, silently counting down on her fat fingers so Pat could wrap things up for the break. Pat was having a Word of Knowledge. That's when God tells Pat things directly, as if he's on the phone calling in information about, say, some woman in Milwaukee with a tumor in her left ovary.

Anyway, that day God gave Pat a "Word" for some lady with deafness in one ear. Pat squinted at the floor director through closed eyelids—he was deep in his healing, we-just-this-Lord-we-just-that, prayer. She was counting down the seconds on her fingers to the out. And Pat wrapped up the Word of Knowledge right on cue! Since a Word of Knowledge is as direct a message from God as you can get this side of the Last Judgment, it interested me to learn that God made sure his Word fit the time slot.

53

Some people literally worshipped my parents. They still do. A lady rushed up to me at one of our seminars and asked if she could shake Dad's hand. I told her that he had already left, which he had, and she grabbed me and blurted "I just want to say I *touched* a Schaeffer!"

After Dad died, a stranger sent me an elaborate hand-carved, laboriously painted, three-foot-tall bas-relief "icon" of my father portrayed as a saint in heaven standing holding hands with Jesus. It must have taken the person months of work to make this curious kitsch monstrosity (somewhat in the style of the nineteenth-century "icons" of George Washington being received by the angels).

Even *Christianity Today* magazine—which, during Dad's lifetime, treated him with suspicion—got into the act some fifteen years after Dad died, with a cover story titled "Our Very Own St. Francis" and a picture of my father dressed like Francis of Assisi. (They talked about his continuing influence and how he shaped the thinking of a whole generation of evangelical pastors.) And I have long since lost count of the number of women who launched into unstoppable gushing sessions when talking about Mom. On the other hand, I have also met quite a few bitter young men and women who tell me that their evangelical mothers "raised me according to your mother's books!"

My adventures in Schaeffer-worship bothered me even when I was profiting from them. A little goes a long way. And the groupie factor also drove my sisters nuts.

Priscilla has made it a mission to disabuse the students who still come to L'Abri of the Schaeffer mythology. She makes no secret of her nervous breakdowns, her dependence on Prozac, her depression and anxiety attacks, her alcohol-related struggles. She will tell anyone who asks that being a Schaeffer child—and the pressure from Mom to be part of the ministry and, above all, from strangers to live up to their "Schaeffer expectations"—didn't help. When I called her to ask if she would allow me to write about her problems, and she gave me the okay, she also said "Mom drove me crazy, but in fairness I would have suffered from stress and depression anywhere. I would push too hard in L'Abri, then crash. If I had been doing something else just as intense, it would have happened, too."

Susan burned out early in L'Abri, too, retired when she was in her fifties, and moved into an assisted-living home with Ranald. (They were both in reasonable health.) Susan told me that when she visits the English L'Abri (the one she founded in Hampshire) that she never goes to any of the meetings and doesn't want to see anyone there except for some members of her immediate family who happen to live nearby.

Debbie, who provides most of the day-to-day care for my aging and fragile mother, says that she struggles with a feeling of rage when she's with Mom—which she realizes is "completely illogical," given that Mother is old and helpless. But she also works hard to include Mom nevertheless. Debby says that she doesn't remember ever having "one real conversation" with my mother during a whole lifetime. "Mom always had her own agenda. She was interested in how we fit into that, not in us."

As for me, if I see someone reading a Bible on an airplane, I'll hurry past in case they look up and somehow recognize me as the "Franky" Schaeffer who they used to watch on the *700 Club*. I'll cross a street when walking past an evangelical "bookstore" for the same reason. And my insecurities—and squirrelly Schaeffer baggage—can be measured by my name changes. I directed *Whatever Happened to the Human Race*? as "Franky Schaeffer," one of my Hollywood features as "Francis," wrote my evangelical books under "Franky," and switched to "Frank" after I left the fold.

To one extent or another, my parents' children have had serious problems that relate to Mom and Dad and their work. And even though everyone can say the same, perhaps there is a little added pressure on the children of venerated saints, saints that in private were far from saintly.

But the fact that I became my father's sidekick was the self-perpetuation of a nightmare. Like most children, I wanted to be independent of my parents and then found myself exacerbating my dependence. Not only was I drawn into my parents' ministry, I was the prime mover and shaker when it came to making sure that Dad got truly famous within the evangelical subculture. If it is tough having a famous father, more fool the son who made him so!

Dad wasn't ever completely comfortable with his new (and very late-in-life) role as a big-time evangelical superstar. He felt out of place when hailed as the "father of the religious right." Was this really what he wanted to be remembered as? And I felt as if I was having a series of out-of-body experiences when

I spoke in front of groups like the Southern Baptists at their huge annual convention. The success of what I was doing made me feel like I was sinking into a swamp.

I would pace around behind the stage before an event, literally praying for escape and cursing myself for having quit painting. I was with people who looked at me squiffy-eyed if I slipped up and said "damn," or "shit," the sorts of people to whom I had to make sure I never mentioned that I loved this or that "godless" movie.

I became lax. I told one homeschool mother (the wife of a pastor whose church I was speaking at) that I had loved *All That Jazz*.

"That's R-rated, isn't it?" she asked, eyeing me suspiciously.

"I guess so," I mumbled.

"Well, *please* don't *ever* say that in front of my children!" she said. "You are responsible for not becoming a stumbling block, and I'm having enough trouble with them already!"

When I later met her "children," I was expecting little kids. They were two pale boys, ages fifteen and seventeen. Having met their mother, I understood why they looked hunted and seemed to be twitching.

Our new breed of Schaeffer followers were the sorts of people who said they adored everything about Dad's book *How Should We Then Live*? "except that naked picture"—Michelangelo's *David*. (I had prevailed in the photograph selections for the book, having lost in the fight over *David*'s nudity in the movie version of our project.)

These were the sorts of people I had to make sure were nowhere around if I ordered a bottle of wine, or talked about my gay friends, or lit up a cigar. And whatever they *thought* Mom and Dad were about, the actual Swiss L'Abri of the 1960s and early '70s would have struck them as shockingly free, a place they never would have let their children visit.

I knew "The Speech" so well, I could think about other things while I delivered it; for instance, about how I wished God had never made any men or women with a "ministry in music." I wished he'd strike them all down so I'd never have to spend another minute listening to another fat lady (even the men were "fat ladies" to me) sing another Jesus-is-my-boyfriend song to synthesized violin playback.

I must have done The Speech over a hundred times in the year or two after *Whatever Happened to the Human Race*? came out, including the time I gave it from Dr. Kennedy's pulpit at his famous Corral Ridge Presbyterian Church in Florida, to over two thousand people who gave me a near-hysterical five-minute standing ovation. (I was also on his TV show several times.)

Shorthand version: Abortion is murder; secular humanism is destroying us; turn back to our Christian foundation; vote Republican.

I learned that the worst audiences, like talking to a roomful of pickled fish wearing down parkas, were in Minnesota. I learned that the best audiences were in California, where people want to have fun twenty-four hours a day, so they laugh at all your jokes and buy a cartload of books and tapes. I learned to leave out fancy French words south of Washington, DC (not counting Miami and New Orleans). And I learned that if you talk "too fast," all those huntin', fishin', shootin', lifetime-NRA-member types, the ones that worry about the United Nations, have their eyes too close together, and have wives caked with about forty pounds of makeup per square inch, start to look at you funny. And if they can't understand what you're saying, pretty soon you feel this suspicious wave of squinty-eyed, do-you-think-you're-better-than-us fucked-upness rolling toward you over the banquet tables and the flower arrangements somebody stuck tinsel and balloons in, and up around the head table and past the lime Jell-O topped with some kind of nameless sweet shit and sprinkled with nuts.

How I hated the trips to and from all those airports! The pastor picking me up always seemed anxious to "share." It was usually about his church and his problems with his congregation or his own "rebellious" teenagers that invariably were "far from the Lord."

"I'll pray for you," I'd mutter, or "The Lord's going to use these times of testing to bring you to a wonderful new place in your walk with him."

What I really wanted to say is that shit happens and that just because I was a Schaeffer didn't make me an expert on his life.

Then there was Miss Piggy at the fund-raiser I did for a chastity-anti-sex-education ministry in Fargo, North Dakota: "We *Can* Wait."

"We *Can* Wait" hired a husband-and-wife "youth minister" team to open my act. They showed up in homemade costumes dressed as Kermit the Frog and Miss Piggy. They sang "Jesus Loves Me," in Kermit and Miss Piggy's voices. They had obviously spent a lot of time on their song-and-dance routine.

After the song, the wife, still dressed in her Miss Piggy outfit, took off her foam rubber trotters and pulled out hand puppets and did a little routine where Miss Piggy (the hand-puppet version) met Cookie Monster hand puppet. The two Miss Piggys—puppet *and* costumed youth-pastor-wife—shared the gospel with Cookie Monster and told him that "love waits" and to *wait* until he was married before "making any li'l Muppets, cuz love isn't a contact sport, sweetie!"

The full-size-Kermit-youth-minister (standing off to one side) was an accomplished ventriloquist and was doing Cookie Monster's voice. Then Kermit accepted Jesus Christ as his very own personal Savior and put on a "chastity ring," after which Kermit said how it was so wonderful that Cookie Monster was now "written up in the Muppet Book of Life."

My children remember my life on the road a bit differently. They had more fun than I did. Jessica writes:

> Listening to my Dad speak was always a pleasure. This may sound exaggerated but it is the literal truth. He was just so good at it. I would wait for the audience's laughter, for the small changes he would make each night, probably to keep it fresh, to keep himself from getting bored. I was never forced to listen anyway, if we wanted to run around we only had to go backstage. My young parents were good at remembering the needs of childhood.

Every moment I spent with our "cobelligerents"—as Dad was now calling the mob of groupies, Muppets, and other evangelical leaders we were in bed with—was sinking me deeper into a mixture of self-loathing and despair. Genie bore the brunt, as did Jessica and Francis. (Soon after John was born, I made my jailbreak, so he had a better time.) I always came back off the road wound-up and angry. I started to despise the people thronging my meetings, and to despise myself for despising them.

I was also planning an escape. My plan was to jump from making evangelical documentaries to directing Hollywood features. From time to time, I would sneak off to Hollywood and have meetings with anyone who would talk to me.

The tension in my life between who I saw myself as, and who I *was* as others saw me—and what I was really doing, no matter how I tried to fool myself—was becoming unbearable. I was working in America, talking about America, living in America but was really a half-assed semi-European just beginning to learn about the real America.

Why anyone listened to me remains a mystery. Maybe it was testimony to the respect my father was held in, maybe something to do with the fact that I was a good speaker, and also perhaps to do with the desperation of the evangelical community, which will latch on to anyone remotely intelligent and follow them, at least for a while.

There were three kinds of evangelical leaders. The dumb or idealistic ones who really believed. The out-and-out charlatans. And the smart ones who still believed—sort of—but knew that the evangelical world was shit, but who couldn't figure out any way to earn as good a living anywhere else. I was turning into one of those, having started out in the idealistic category.

I remember a day that my predicament become clearer. I was in the Southern California studios of the Trinity Broadcasting Network (TBN). I had just been on their annual telethon. Then I did Dobson's program *Focus on the Family* (yet again) via a phone interview between setups for the TBN telethon. I'd suffered through several hours of on-air fundraising along with some sleazy gospel trio and the flagrantly flaky (and apparently embalmed) hosts. We'd been hanging around their set for what seemed like a lifetime. (It looked like something Donald Trump's decorator might have rejected as too tastelessly garish.) The thrust of the TBN show (and also Dobson's "phoner") was that we needed to save America from decadence, corruption, and evil. The examples of all this "evil" included sweeping generalizations about public schools, the media, movies, the arts in general, and the gays. I came home to raving.

"If we win, the first person they'll put against the wall and shoot will be me!" I yelled at Genie.

"Then why are you doing this?" asked Genie.

"I'm fucking *stuck*! How are we supposed to earn our living if I quit? I've never even been to college! I don't know how to do *anything*!"

"What about going back to painting?"

"How will we live?"

"You'll have shows."

"It isn't that simple. I've let all my contacts go cold. And anyway, I wasn't even making that much. We're stuck!"

"We can live more simply."

"I just don't know how to get out!" I screamed.

Genie saved me. I didn't know it, but what she said next was my door back to sanity.

"Why don't you just quit and write a novel, you know, tell all those stories you tell the children about your vacations in Italy, something like that?"

I didn't act on Genie's advice right away.

54

Where we had once had art festivals, the evangelicals we were "part of" wanted to ban books. Where we inhaled Altman and Bergman, they wanted to protect their children from "filthy movies" and stop their teens from seeing anything R-rated at all!

Where homeschooling had meant freedom for me—albeit chaotic, crazy freedom—homeschool leaders like Mary Pride (whose books I got published and who owed me her platform) were pushing homeschooling as a means to isolate and brainwash a generation of children.

The evangelical homeschool movement was becoming profoundly anti-American. And Dad and I had done our part to empower them. The biggest laugh of all was that my home "school" experience was held up by some as proof that homeschooling was a great thing! Edith Schaeffer had homeschooled the great pro-life firebrand Franky, so this *must* work!

The Evangelical homeschool leaders were doing all they could to undermine the credibility of the public school system. The public schools taught sex education! The public schools taught evolution! The public schools had no values! In fact, you were a bad parent if you *didn't* homeschool, or at least send your child to a "Christian school."

The idea of public space, the ideas that led to the building of my father's and my favorite places, for instance all those civic works in Florence and the piazzas we so happily strolled, was the very idea that the evangelical homeschool movement unwittingly wanted to destroy. They wanted no public spaces (physical or intellectual) to be shared by people of all beliefs. They wanted only *private spaces,* where they could indoctrinate their children free from "interference."

Of course, many parents were also driven to find all sorts of solutions for educating their children in the face of a very broken public school system that in places was so minimal, unimaginative, and awful that putting a child in a public school amounted to abuse. (One only has to read the post-1960s statistics on the drastic decline of classical music record sales in America to see that something has gone terribly wrong with public "education.") The problem with the evangelical homeschool movement was not their desire to educate their children at home, or in private religious schools, but the evangelical impulse to "protect" children from ideas that might lead them to "question" and to keep them cloistered in what amounted to a series of one-family gated communities.

There were many parents I knew (including many evangelicals) who were homeschooling who used their daily contact with their children to expand, not diminish, their children's exposure to the bigger world. That said, by the 1970s the evangelicals as a whole had come up with an alternate "gated" America: "Christian" education, radio, rock, makeup, publishing, schools, homeschools, weight loss, sex manuals, and politics. It wasn't about *being* something but about *not* being secular, about *not* having nudity, sex, or four-letter words. What it was *for,* no one knew.

What was so strange was how evangelicals learned to use all

those worldly tools that their fundamentalist grandparents stood against and that, as a child, I was forbidden from even knowing about. They were now using rock, TV, and movies to construct an alternate reality. But they were using these "worldly tools" in a way that was odd: it was not to involve themselves with their culture and learn from it, but to hide from other Americans and create private space.

Mom may have banned "jazzy music" when I was little, but our bookshelves were full of real books. I was never warned away from reading anything I wanted (except from schmaltzy Disney crap). A good book was a good book, and so what if Mark Twain didn't like Jesus? Twain was still a good writer. I was never protected from the wrong people either. L'Abri *welcomed* the wrong people. Mom and Dad's idea of the Christian life was *not* to retreat behind high walls.

I was getting queasy. I had gone from wanting to be an artist and movie director, to helping empower the types of people who would burn my paintings if they ever saw them. Some of them were even planning to stone some of my friends to death—*literally.*

At a second secret strategy meeting (also related to founding the Rutherford Institute), Pat Robertson told us proudly about burning a reproduction of a nude by Modigliani that he used to have over his fireplace. He said that as soon as he got saved, he'd taken it down.

As Pat told us his art-burning story with many a shiver, as if he was confessing to have once been a mass murderer before he "met Jesus," Dad squirmed. I stared in his direction, but he wouldn't meet my eyes. My father loved Modigliani, and sometimes talked about how Modigliani "retained the human" in his art, in contrast to Marcel Duchamp. (I had often seen Dad's Modigliani art book open on his chaise longue.)

At that meeting there was also a character named Gary North in attendance, one of the twilight-zone religious-right strategists I'd run into once in a while on the road, someone Dad felt was a nutty gold-standard fruitcake. North was a leading Theonomist in the so-called Reconstruction Movement, led by Rousas Rushdoony, who happened to be North's father-in-law.

The Theonomists—otherwise known as Dominionists; in other words, people who believed in taking "dominion" over society and the world in the name of Jesus—believed in restoring American law to its strictest Puritan origins. They wanted to make America into a modern-day Calvin's Reformation Geneva. They were our version of the Taliban. They were antitax, antigovernment libertarians (when it came to economics), but on social issues were working to replace secular law with Old Testament biblical law.

The Reconstructionists were releasing a steady stream of position papers, books, and magazines and holding conferences all over the country. They had a national following that included Howard Ahmanson (heir of the Home Savings bank fortune) who would later help bankroll the "Intelligent Design" movement.

John Calvin, Oliver Cromwell, and the nastier Old Testament prophets were the Reconstructionists' heroes. And according to the law in John Calvin's Reformation Geneva, women pregnant out of wedlock were to be drowned along with their unborn babies, and of course homosexuals were to be killed and heretics burned at the stake.

Dad regarded Rushdoony as clinically insane. And Rushdoony's program, if realized, would have included the execution of homosexuals and adulterers.

Dad never had liked John Calvin. In fact when L'Abri

became more formal and added a study center where students could listen to taped lectures, Dad named it "Farel House" after the French/Swiss Reformer Guillaume Farel, who was principally responsible for bringing the Reformation to the French-speaking part of Switzerland. As Dad always said, "Some people wanted to call it 'Calvin House,' but Calvin was too harsh. I like Farel better. He was gentler and less reformed than Calvin theologically."

The Theonomists, Reconstructionists, and Dominionists were the theocratic/authoritarian-party-in-waiting of American Christendom. And we Schaeffers were helping them expand their national base, because they were showing up at our events and using some of our books to give their views a little more credibility. And *I* was on the Rutherford Institute board as a founding member, along with Gary North.

We were supposed to be strategizing on how to fund the Rutherford Institute. But that day all North wanted to talk about was buying and hoarding gold as a hedge against the inevitable "complete collapse" that was about to engulf the world economy, that and patterns of radiation distribution from our major cities that would soon—and inevitably—be bombed by the Soviets. (North wrote a book—*Fighting Chance*—advocating the building of backyard bomb shelters, and later he predicted a worldwide catastrophe at the so-called Y2K.)

John Whitehead, who in private life wasn't such a bad guy—he was a closet Beatles and Who fan and kept posters of works by Edvard Munch in his office—was looking slightly crazed and trying to keep the meeting on track. But Gary North kept quoting his latest study about which Western states we should all buy land in, given the prevailing wind direction from the big cities.

Dad seemed lost in a depressed daze. He had recently been saying privately that the evangelical world was more or less being led by lunatics, psychopaths, and extremists, and agreeing with me that if "our side" ever won, America would be in deep trouble. But by then Dad was dying and knew he had very little time left. There was no time to change his life or his new "friends."

All I could do was to bitterly regret what I'd gotten him into. I still do.

Dad was rudely shocked by the true state of American "mainstream" evangelicalism. Before Dad got famous in the early 1970s, those evangelicals who came to L'Abri were usually not so typical. They were self-selecting, often the cream of the crop of more open-minded believers. That was also true of schools and churches that had invited Dad and Mom to speak, before my parents became so powerful and before evangelicals got so politicized. For instance, Dad used to speak at the relatively moderate Wheaton College but was never invited to far-right and racist Bob Jones University and would not have gone if he had been invited.

It must have come as a shock to Dad to be plunged into the heart of the American evangelical scene in the 1970s and 1980s, and to suddenly see just *who* he was urging to take power in the name of returning America to our "Christian roots." Who would be in charge? Pat Robertson? Jerry Falwell? Gary North? Dr. Dobson? Rousas Rushdoony? And what sort of fools would "our people" elect as president or for Congress, given that they had so easily been duped by the flakes, madmen, and charlatans they were hailing (and lavishly funding) as their spiritual leaders?

55

I had such a reputation as a hard-assed pro-life fundamentalist that in the early '80s, the editors of an evangelical satirical youth-oriented magazine, *The Wittenberg Door,* put a picture of a mud-throwing child labeled "Franky Schaeffer" on their cover. What they were accusing me of (accurately) was that I had been attacking other evangelicals for their lack of commitment to the pro-life cause. For instance, I had been going after *Christianity Today* magazine in a series of articles in my newsletter *The Christian Activist*—we had about 150,000 readers—that generated hundreds of critical letters to the *Christianity Today* editors. By then, Dad and I were both saying that evangelicals who would not take a stand on abortion had denied their faith.

By the early '80s, most evangelical leaders (who wanted to keep their jobs) came over to our side on "the issue" or were intimidated into silence if they still had doubts. But the spiritual-versus-political debate was over. Billy Graham might be maintaining his nonpolitical stance, but we activists had won. Evangelical Christianity was now more about winning elections than about winning souls.

After I read the *Wittenberg Door* cover article, I sent the editors a photograph of myself throwing fistfuls of mud while dressed the same way as their mud-throwing cover model. They ran the picture, along with an editorial comment that my sense of humor surprised them.

Their surprise was a wakeup call. I'd never thought of myself as some kind of square jerk that other people would presume had no sense of humor! What, or who, was I turning into?

I was at the annual Christian Booksellers Association convention (CBA). Dad was very ill. (I think this was in 1983.) I had recently delivered a keynote address at the National Religious Broadcasters (NRB). I was at CBA signing copies of my evangelical books for eager bookstore managers and their wives, who were lined up for several hundred yards at the Crossway Publishers' booth.

Everything was for sale. Everything was copied from the secular world but made bizarrely religious. Everything was taste-in-your-ass horrible, including the evangelical version of the "Budweiser" towel, a rip-off of the then-popular Budweiser commercial "This Bud's for You!" There was a lookalike beer can on it with two crucified hands and the logo, "This *Blood*'s for You!" being offered at the convention. It was very popular.

A few days after my book signings at the CBA, I wrote a scene for some future movie I was thinking of making. It reflects the split personality I had developed. One moment I was meeting and greeting, and the next scribbling a poisonous little fantasy about the people I was such a hero to who, in my mind, I was calling "the low IQs." I was referring to myself, and other evangelical leaders, as the "Famous Christian of the Hour." The fictitious conversation takes place between Allison and Andy. Andy has never been to an NRB or CBA, and Allison is explaining these evangelical trade fairs to him:

"Okay, Andy," Allison said, "I'll explain it all to you. At the National Religious Broadcasters, the point is the herd of low IQs try and get *close* to the Famous Christian of the Hour, like people do sucking up to movie stars. And then there is this dance number where the 'little people' low IQs surge around the Famous Christian and tell the asshole how great he or she is. And the Famous low IQ has to *pretend* he is *just so glad* to see each and every precious nobody low IQ and pretend that he is in no hurry to get away from the scum, and back to his six-room, luxury hotel suite. So his 'people,' the little knot of assholes around him, are forced to keep tearing the Famous Christian of the Hour away from the flock of nobody low IQ ass-kissers, that he keeps hugging like they're his mother, because the Famous Christian of the Hour still has fifty meetings to do that day upon which the fate of the Lord's work on this earth depends, in other words whether or not the Famous Christian of the Hour gets his syndication deal renewed for another year on a thousand Christian radio and TV stations.

"See in most trade shows they're only trying to sell you some regular harmless shit, computers or guided missiles, whatever. But at the National Religious Broadcasters and/or the Christian Bookseller's Association, what's getting sold is God. And since God won't show up and get franchised, the assholes with the booths have to kind of make up a bunch of God-awful shit to sell in his place."

56

When Dad died, Ronald Reagan wrote this note to Mom:

Nancy and I express our deep sympathy to you and your family on the death of your husband. We want you to know that you are in our thoughts and prayers.

While words are inadequate to console you on your loss, you can take comfort in knowing that Dr. Schaeffer will be greatly missed by all who knew him and his work. He will long be remembered as one of the great Christian thinkers of our century, with a childlike faith and a profound compassion toward others. It can rarely be said of an individual that his life touched many others and affected them to the better. It will be said of Dr. Schaeffer that his life touched many and brought them to the truth of their Creator. In June of 1982, Francis last wrote to me and enclosed a copy of an address he had just given which described in moving terms that "final reality" which is God. Dr. Schaeffer drew all his strength and spirit from that source and shared that message with a waiting world. Now he has found his final home.

> May God grant you his peace in serenity which is only His to give. With our sincere condolences.
>
> Sincerely, Ronald Reagan,
>
> The White House, May 17, 1984

Author, former editor of *Punch* magazine, and Dad's friend Malcolm Muggeridge wrote: "Francis was a great Christian doing a great Christian work. I'm glad to think that the last time we saw one another—at the great pro-life rally at Hyde Park in London—perfect harmony and affection united us." (Dad and Muggeridge had led a pro-life rally in Hyde Park a year or two before Dad died.)

Sir Bernard Brane, Member of Parliament, wrote: "On behalf of the British pro-life members of Parliament, and peers of the realm, we join in paying homage to the memory of Dr. Francis Schaeffer, who did more than any individual throughout the world to rally the Protestant conscience on abortion. We salute him."

Bill Buckley, writing in the *National Review* magazine (June 15, 1984), said "It was his commitment to the truth of scripture that made him such a foe of totalitarianism and relativism, and caused him to champion freedom and the sanctity of human life."

Jack Kemp inserted this in the Congressional Record (May 15, 1984): "Wherever he went, Dr. Schaeffer had a profound influence on people. Dr. Schaeffer was not an 'Ivory Tower' theologian but a great prophet and a great Christian leader."

Time called Dad a "leading evangelical scholar," in their obituary.

Dad's funeral embodied all the chaos, make-it-up-as-you-go insanity of evangelicalism. It was to funerals what "personalized" weddings are to marriage, ones where the young couple compose their own vows while some friend "really like into guitar" provides the music.

There is a good reason we humans take refuge in the collective wisdom accumulated over time as expressed in liturgies and cultural habits of long practice. And the arrogance of the Protestant notion that one's individual whims are equal to all occasions manifests itself in innumerable bad hair moments and in dreadful church services, let alone at innumerable do-it-yourself weddings. But funerals are supposed to be serious. Creativity isn't always good.

How do you bury a Protestant pope? There was nothing to fall back on. When Mom decided to use his funeral as a "witness," throw open the doors, and turn the-burying-of-Francis-Schaeffer into what amounted to a farewell seminar/trade show, no one could stop her. How do you say no to a grieving widow? Only Mom wasn't grieving. She was folding Dad's death into The Work, and rather cheerful about the whole thing.

Dad was our "holy tradition." He was bigger than any church. We set trends; we didn't follow them. As Mom said, "He meant so much to *all* Christians, it just wouldn't be *fair* to have the funeral in any one particular denomination or with any one particular pastor." So we rented a high-school gym in Rochester, Minnesota, where Dad died. What other building could hold the throng? And we didn't ask a pastor to officiate. Who would be good enough? We would make this up as we went along, and showcase our family.

"Mom, how about a private funeral?" I asked.

"Of *course* we can't do that! We can't waste this opportunity! Besides, these are *our* people!"

There was a parade of family, friends, and associates, high-powered leaders, and many hundreds and hundreds of groupies and assorted hangers-on—"our people." The atmosphere was a cross between a farewell Beatles concert and a more solemn than usual NASCAR event. An episode of *How Should We Then Live?* was shown—"How nice he got to preach his own funeral sermon!" (Ruth Graham)—and my brothers-in-law all spoke. I declined Mom's urging me to "use this great opportunity." (Though I did say a few shaky words at the grave when the crowd had shrunk to a mere fifty groupies and a dozen or so L'Abri workers.)

In the gym, the coffin was placed between looped-back ropes on a basketball parquet floor and lined up with the three-point line. A local baroque music ensemble of semiprofessional Mayo Clinic doctors' wives played, and played, for so long it seemed as if we were in a concert. The music was not helped any by the high-school gym "acoustics," or the socks, sweat, and sperm locker-room smell.

Movies, music, and rambling freelance tributes from Dad's sons-in-law were punctuated by tributes read out loud, seemingly forever, that had poured in from the White House, Congress, and every semifamous evangelical in the world, interspersed with yet more music from the ubiquitous quartet. And Mom was greeting all the you-have-no-idea-what-your-books-mean-to-me throng.

It was a nightmare.

Ten years later, the first Greek Orthodox funeral I went to filled me with envy. I decided that whatever else happened, I didn't want to die as a member of a religion that has no clue about what to do with the most sacred moments of life, and death.

The Greek Orthodox do what they have always done. The open casket faces the altar feet first. The priest performs the short and solemn liturgy. The ancient prayers of the Church are prayed, and everyone knows what will happen next. The family is not on display but folded into the seamless tradition of mourning, one their great-great-grandmothers would know as well as they do, one that has long since been worn smooth as the path between a playground and a road made by thousands of feet.

I had said my good-bye to Dad a week before he died. We were alone in St. Mary's Hospital. I would have stayed to be with him, but it conflicted with an "important" speaking engagement (I forget where) that Dad had told me to take in his place. I helped Dad shave, then clambered up beside him. We sat side by side and talked about skiing.

"Remember, Dad?"

He had seemed so strong, so absolutely trustworthy, so permanent when I followed him down the slope. About the second or third day of the Zermatt vacation, we would skip breakfast and leave at first light, heavily muffled against the cold. Because we stayed in Riffelberg, a few miles above Zermatt, we could ski right out the door before the lifts opened and be on our way to the valley where the big cable cars were that would take us up the mountains.

We had to be extra careful. The bluish predawn light flattened out all the contours of the *piste*. What looked smooth might be a series of bumps that would unexpectedly send me spinning out of control, legs thumping up and down like pistons as I flew over ridges. But Dad went ahead. He would call back a warning if he hit ice or deep ridges.

We skied in silence. The only sound was made by the metal edges of our skis slicing into the icy slope. By the time we arrived in the Zermatt Valley, the wool mufflers in front of our mouths were crusted white with moisture from our frozen breaths. Soon, my father and I were waiting at the cable car station, munching on the chocolate bar Dad always brought.

Dad told me not to turn back at his hospital room door. He wanted no maudlin parting. We hugged and then shook hands.

"I love you, Dad."

"I love you, boy."

"Good-bye."

57

I still regard abortion as an unmitigated tragedy. But I no longer think that it should always be illegal. On the other hand, I don't think abortion should always be legal either.

Evangelicals weren't politicized (at least in the current meaning of the word) until after *Roe v. Wade* and after Dad, Koop, and I stirred them up over the issue of abortion. More than thirty years after helping to launch the evangelical pro-life movement, I am filled with bitter regret for the unintended consequences.

In 2000, after a close and disputed contest, settled by the Supreme Court, we elected a president who claimed he believed God created the earth and who, as president, put car manufacturers' and oil companies' interests ahead of caring for that creation. We elected a "born-again" president who said he lived by biblical ethics but who played the dirtiest political games possible, for instance in the filthy lies his people spread to derail Senator John McCain's presidential primary bid. We elected a pro-life Republican Party that did nothing to actually care for the pregnant women and babies they said they were concerned for, but rather were corrupted by power, and took their sincere evangelical followers for granted, and played them for suckers.

The so-called evangelical leadership—Dobson, Robertson, Falwell, and all the rest—also played the pro-life community for suckers. While thousands of men and women in the crisis pregnancy movement gave of themselves with tremendous and sincere sacrifice (to help women and babies), their evangelical "leaders" did little more than cash in on fund-raising opportunities and stir the pot so they could keep their followers motivated. That way, the evangelical leaders could represent themselves as power brokers to the politicians willing to kowtow to them.

To the extent that the Republican Party benefited from the pro-life movement, my efforts and those of my father contributed to making the Republican congressional majorities of the 1980s and 1990s possible. We also indirectly helped make the elections of Reagan, Bush Sr., and Bush Jr. possible.

Bush Jr. was the "Christians' " president. So it was bitterly ironic that Bush Jr. was personally responsible for, amongst other self-inflicted horrors, the persecution, displacement, and destruction of the one million, three hundred thousand-person beleaguered *Christian* minority in Iraq. They had fared much better under the secular regime of Saddam Hussein than they did once Bush Jr. unleashed the Islamic militants.

It bears repeating: Bush Jr., the Bible-believing, born-again president, delivered up his Iraqi *fellow Christians* to be destroyed. They fled, died, or went into hiding because a "faith-based" evangelical American president stupidly unleashed a civil war. And of course Bush Jr. was also responsible for the killing of countless other innocent civilians caught in the sectarian strife.

The puny "president" I indirectly helped elect sent my son John to an ill-conceived, ineptly carried-out war, a war where my son's friend Alex Del Rio got his legs blown off, where Mark, the only son of my friend Mindy Evnin, was killed. And Bush Jr. was elected with the help of millions of evangelicals that Dad, Koop, and I—directly or indirectly—helped galvanize.

How could such a little man—a towering mediocrity—so clearly overmatched by the job ever have become president? One reason is that single-issue politics deforms the process and derails common sense. It facilitates the election of leaders just because they are "correct" on "my issue."

Roe v. Wade has given us more than thirty years of culture war. The results have been tragic. For one thing, *Roe* has given us some terrible leadership. This works both ways. The Democratic Party has, until recently, also limited itself to candidates who are rigidly correct "theologically" on abortion and other social issues.

It seems to me that by demanding ideological purity on abortion (and other single issues as well), both parties have worked to eliminate the sorts of serious smart pragmatic people who make competent leaders. What we are left with are those willing to toe the party theological line, who are talented at kissing the asses of their party's ideologues, raising money, and looking good on TV, but not much else.

But what if absolute consistency on any issue from the left or the right, religious or secular, is an indication of mediocre intelligence and a lack of intellectual honesty? What if the world is a complex place? What if leadership requires flexibility? What if ideology is a bad substitute for common sense? What if ideological consistency, let alone "purity," is a sign of small-mindedness, maybe even stupidity?

Logically there was no forgone conclusion that the left would take the pro-choice side. Margaret Sanger, founder of Planned Parenthood, had called abortion murder and, following her lead, so had Planned Parenthood in their literature, right up to 1968. But since the left (and hence the Democratic Party, at least the public's perception of that party) embraced the sexual revolution, the way it fell out was that the right, especially the so-called Christian Right, became the "defenders of unborn life." And we did this while often supporting capital punishment. And the Democrats supported abortion on-demand, while often being against the execution of convicted criminals, and while the Democratic Party included a strong traditionally pacifist wing.

America was entering an ethical twilight zone of contradictory theological absolutism that bled into all walks of life and into many unrelated political issues. Both sides were relying on their respective "faiths," feminist purity of heart on the one hand and so-called biblical ethics on the other. America was involved in yet another "church split" masquerading as politics.

Meanwhile, the left (and hence the Democratic Party) seemed to be encouraging abortion, even the abortion of the same "imperfect" babies who, on other days, liberal Democrats, were legislating on behalf of, to have ramps built giving the handicapped access to libraries, hotels, and restaurants.

One would have thought that some on the left might have noted these inconsistencies, or at least been a little nervous about abortion being made legal for any reason at any time in pregnancy, in view of the exploding potential of genetic screening for "undesirable" humans that might someday include screening for the "gay gene" or the "criminal gene" or even the "hyperactive child gene." In fact, some civil libertarians, like *Village Voice* editor Nat Hentoff, spoke out vehemently on the pro-life side on just such grounds, and he quit the board of the ACLU over its lopsided support of abortion advocates.

If it had been the other way around and the left had championed the unborn, perhaps against corporate medical industry interests, or in the name of equality—or because of the lessons taught by the rise of the eugenics movement of the 1920s and 1930s, or because of being queasy over a recently slave-owning society once again deciding who was more equal, even more human "legally" than others—my father would have been embraced as a religious leader on the left. And if Dad had been allied with the left, it would have ultimately been a much better fit for him—and for me.

The battle lines were drawn when *Roe* not only became the law of the land, precluding further debate and democratic process, but also became the most permissive abortion law in the world, outside of what was then the Soviet Union. What Dr. Koop, Dad, and I helped start was a slow-motion civil war of reaction that has morphed into "red"- and "blue"-state America.

We Americans—secular, religious, of the left and the right—like to think of ourselves as good. This national delusion is our real religion. We think we know something special about virtue, the way the French believe they have the inside track on food and wine. When we do bad things, we like to dress them up and call them good, for the same reason no Frenchman will admit to being a bad cook. We can't just hit an enemy, we have to call it "spreading democracy." We can't just abort a baby, we have to call it "reproductive rights." We can't tolerate human frailty, we have to fight to outlaw all abortion as "murder," declare victory over "evil," and leave some young woman paying the price for our self-righteousness.

For most Americans, thoughts about the rights of the unborn were blessedly fuzzy before *Roe* and allowed plenty of room for hypocrisy of the kind that makes life bearable. They would have preferred that some abortion be legal and be done quietly, but that there be a line drawn that would provide us with moral cover, something to feed our delusion of goodness.

Roe was too extreme for our American sense of the virtuous self, and it provided no moral cover, say of the kind most European governments provided when it came to legalizing abortion, by strongly discouraging abortion past the earlier stages of pregnancy. *Roe* was too sweeping. It was absolutist—and bad public relations, too.

To most Americans—including me these days—it is gut-check self-evident that a fertilized egg is *not a person,* because personhood is a lot more than a collection of chromosomes in a Petri dish or in the womb. To most Americans—including me these days—it is also gut-check self-evident that an unborn baby is *mighty like one of us,* and that a lot of fast talking about reproductive rights and choice or a woman's mental well-being doesn't answer the horror of a three-pound child with her head deliberately caved in lying in a medical waste receptacle.

Perception is reality in politics, maybe in ethics, too. And to many Americans, the Democrats, at least in perception, adopted an absolutist pro-choice platform, guaranteed to alienate many reasonable and compassionate people. When it came to defending *Roe,* the Democrats seemed to have replaced the right to life, liberty, and the pursuit of happiness with the right to fucking.

Roe was an answer to the "by-product" of sex, and, most particularly, of the '60s sexual revolution. The sexual revolution was just one example of the individualistic "I want" replacing the moralistic "you should." But as the sexual revolution part of the "I want" revolution was overtaken by AIDS and by an STD and teen-pregnancy epidemic, it started to look idiotic.

It turned out that personal preference is not always the best guide. And there were plenty of women of all political and religious persuasions who, post-*Roe,* woke up to the fact that male sexual "ethics" now separated sex, commitment, and responsibility into watertight compartments. A lot of people had the uneasy feeling that things had gone "too far." That included many liberal parents who were appalled by a culture wherein it was considered "normal" that their young teenage (even preteen) daughters dispensed casual oral sex to cement "friendships" with boys they hardly knew. In the public mind, this moral slide was somehow linked to a loss of moral focus, and (fairly or unfairly) the legalizing of abortion was perceived as a big part of that slide.

Up to the 2006 elections, the Democrats were saddled with the public's perception of being the party that had aggressively gone to bat for *Roe*. Then in 2006, when the Democratic Party began to include a few outspoken pro-life candidates in their national congressional races—and some won—they seemed to be correcting an error, because it wasn't long ago that Democratic candidates who did not pass the pro-choice theological litmus test were barred from even speaking at Democratic Party conventions.

Where the pro-life movement seemed nutty when saying that a fertilized egg is fully human, at least pro-life nuts had genetic science on their side. But when the pro-choice proponents found themselves trying to explain why a six-month-old unborn baby deserved no protection, and was a mere "part of a woman's body," subject to her "choice," they defied both common sense and science. And how could a country hooked on notions of its own goodness feel warm and fuzzy about "procedures" involving the killing of almost-viable, sometimes even viable, babies?

Defending such horrors was awkward. It pushed otherwise moderate people to extremes. The extremes persist. After the Supreme Court upheld the federal Partial Birth Abortion Ban Act (April 18, 2007), the next day the *Times* reacted predictably saying that to ban even extremely late-term abortions, "severely eroded the constitutional respect and protection accorded women." The paper also stated that the decision "threatened the rule of law." What the editors didn't mention was that all the Court had done was to bring American law a bit closer to European and other countries less extreme abortion laws.

A paper like the *Times* looks philosophically unimaginative and ethically challenged when it doggedly sticks to the party line at the extremes of the argument. They look as silly and theologically dogmatic as the nutcase pro-lifers who want to hold funerals for fertilized eggs and ban stem-cell research.

How do we make our society better when it comes to protecting the right to life, liberty, and the pursuit of happiness? This is about more than one issue. For instance, it seems to me that capital punishment is a terrible idea. Our society would be a better place to live if the state could rise above acts of vengeance. Symbols matter. On the other hand, if a policeman is dealing with a criminal who has taken hostages and has started killing them, and will not surrender, I hope the cop shoots him before others are killed. This is not an act of vengeance but one of need, to protect society when other means aren't available. And I'd rather live in a society that is willing to sometimes kill out of necessity than follow some theological "sanctity of life" ethic to an absurd extreme.

It seems to me that there will always be a need for some abortions to terminate some troubled early pregnancies. But this is no small thing. It is a sad reality. But compassion for women facing a tough pregnancy has to be balanced by the greater good. Sometimes compassion for the innocent means saying no to a couple that wants to abort their child because their unborn daughter is going to need surgery to correct a harelip and they want a "perfect" designer baby. Sometimes it means saying yes to a thirteen-year-old who has been molested or raped.

I think there is a difference between killing in cold blood, when there are other alternatives, and killing out of necessity. And I don't think this difference is always clear. But executing a criminal who is no longer a threat to anyone is different (practically and symbolically) from shooting a hostage-taker who is about to kill innocent people. Fighting Japan after it attacked us was different from attacking an Iraq that was no threat to us.

I want to live in a society that is willing to *struggle* with these balancing acts. I want to be in a society that values human life, because I am human, and far from perfect, and I want to be valued.

What I *don't* want to live in is a culture that makes sweeping and dismissive secular or religious "theological" one-size-fits-all decisions that oversimplify complex issues. And ideas of the good life based on perfection are a trap, a trap that prophetic books like *Brave New World* gave us fair warning about, and that films like *Blade Runner* explored. We have been warned.

What kind of insanely individualistic culture do we become when the words "I want" trump all other considerations? What happens to all our rights in such a world? What happens to our sense of community? *Roe v. Wade* was no better than the total ban on all abortions was. *Roe* painted us all into a corner.

And *Roe* should be overturned and replaced with a far more nuanced set of laws.

Some abortions should be legal; and under any conceivably realistic scenario post-*Roe,* they would be. But advances in science and the exponentially exploding possibilities of human engineering have to be included in our thinking. The situation is not static, and therefore *Roe* "settled" nothing. The reality is constantly changing: for instance, what "viability" is. *Roe* was merely a snapshot of one moment in time, a pretty extreme moment. It was a sledgehammer where a scalpel was needed.

We will never find a "good" solution to the question of abortion. What we need to do is to back away from the idea that there is an ideological "fix" to every problem. Then again, that's just one opinion. And I could be wrong. I often am.

58

Before I settled for less—before I fell to depths I could have never anticipated in my wildest nightmares—I caught a break. The twenty-minute reel I cut from *Whatever Happened to the Human Race?* almost got me in the door at United Artists. Only later, when I squandered this promising start by making four mediocre Hollywood features, did I come to realize that, ironically, my best work in film was what I did within the evangelical context that I had so longed to escape to make "real movies."

John Kohn, my Hollywood mentor, a World War II vet, friend, producer, lefty screenwriter, and former president of EMI, set up a meeting with Steven Bach, head of production at United Artists. (I had first been introduced to John Kohn by his vice president at EMI, whose brother had seen one of my documentaries.)

Steve Bach and I met twice and had several conversations on the phone. Steve (like most people outside of the evangelical ghetto) had never heard of my father. (At least if he had, he never brought it up.) And I was careful to cut my reel in such a way that none of the controversial pro-life material was there. It looked like the footage had been pulled from a high-end dramatized BBC series on medical ethics.

Steve liked my reel and gave me a book about the Dutch art forger Han van Meegeren. Meegeren specialized in painting and then "discovering" fake Vermeer paintings. He fooled the Dutch art world and even the invading Nazis. Ironically, he was arrested after the war for collaborating with the Nazis, because he had sold them several "Vermeers," thus passing "national art treasures" to the enemy. His only defense was to prove that they were fakes. Since the ego and reputations of the top Dutch art experts were on the line—they had authenticated Meegeren's work—he was put in the weird position of having to fight to expose his own criminality to save himself.

John Kohn called me after my first meeting with Steve to say he thought, based on what Steve told him, that it was close to a done deal. Steve—who John always described as "too nice to be in the movie business"—had liked me, John said. And given that I was both a painter and a filmmaker and more or less a European, Steve thought the Meegeren material was a good choice for my first feature. So did I.

Steve was a kind and genuine person, and the idea of making a movie for him, about someone passing himself off as one thing when he was another, fit my situation perfectly! To say the least, I had a "feel" for the material!

After a second meeting, Steve asked me to write a treatment, and ten pages of script, then to come back in three weeks. Maybe he'd make me an offer for a development deal to write and direct a movie. I was ecstatic!

Several weeks later, I was back at United Artists. The door to Steve's office opened, and a security guard asked me why I was there. (Steve had put me on the list at the gate so I could get in.) More security guards arrived. Someone asked me if

Steve had sent me "back to get something." Later, when I read Steve's book *Final Cut,* I figured out that this was the same morning (or near to it) that he was told to clear out his desk after he was fired because Michael Cimino's *Heaven's Gate* fiasco took down the company.

It was soon after this that I decided to try my luck at raising the money for a low-budget feature film. I wanted to try to get in the back door to the movie business, having struck out on my best try at the front door. Meanwhile, Schaeffer V Productions (my evangelical nonprofit documentary company through which Jim and I had produced *Whatever Happened to the Human Race*?) was a going concern with several million dollars passing through it every year from donations we had used to make the films and run the second seminar tour. We had produced several more evangelical films since working with Koop and Dad, including one to launch the Rutherford Institute, published our free, widely distributed newsletter, and sponsored my speaking tours and other events.

Now I wanted out of the evangelical world. But I waited to bow out until I had my first feature film going. To my discredit, I played the game until then.

Within two years of Dad's death, and at the height of our success, Jim and I shut down Schaeffer V Productions more or less overnight. We closed so fast, Jim had to get the office staff to send back unopened mail to some donors.

I was surprised by how quickly I was forgotten, how calm the waters were, as soon as I paddled out of the center of the evangelical right-wing whitewater. From one day to the next, I went from daily calls to be on some TV show, or be on the radio, or to be a participant in this or that symposium, march, seminar, or publishing venture, to blessed silence. It was a relief. It also confirmed what I already knew: that evangelicalism is not so much a religion as a series of fast-moving personality cults.

As soon as a leader steps aside, or is shoved aside, or stumbles, the crowd looks for the next man or woman to briefly follow. There is always a bigger show down the street, another even better Bible-study leader or congregation to try, another hot author/guru to read, another trend, from speaking in tongues to giving homeschooling a try. And most evangelicals spend a good portion of their time wandering from church to church, from leader to leader, even from one radio and TV personality to another, in the same way that when I was a teen I'd switch my loyalty from one rock band to another. It's all about who is "hot."

In 1984–85, I directed *Booby Trap* (released as *Wired to Kill* in the United States and under the original title in the UK and other countries). Our movie was a *Road Warrior* ripoff with a twist: A young couple is preyed upon by a futuristic gang, and the couple sets a series of traps to kill them off.

Jim and I raised $1.3 million from about thirty or so investors. These investors included several evangelical heavy hitters I knew from my nonprofit work (like Mary Crowley). Most of the investors were just people who wanted to make money and get near the movies, and who had money to spare.

Jim and I worked without pay, fees, or salary, all the better to convince our investors that we had faith in our projections of profits. *Wired* was a bust. Then the money I had made in the evangelical subculture off my book royalties began to disappear, leaving Genie and me more or less living hand-to-mouth.

If only we had opened on a better weekend! If only we had cast a "name" as one of the leads! If only I had had the talent to match my ambition! If only I'd *paid* myself! The real problem was that we never had a good script.

During preproduction, I had concentrated on raising the money, not the script writing. And I lacked the discipline that can only be honed in the struggle to write well. "Writing" and "publishing" had been way too easy in the evangelical world. I brought all my bad habits to my screenplay: hasty-first-draft-get-it-done-someone-else-will-fix-this-later "writing."

And there was another problem: I was infatuated with Emily, our female lead, a petite, unknown, winsome blond nineteen-year-old I tagged around after like a lost dog. After I neglected the script, shooting *Booby Trap/Wired* became about flirting with Emily. It also became about acting the part of a hot young director, of living in LA with Genie and the children, long afternoons during preproduction and postproduction by the Oakwood apartments swimming pool in Burbank, trips to Zuma Beach with the kids, followed by the sunburn-cooling chill of the Chinese Mann Theater where we watched movies.

My son Francis, who was about eleven then, remembers:

> The apartment in LA had a pool. The apartment was nice enough, but a bit small. Happily we could spend huge amounts of time outside. Jessica and I basically lived at the pool when we were not at the shoot. It was large and warm and had barbecue grills near it that were for the use of the residents. I swam so much that I constantly had irritated eyes and ears. Dad, Jessica, and I played in the pool together all the time. Dad played too rough, so frequently one of us ended up in tears and we used to hit him as hard as we could to get away.

> Dad was over the top, funnier, louder, scarier, more loving, more demonstrative, smarter, more informed, than other kids' dads. He was bigger than life, terrifying, mercurial in mood. Mom kept it all going, was the calm force, steady, gentle, and so loving.

Genie knew I had a crush on my star and put up with it because I told her about it, lamented the distraction; and she trusted me—or pretended to. Genie would even tease me. And when we were all living in a motel out at the Fontana location with the cast and crew, Genie would look out the window sometimes and say "She's in the swimming pool wearing a really cute little bikini. You don't want to miss this."

Even presuming that Emily would have let me—and there was no reason to believe she would have—I never touched her. She had a boyfriend. It was all pitiful and distracting lust from a distance. Genie was right to laugh at me.

My only lasting regret is that we had one terrific actor in the movie, Merritt Butrick, who played my Shakespeare-quoting villain, the leader of the gang. I didn't know it, but he was dying of AIDS. Back in 1984, none of us knew what the illness was about. There were only rumors about a "gay cancer."

Merritt kept coming to work ill and never missed a day of shooting, even when he was horribly sick with a high fever. Merritt deserved a better movie to be his last film. He was barely thirty when he died. He was hard-working, a real actor, a real friend. He did all he could to help me run the set—he had some clout with our cast and crew, since Merritt had just played Captain Kirk's son in several of the *Star Trek* movies. And everyone who knew him thought Merritt was going to be a star. Merritt helped me survive many self-inflicted disasters, like the time one of the other "gang members" inadvertently sliced open Emily's hand on our first day of shooting, in a scene wherein she'd been "captured."

The actor was supposed to be cutting Emily loose and instead sliced down on her wrist and palm. At first we didn't know anything was wrong because her real blood just mixed right in with the blood-mix. And the script called for her to scream, which she did. When everyone blamed the idiot first-time director for asking the actor to use a razor-sharp knife in a wide shot where close-up details didn't matter, Merritt stuck up for me and shut them up. (She got sixteen stitches and we "wrote" a bandage into the rest of the story.)

Merritt's moments on screen are a window into the better movie that *Wired* could have been, if I had had the discipline, skill, and dedication he brought to our movie. I betrayed Merritt's talent by settling for making exploitation crap when I should have had the courage and foresight to try to make a good movie, rather than something "easy to sell as a first film." And by not writing a good script, I doomed the project, such as it was.

I was so impressed with myself and so in love with the process and, above all, just so relieved to be *out* of the evangelical world!—I had finally gotten to direct a *real movie*!—that I lost myself in the production details, the art direction, the musical score (which was being written and performed by Jim's old friend Russ Farante and his "Yellow Jackets" jazz band), and everything else. I got lost with the special effects guys, spending hundreds of hours on the minutiae of the design of our robot, glorying in details that made no difference to the picture, that would never be on the screen, like the fact that our robot worked! I got lost working with the costume designer, wandering around the closed steel mill at Fontana—our principal location—picking up industrial waste that she crafted into the gang's wardrobe. Mostly I got lost drooling over Emily.

Francis remembers:

> Fontana was huge. The dust stuck to everything and had an acidic smell. There were different shades of dust, brilliant silver flecks, rust colored, orange, reds, even some greenish colors. Dad gave us white environmental clean-up suits that were way too big. As time went on we wore them less and less. Anything you touched would leave a mark on your suit, so there was no point trying to keep them clean. If you walked down one of the endless abandoned production halls you could look behind you and see clouds of dust hanging in the shafts of light, glinting and shimmering. Little metallic flecks slowly spinning. These clouds never seemed to settle.

Jessica, who was about fourteen, remembers things a bit differently:

> Dad had passed through the evangelical world and become sickened by it. *Wired to Kill* was a movie but it was also an act of rebellion. And he was giving up a lot to do it, a high and stable income for one thing and acclaim and acceptance in the only world he had ever actually been a part of—like it or not. He was afloat trying to remake himself as someone other than Dr. Schaeffer's son.

My brother Francis and I had the run of the set. I watched the makeup artist. I still remember that she offered me a job if I wanted to come train under her when I got older. We made friends with the special effects guys and were in on the joke when they blew up my dad's birthday cake as he bent over the candles.

Dad would stomp around on the huge *Wired* Fontana location till his feet hurt so badly in the evening that his body would twist with the pain as he hobbled into the hotel pool for a soak. Dad has made a do or die agreement with his body—it is either to do what he wants or die in the attempt.

The one time of day Dad would get a truly desperate note in his voice was at magic hour. "The Light! We're losing the light!" he would shout. Dad is always dealing with forces wildly beyond his control—the will of God, Supreme Court rulings, or the tilting of the planet. At sunset it was the movement of the universe that was the main problem. The universe was in motion and if your head grip hadn't laid the dolly track correctly, the focus puller was slow, or the actress not present, the planet continued its planetary journey and you were screwed. No Magic Hour shot for you that night! "The golden hour," that moment at sunset when for a few precious minutes the light is golden and objects glow from within, the hour created for cinematographers and harassed directors everywhere, would pass and you were left—in the gray dead light of late evening. But Dad always got his shot.

59

Where, as a painter, doing anything but my best had once been unthinkable, not as a matter of principle but as a matter of gut instinct and pride, all I was interested in on the movies I directed was to get the job done and move on to something better. But there was nothing "better."

I woke to the fact that I was losing everything: my faith, my art, my ideals about art, my pride. I was also treating my family like crap. I wanted a fresh start, any fresh start. I didn't want to be me any more. I kept sinking—a prodigal son, minus the father to return to.

In 1988–89, Genie, the three children, and I lived in South Africa and Namibia while I directed two movies, *Headhunter* and *Rebel Storm*. I was in Africa for a little over a year. My agent (*Wired* had at least gotten me an agent) snagged me a job directing *Headhunter*, a horror film (in every sense of the word). *Rebel Storm* was a bigger film, but not much better.

For most of the *Headhunter* production, I was alone, with my family only coming out about halfway through, when we were about to go into postproduction. By then, the producers had hired me to stay on for another six months to direct *Rebel Storm*, a sci-fi thriller about a future wherein everything is run by the religious right, when rock music has been banned.

The fact that they hired me to direct this picture was just a weird coincidence. They had no idea about my religious background, let alone that I'd spent the better part of several years helping to make the non–science fiction version of their paranoid-lefty story a reality.

The American producers of my two African productions were generous, fair, kind, and decent. They rented my family a lovely house and flew my wife and children out.

I picked up Genie and the children at the Johannesburg airport. A few moments later, they were staring wide-eyed out the window of my rental car as we sped along thousands of yards of rusted chain link fence. Behind it were tens of tens of thousands of shacks in the Alexandra black township.

Thick haze hung over the whole place. I explained that it was the cooking fires that made the smog. Sunlight cut fingers of pink out of the smoky air, but otherwise it was almost dark. The last of the sun glittered red on the muddy puddles. Mothers, with babies tied to their backs by blankets twisted above their breasts, never looked up. Some squatted next to fires. Others walked on the road, carrying bags of groceries on their heads; some picked their way between the shacks, stepping over ditches. Black men ran up the roads in long lines, ran down through gaps in the fence, ran into alleys full of women and children. The children had on school uniforms, black skirts, white knee socks, white blouses, or shorts, shirts, and ties. A few moments later, we pulled into our whites-only swanky neighborhood, through the gates of our lovely home.

Trevor, one of our local South African producers, and his pleasant wife Veronica were drunks. I never saw them sober for the better part of a year. It was as if what was happening to apartheid South Africa was just too hard to take sober. She had lots of makeup, chain-smoked, was always pulling cigarettes out of packages of Benson and Hedges Gold that were all over the patio, on chairs, tables, and the bar. Her hands shook when she lit her cigarettes. I had never seen people drink or smoke so much.

At night in the winter, the skyline flickered with flames, as farmers burned off the dry stubble and hay in the fields, and the veldt would catch fire. The whites on the crew, and my American producers, carried guns when they went out at night. I got chased by cops in an unmarked car while I was driving home from a night shoot. When they learned I was an American, they were apologetic. Another night, I saved a man and two women in an overturned car, pulled them out before it caught fire. Then I raced back to the production office to call an ambulance. When it came, the white driver yelled at me for calling a "white ambulance" for blacks. They left, and the black injured man and dazed black women sat waiting until a "black ambulance" arrived. It was an old van with no stretcher. (The white ambulance was a fully equipped American-style EMS unit.) One of our white effects guys set himself on fire after he rigged an explosion wrong. My son Francis nearly had his head blown off when the "weapons master," another white drunk, brought live shotgun shells onto the set and was shooting with our picture guns "just for fun," then forgot a round was in the chamber, pulled the trigger and blew in the car door Francis was standing next to. A white production assistant committed suicide. Someone said they thought he had discovered he had AIDS.

It was as if somehow the metaphysical doom and gloom of imploding, last-ditch apartheid was infecting our productions. As Mom would have said (accurately, for once), the whole country seemed filled with spiritual despair.

John remembers things more positively:

> Being seven years old I was oblivious to the fact that my parents were in real financial trouble, that my father was stressed and exhausted, that we were living within a few miles of a black township that had one of the highest murder rates in the world and that we were living in the midst of the last moments of one of the most racist regimes on earth. For me South Africa was a new place with lots of frogs that were easy to catch and movie sets where I could pretty much do what I pleased. The crew was indulgent. I spent a lot of time in the back of the effects truck rigging explosives. Almost all of my memories are good.

Francis writes:

> I was fourteen. One event made a big impression on me, the near death of one of our stunt men. He was meant to ride his motorcycle in front of the vehicle that had the camera on it. He timed it wrong, or there was some miscommunication, whatever the cause, he ended up going under the tire of the camera vehicle, which was a mockup of a Soviet troop transporter. I happened to be in the truck at the time and felt us hit him. I remember being surprised that we could have hit such a big bump given the flatness of the desert. The visibility was not good, so I did not know what had happened until I got out.
>
> Dad told me to run back to the base camp to tell one of the producers what had happened. This was smart of Dad as it kept me from sitting there and watching the stuntman

die. Though he did not actually die, he came very close and spent many months in the hospital. I knew that this was bad by the way everyone reacted to the news.

Jessica remembers:

By South Africa our father-daughter relationship had more or less fallen apart. Not that it was going well with any other member of the family, we just weren't very happy and that was that. Dad's movie directing career wasn't going well, the people he was working with were brutal, our finances were in shambles, when we left South Africa my parents didn't even have the money to pay our school.

Even Mom, our family pool of healing, was struggling to keep her equilibrium. I was seventeen turning eighteen, a plump, spacey teenager girl, the very sight of which irritated my Dad. There is a double edge to having parents who are too young to cope with you happily. Eventually your presence makes them feel guilty and it's hard to enjoy your company.

Having said that, South Africa was our family's last great adventure when we were all together and we did enjoy it. Some experiences were larger than my personal difficulties. South Africa was bleeding internally, like a body hemorrhaging from poison but we children wandered through as charmed beings. I headed off with a stunt man and learned how to change places on a moving motorcycle driving through the desert sand. Francis and John made bombs for the movie explosions, we wandered in a deserted gem mine picking bits of sparkling stone from the walls.

The head grip (he was white) was stealing film equipment, lots of film equipment from the production company. When my brother's souvenir—John's Zulu spear—went missing, my dad told the grip that it had better be found. The grip looked furious and John's spear reappeared.

We met a black pastor who had been tortured almost to death by the police and we met a white police officer who tortured black prisoners and bragged about it. Meanwhile our black pastor friend told us that Winnie Mandela was burning blacks to death who didn't agree with her.

Five months later I would graduate from high school and move to New York City. The next time I visited home it was to prepare for my wedding.

Dad did get back from South Africa more or less in one piece. Three of his neighbors had been murdered in their homes on separate nights and two production crew women were raped. He had ended up sleeping holding his only weapon, John's Zulu spear. On the plane ride back he had decided to *really* rest, took a large dose of sleeping pills and mixed them with alcohol just to make sure they did their job. He arrived home sick, stunned with exhaustion, and more dead than alive—as usual.

One night on the *Headhunter* shoot, we had a hundred or so black extras out in an old abandoned rail yard in Pretoria, South Africa. The "demonic monster" was going to appear after they held a ritual around a huge fire. The extras would then chase Kay Lenz, who was playing our "Miami cop"—the picture was set in Miami, although shot in South Africa to save money—through some abandoned rail cars.

The extras gathered around the fire. It was part of the scene but was also keeping them warm between setups. As with all movie making, most of the evening was taken up waiting around for things to be fussed with, lights, dolly tracks, makeup. I asked the extras to sing something, anything, and to march around the fire in their "demonic" ritual.

"What shall we sing?" they asked.

"Anything you want," I said. "As long as your lips are moving. Later we'll dub in some sort of chant or something."

The choice was "Shosho Loza," a hymn that was once sung by the black gold miners about missing their homes. It had more recently been adapted by the ANC as a kind of unofficial hymn of resistance. "Shosho Loza" was considered subversive. And it was very beautiful.

The extras, none of whom knew each other before we hired them, sang as if they were in a choir that had rehearsed for weeks. The song, in several parts harmony, somewhat in the style of the Soweto Gospel Choir, echoed around the derelict rail yard. Some of the white crewmembers, our production manager Trevor in particular, seemed nervous and said we'd better get them to stop this pretty soon. But other whites on the crew joined in.

I was so ashamed. The most beautiful thing in our shit film was going to be some incidental music on the guide track, which later we'd replace with some bullshit incantation. We were with a group of mostly indigent people our production manager had picked up off the street. They were working for a few rand and a hot meal. And they sang like angels, the bass voices sounding sweet as French horns, the women's voices harmonizing in keening tones to break your heart. I withdrew to a corner where no one could see me. I was in the dark crying.

60

I thought I had hit bottom with the African pictures. But I had one further step to fall.

In 1991–92, I was directing what turned out to be my last feature: *Baby on Board*. My final movie entanglement ended with a pathetic whimper, actually more like a runny sneeze.

I was living in the Canadian producer's guest room in his Toronto townhouse. He was too cheap to pay for a hotel room or rent me an apartment. The only food he kept was an assortment of green teas and vitamins. He had taken over the production of *Baby on Board* from Sandy Howard, a former B-movie mogul, producer of one real movie: *A Man Called Horse*.

Genie only met the Canadian once. She didn't like him. He reminded her of too many of the televangelists we knew.

"This man's given me a break, okay?" I said.

"Is that right?" asked Genie. "Then why did he defer your fee? Keep him away from me."

But when I crashed a limousine in New York City, while we were shooting some scenes to cut into the footage we shot in Canada, shooting Toronto-for-New-York, the producer did wire down $2,700 to cover my credit card debt.

I crashed the limousine because the driver kept screwing up the take by getting the cue wrong as to when to come around the corner of an alley near West 66th Street and Broadway.

Fool I that was, I jumped into the driver's seat and tried to direct via walkie-talkie while driving the picture car.

We were in New York for a week of pick-up shots with just the stars and me. I was shooting without a permit, just running around New York City trying to get little pieces of film, to cut into the picture so it would look as if the action was taking place there, not in Toronto. Our stars, Carol Kane and Judge Reinhold, were gamely traipsing around with me.

By that time, the Canadian production had run out of money, so I was directing and shooting, operating the 35-millimeter Arriflex, lugging equipment, and hiring cabs. We kept hiring cabs that looked like "our" cab, the one we had as a picture car in Toronto.

The story was about a five-year-old girl left in a New York taxi, and the cab driver's attempt to get her back to her mother, while the mob chases the mother around New York, for whatever implausible reason. Judge (the driver) and Carol (the mom) hated each other by the end of the shoot and wouldn't film scenes together. I don't know why they didn't get along. They were both lovely to work with. Maybe it was just a case of depression at being stuck on such a shit movie. By the end of the shoot, they did lines in the master shots together, then the close-ups with a stand-in. We'd switch and shoot the close-up of the other actor with another stand-in.

Most of the movie took place in a moving vehicle out of doors. And we had two five-year-olds. (One would "act" while the other rested.) We were shooting exteriors in Toronto, in winter, a record-cold winter, for a movie written to take place in New York City in the summer. I got pneumonia. I wasn't getting paid more than a fraction of my fee. Other than that, the whole thing was great. As Sandy Howard would say, more than once, when I'd call him to whine: "It's fucking not a fucking movie but a fucking deal!"

After ABC watched the rough cut, they flew me to LA to re-cut the movie under their supervision. I recut with Candice Bergen's brother, a film editor with a reputation for being able to "save" movies. I still wanted to try to make the movie work, make my career succeed. And finishing the picture was my only chance of getting another job. But I wasn't getting paid, not even a per diem. And I had never caught up financially from not paying myself when I directed *Wired.* But, as the Canadian producer said, "Your name will be on this piece of shit, so if you want someone to fuck it up even worse, then go the fuck home."

Then the really bad times began. I started to steal.

It was after I had written my first as-yet unpublished novel *Portofino.* I still went crazy. At Genie's urging, I had started writing the book the year before I went to Canada. I began writing it on the back of an airline ticket envelope. I finished the first draft in about five months and found an agent. I had told no one besides Genie that I was writing. I read the new chapters out loud to her as I completed them. She laughed and loved it. The book was the first thing I had made since I quit painting that Genie really liked.

Macmillan bought my novel. And then, except for some minimal editing exchanges carried on by mail, I more or less forgot the book. It wasn't going to come out for almost a year. As I sank deep into the Canadian production, I hardly thought of the novel.

I was in LA, living in a tiny squalid rented room on Hollywood Boulevard near the Chinese Mann Theater, where my kids and I had watched so many movies back when I thought I was on the cusp of success. I was editing and reediting, and still trying to put together more movie deals.

The edit ended, but I didn't dare go home. I felt as if my only hope was to stay in LA and do meetings, look for work, read more horrible scripts, anything but go home in total defeat. And then what? Get a job washing dishes? Genie was talking about getting a waitress job.

Of course I wasn't sending any money home. And I didn't want to ask Genie to deplete our savings by sending me money. The only cash I had on hand was reserved for gas. (I was driving the old Schaeffer Productions Honda. It had 230,000 miles on it and only worked in second gear and reverse.) I hadn't paid the rent for two months.

I was convinced that I'd never earn another dime, that somehow I had to make our dwindling savings last forever, that my life was more or less over. I felt as if I was viewing a wasted life from the grave. But I was *not* going to pretend to reconvert to my evangelical faith and hook up with the old Jesus cash-cow again, no matter what, though it would have only taken two or three phone calls to line up a speaking engagement or two.

This wasn't a matter of high principle; I just couldn't take the bullshit any more.

Long after the edit was done, I lived for the better part of four months by eating off the craft-services table in the editing suite. No one cared. By then, I was like some ghost that haunted the place. Maybe they thought I had become homeless. I ate doughnuts and stale cereal. When I craved protein, I shoplifted pork chops from Ralph's grocery.

Most of the time I sat next to the phone in my room, looking at other people's fingerprints on my yellow wall. When I figured that the producers, who rarely returned my calls, were on their way back to Beverly Hills, the Valley, or Santa Monica, from their Hollywood, Century City, and Westwood offices, I turned on my answering machine and went to Ralph's.

Ralph's, on Sunset Boulevard at La Brea, was a good place to shoplift. It was a five-minute walk from my room, down Alta Vista Boulevard. I always went the same way. I'd walk past rubber plants with dusty leaves and benches covered with advertisements for the Jewish cemeteries. They were vandalized by people who misspelled their profanities.

"Fuk Yous."

"Deth."

"Asole."

The heavyset Mexican security guard at Ralph's was no problem. He spent his time playing with his keys or fingering the mace strapped to his shiny belt. Once in a while he would do his security guard stuff and keep the homeless, who hung around the boarded-up, frozen yogurt bar across the street, from panhandling Ralph's customers. But mostly he didn't do anything. Anyway, he never bothered me. I was convinced it was because Jesus was protecting me, an odd, mad mixture of faith and larceny.

Besides, my Reeboks were new-looking and I kept my hair combed. When my Reeboks got dirty, I touched them up with typing white-out. Sometimes I would think about the fact that I was the same person Billy Zeoli had given company credit cards to, and who had flown my family all over America in a private plane during the seminars. Sometimes I'd wonder how Rich DeVos and the other evangelical billionaires that I'd raised millions of dollars from would view my present state. Mostly I just sank into a trance. I didn't even have the energy to jack off.

Once in a while I'd fantasize that I'd re-re-reconvert, go back on the *700 Club*, cry, come home to Jesus, and even pull a Chuck Colson! He got out of jail after serving time for Watergate, wrote a best-seller, founded a prison ministry, hired ghost writers (who wrote best-sellers for him), and he never looked back! He was even being hailed as the "next Francis Schaeffer" by *Christianity Today* magazine!

I'd be tempted if some dire need came up, say I needed a new pair of shoelaces or a script copied. Then I'd catch a bit of Christian radio wafting out of some car window at a traffic light, or spot Pat Robertson's grinning face, or hear some street preacher ranting on the sidewalk. I'd remember that if it came down to it, I'd rather be arrested for shoplifting than ever be an evangelical leader again. There was a certain basic and decent honesty about stealing pork chops that selling God had lacked.

Even with two extra-thick cut pork chops stuffed into my underpants (the cold meat made my testicles ache), the guard didn't seem to notice or care. I was a white guy. And for my neighborhood, Hollywood Boulevard at Curson, I looked fairly honest compared to the homeless crazies that hung around the sticky sidewalk and scrawled their names on the hacked trunks of dying palm trees.

I usually fried my chops. Then I'd add two drops of Liquid Smoke for flavor. I ate in front of my TV, which sat on the floor at the end of my mattress. I kept my electric frying pan, phone-answering machine, reading lamp, and pile of scripts next to the TV. I was seriously contemplating moving up to stealing steaks.

Once in a while—usually via relayed messages from Genie—I'd hear from Dr. Koop or Dr. Kennedy, or Lane Dennis (the publisher at Crossway), asking what I was doing. The messages seemed totally surreal and got farther apart. I fell out of touch with my old partner Jim. I was just too embarrassed to talk.

Meanwhile, I was offered a job directing *Halloween Four* (or was it *Five*?). Then somebody at Creative Artist's Agency (CAA) said something about me directing a script I'd cowritten with Calder Willingham a few years before . . . more meetings. (High and mighty CAA were *his* agents, not mine.) Sandy Howard was about to be evicted from his apartment. I shoplifted a few more pork chops. *Halloween Four* (or *Five*) fell through. CAA didn't call back. Sandy invited me for dinner. We ate a can of split pea soup. He was in even worse shape than me.

Then *Portofino* was published.

PART IV

PEACE

61

I had been hiding in plain sight. One person I met in Hollywood—Frank Gruber—became a best friend. He explains:

> I'm an entertainment lawyer and I met Frank Schaeffer sometime in the mid '80s when a few long forgotten clients wanted to buy a screenplay Frank had commissioned. It was a cheesy horror story Frank had wanted to direct but was then willing to give up. We did the deal and nothing came of it. But then a couple years later Frank had another screenplay he had written and he wanted a Hollywood lawyer.
>
> Frank remembered me from the other deal. He told me about his screenplay and I read it. It was a true story about Italians, both religious Catholics and Communist partisans, who save 92 Jewish orphans from the Germans. I read it on an airplane, and I remember being so moved, I teared up.
>
> I also remember thinking it was amazing that someone could write a story about saving 92 Jews, and yet there was almost nothing about Jews in the script. It was all about Christian faith. That began my association with Frank Schaeffer.

The Foreigners was one of those film projects that "almost get made." But it had an effect on me, because it was the first time I worked so closely with a client that, after dealing with the ethical niceties being a lawyer requires, I became his producer/partner.

I'll never forget the first time Frank visited in Santa Monica. We had a little guesthouse in the back and he stayed there and we worked on the screenplay. My son Henry was about three and he and Frank hit it off immediately, as Frank loves to read books to children.

The next big moment in our relationship came several years later when Frank asked me to read the manuscript for his first novel, *Portofino*. I was the first person, other than Frank's wife, to read the book. Because those of Frank's screenplays that I had read had been wildly in need of rewriting, I expected the manuscript to be a mess. But the opposite was true. I read the whole thing over a July 4 weekend, laughing out loud, and reading passages out loud to my wife, Janet. The published version of the book differs from what I read in the first draft by at most one percent.

It was in connection with *Portofino* that I learned that Frank was not what he seemed to be when it came to religion and politics. Frank had told me vaguely ("hiding his light under a bushel" to the end) that his father had been a Protestant theologian, but after reading *Portofino* I learned that there was more to it than that.

His literary agent at the time mentioned casually that "of course a lot of Christian bookstores" might want to carry the book. Given *Portofino*'s jaundiced view of Christian fundamentalism, that surprised me, and that's when I learned that Frank's father, Francis A. Schaeffer, was a famous evangelical, and his mother, Edith Schaeffer, was equally prominent.

I like to think that Frank is still the boy, Calvin, in his novels, who is afraid that if he gives the English girl he loves a pamphlet about predestination, she will be "predestined" not to want to be with him any more. But then perhaps I'm one of the liberals Frank complains about who assume that anyone who lives near Boston, writes novels, and has good art on his walls has the same views they do. Maybe that intimidated him. As close as we became over the past twenty years as we wrote screenplays together and traveled to locations for films for which the money always seemed to disappear, as we read each other's work, as we visited each other's families, it took years for Frank to gain the confidence that I would still be his friend if he told me about his deep Christian faith.

As Frank grew to trust me more, and more freely shared his opinions, we began to enjoy our conflicts. I remember one trip to New York when I met Frank and Genie at the Metropolitan Museum of Art. We were there to see the big Byzantine show they had in the late '90s. In the cafeteria, we had a long argument about abortion rights. We were there to see the art, but we couldn't stop arguing.

Portofino got a rave six-column, half-page review in the *Los Angeles Times* by Richard Eder. It also got wonderful reviews in twenty or so other newspapers. I didn't get one bad review in America (or in Great Britain when it was published there, or, to my knowledge, in the nine other countries where it was translated and published). And not one reviewer connected me to either my family, to L'Abri, or to "Franky," the author of those crazy right-wing screeds.

At last I wasn't making lame-ass excuses: "The budget got cut. . . .The producer put his girlfriend in the movie. . . . I never did like the script. . . ." I hadn't felt so happy about anything I'd done professionally since I was nineteen and I walked into the Chante Pierre Gallery and saw my name in the catalogue and fifteen of my paintings framed and beautifully lit.

A few months later, I started writing a second novel, *Saving Grandma.* And though our financial situation was still dire, I didn't feel broke any more. (In fact, I had never been as "broke" as I had imagined when sinking under my depression out in LA. My belief we were broke was a depression-fueled fantasy.) We were having financial troubles, but not anywhere near as extreme as I imagined. I was also no longer looking for those main-chance shortcuts, for the next steppingstone, rather than having the discipline and concentration to do what was right in front of me well.

At last I was *really working* at my writing. I found that I had stumbled on something I possessed the patience to do well. When I wrote fiction (and secular nonfiction), I didn't run out of steam. It seemed normal to do ten, fifteen, or twenty drafts. Mr. Parke would have been pleased. I was finally bucking up, showing a bit of spine!

My learning curve was steep and slow. Since I never had much formal education, I learned by doing. My evangelical books were hastily written (or dictated). And they were merely propaganda. But at least I was forced to start a process where I learned to write a bit better with each project, a process that—when I began to take my writing seriously *as writing*—began to pay off. In any case, I was thirty-nine before I finally wrote something I was proud of.

I snapped out of my funk, turned down an offer to direct some crap picture in Hong Kong, framed the *L.A. Times* review, and changed my phone number. Since I had screwed up our money matters completely, Genie insisted on taking over our family's finances. I should have begged her to do that many years before but was too proud to admit that there are things—many things—that I'm not good at.

Genie mortgaged our home. (We had paid cash for it in the flush old evangelical days.) She did a brilliant job of managing our money, paid off our debts, started a successful small business, and, over a few years, pulled us out of a steep financial nosedive.

After my second novel was published, I was starting to feel almost sane. On a visit back to LA (I was there doing a reading at Dutton's from *Saving Grandma*), I went to a nearby Ralph's, bought fifty dollars' worth of pork chops, and then put them back into the meat display case. I could have just sent the company a check, but I enjoyed the symbolism of this theatrical bit of penance.

Where my evangelical books had once sold a hundred thousand copies in weeks—for instance, during the period when Dobson bought, then gave away, tens of thousands of copies of *A Time for Anger*—*Portofino* sold a mere several thousand over several months. Nevertheless, it had good hardcover (and later paperback) sales for a first novel by an unknown writer (unknown to the fiction-buying secular public, that is). *Saving Grandma* did fine, too. And over the years since, some books have done better than others. (Oprah helped one make the best-seller list.) But the earnings from my secular writing feel genuine, not like some sort of Monopoly money, which was the way my Jesus-dollars always struck me.

There were a few final and strange little moments on my

way out of the evangelical world. At first, Macmillan (who published the original hardcover) foolishly thought they could sell *Portofino* in the Christian Booksellers Association market, given the family name and my evangelical "track." As soon as the word got out that *Portofino* was funny at the expense of the fundamentalist subculture, not to mention that there was sex in the book, Macmillan got cartloads of CBA returns. I received a handful of irate letters from a dozen or so evangelical bookstore managers, all of whom, a few years before, would have killed to have me come to their stores for an event.

When *Portofino* was published, my sister Susan was very upset and wrote me a barely coherent seven-page letter. She faulted me for both making my novel too fictional—"We never did anything like that!"—and not for not being true to life—"*Why* don't you tell what it was really like?" Her reaction was couched in pietistic terms.

I didn't feel like explaining that writers write about what they know and that if I'd been the son of a steelworker, I probably would be setting my novels in a steel town. I also knew I wasn't alone. François Truffaut infuriated his family when he made *The 400 Blows*. His relations with his parents became intolerable as the autobiographical film was released in the early '60s. Artists are like creatures who swallow themselves. We process our lives into what we make.

Susan and I didn't speak for a while. We had no dramatic reconciliation, just began talking about our mother's needs. I think we are friends again.

Debby didn't like *Portofino* either, but her reaction was mild since she is an inveterate reader of fiction and appreciated my writing, if not the thinly veiled biographical side of my novel. Priscilla had no problem with the novel, laughed, and at one point said "Be *sure* you *don't* show this to Susan!"

My mother and I never talked about my first or subsequent semiautobiographical novels, but I did learn that she'd given away half a dozen or so copies of *Portofino* to friends. So I think she was at least as proud of me for my "secular success" (something she had always wanted for her writing that eluded her) as she probably was annoyed to find herself reincarnated as the character "Elsa."

My children were tracking, too. I think they were glad that the years of turmoil were winding down. John writes:

> I can remember sitting down to read my dad's first novel, *Portofino*. It was during the summer of 1992 and I sat outside on the deck eating bread dipped in hot chocolate. (Dad has a picture on his desk of me sitting there reading his novel.)
>
> If I remember correctly I finished the book that afternoon having sat there for the better part of the day. I knew that *Portofino* was based on his childhood and not completely biographical. But it was much more fun for me to treat it as a strict family history. It was an eye-opening experience for a twelve-year-old.
>
> I think most people have a moment in their lives when they finally see their parents for the first time outside of a selfish utilitarian worldview. Reading *Portofino* was the first time I saw my father. I saw him as a child through Calvin Becker (the protagonist of the novel) and for me Calvin will always be the picture of my father as a child, sitting between his parents with the look of thinly veiled mayhem in his eyes. Perhaps more importantly, I saw my father as a man for the first time in the way he worked on and promoted his book, as someone who deeply wanted to create something that was artistically valid and that would outlast him.

62

After Jim Buchfuehrer and I quit working together (and shut down Schaeffer V Productions in the mid eighties), and after I left the evangelical fold, Jim joined an Orthodox church. I would call him and complain about how lost I was feeling. Then in 1989, I visited Jim in Los Gatos and went to church with him. (There are Greek, Russian, and Antiochian Orthodox in America, as well as some others. The Orthodox groups all share the same liturgies and theology but happen to come from various national emigrant backgrounds. Jim was going to an Antiochian church.)

I loved the liturgy. Somehow, in my mind it connected to everything I had loved most about Italy. There was nothing logical about this. For whatever reason, the liturgy made me feel as if I was standing in a warm piazza surrounded by milling friendly crowds. Sermons didn't seem to be the point. The liturgy wasn't an exercise in theology, but an unexplained and mysterious act of worship. In Orthodoxy, in the saints' lives, in the beauty of the liturgy, in the respect for tradition I rediscovered what I had briefly experienced in my earliest childhood: faith couched in the most beautiful terms.

When I converted to the Greek Orthodox Church (around Christmas of 1990), I was chrismated: anointed with oil, had a bit of hair trimmed off, and a gold cross put around my neck.

I read the Nicene Creed out loud, spit on the Devil, renounced some things, affirmed others.

My family reacted to my conversion in different ways. Genie, Jessica, her husband Dani, Francis, and John joined the Orthodox Church at different times a year or so after me and for their own reasons. John was ten, so he grew up serving at the altar. Jessica was already living in Finland and started going to the Finnish state Orthodox Church there. Francis sometimes drives up from where he lives (about forty-five minutes away) and joins Genie and me for church. These days, I don't know what my children believe or don't. I don't ask. It's none of my business. Genie's family was pleased when we left the evangelical world and joined something that seemed more "Catholic" and therefore more familiar. My sisters and brothers-in-law were dismayed. Udo wrote several pointed articles about the "failures" of the Russian Orthodox Church and put them in the newsletter of the Francis Schaeffer Foundation. Susan dropped out of sight for a while. John Sandri was kind. I never heard a word from my oldest friends within the evangelical community.

For a couple of years, I had the zeal of a convert and stuck my conversion in my sister's faces. I was obnoxious. Of course, my ranting was ironic since Orthodox tradition teaches a transcendent mystery of faith, so that the type of heated historical (hysterical) "theological" arguments I was having were far more Protestant than Orthodox. Obviously I had missed the point.

My conversion didn't instantly turn my life around or fix every problem. Soon after I joined the Greek Orthodox Church, I was making *Baby on Board* and then marooned in Hollywood stuffing pork chops down my pants. And this was *after* I had spit on the Devil! On my sorties to Ralph's, I'd sometimes wonder how my new Orthodox friends would take it if Genie had to ask them for bail money.

The Greek Orthodox have access to the sacrament of confession. As the years went by I found that confession helped me draw a line under sins that had more or less tortured me. For instance, I confessed about the times I had slapped Jessica. Then Jessica and I had several talks that ended in tears, forgiveness, and all those things that faith is supposed to do.

I received more spiritual edification out of working on the annual fund-raising food festival, shoulder-to-shoulder with some remarkably lovely people, as we prepared lamb shanks and trays of pasticcio and swept up the church hall, than from speaking, let alone being a "Christian leader." It was better than parading around in front of audiences, talking about things I barely understood. And I liked deepening my relationship with the people I passed on the street every day in our town. I felt as if in some ways I was back living in my old village. I had a deep local connection to my time and place again.

Genie is the "Ladies' Aid" treasurer. I'm just her husband. There are a few people in the congregation who read my novels and, at coffee hour, sometimes ask me questions. Unlike my old evangelical friends, real life doesn't seem to upset them. I never have to "explain" about why I put sex in my books, swear words, or characters who don't seem to be able to find Jesus.

Genie and I like the fact that in our community, half the congregation comes to church late, so we can wander in at any time and still feel like we participated. And I don't have to go to church more often than I can stand. When it starts to feel like religion again, I just drop out for a few months, then wander back.

Perhaps I converted to the Greek Orthodox Church (rather than simply abandoning religious faith) because spirituality is a way to connect with people and might even be part of a journey toward God. (If there is a God.) According to Jesus, community *is* spirituality: "Love one another."

To me, the Greek Orthodox Church is not *the* community but *a* community. Community is an antidote to the poisonous American consumerist "me" and "I want" life that leads to isolation and unhappiness.

Even if spirituality is an illusion that doesn't resolve our longing for transcendent meaning or our need for other people, maybe the fact that we hope for more means that there is more. Perhaps we are somehow more than the sum of our brain chemistry. Maybe science explains the "how" of the brain but not the "why," in the same way that a chemical analysis of the pigments used by van Gogh only explains what a painting is made of, not why we like it, much less what it *is*.

When I left evangelicalism, it certainly was not because I was disillusioned with the faith of my early childhood. I have sweet (if somewhat nutty) memories of all those days of prayer, fasting, and "wrestling with principalities and powers." We might have been deluded, but we weren't unhappy. And there are a lot worse things than parents who keep you away from TV, grasping materialism, and hype, and let you run free and use your imagination.

I think my problem with remaining an evangelical centered on what the evangelical community became. It was the merging of the entertainment business with faith, the flippant lightweight kitsch ugliness of American Christianity, the sheer stupidity, the paranoia of the American right-wing enterprise, the platitudes married to pop culture, all of it . . . that made me crazy. It was just too stupid for words.

The Greek Orthodox Church is the least-changed continuous body of Christian worship and tradition. So what? The average pebble in my driveway predates human existence by a hundred million years or so. On the other hand, if you want to try to live as a Christian, maybe it makes sense to attach yourself to a body of faith that bears at least a passing resemblance to what Christians everywhere, from the beginning of the Christian era, believed and, more importantly, did.

Perhaps there is a more substantive point: Once you buy the evangelical born-again "Jesus saves" mantra, the idea that salvation is a journey goes out the window. You're living in the realm of a magical formula. It seems to me that the Orthodox idea of a slow journey to God, wherein no one is altogether instantly "saved" or "lost" and nothing is completely resolved in this life (and perhaps not in the next), mirrors the reality of how life works, at least as I've experienced it.

One thing I do not regret is that I missed the "opportunity" to be the so-called big-time evangelical leader I could have been. I was good at speaking. We would never have run out of paranoid delusions with which to stir up the ever-fearful and willfully ignorant. But the idea of "passing up" a chance to become a cross between Pat Robertson, Elmer Gantry, and Ralph Reed never bothered me.

The basic prayer of the Greek Orthodox Church, "Lord Jesus Christ, Son of God, have mercy on me, a sinner!" has become a personal mantra. It is almost like breathing, an answer to any situation, from waiting for a call from a son at war, to hoping I'll sell a book, to moments when I have, for the hundredth time, been rude, mean, and a bad husband. The prayer belongs to the historic church, but the impulse that drives me to say it was bred into me before I could talk.

It doesn't matter what I think. It is a question of what I am. And I am grateful. There is plenty to feel guilty about. I don't see guilt as a hang-up to be cured, but a truthful statement of my condition. And prayer seems to me to be the only logical response, not the cure but an answer.

63

Honesty is the only thing that is satisfying about writing. And honesty is always filled with inconsistency. Since our opinions change, to be "sure" about anything—as if that opinion is fixed and will last forever—is to lie. Anything we say is only a snapshot of a passing moment.

Honesty is what was missing from my evangelical writing and my evangelical and secular movies. How could I make an honest documentary when I had to replace stunning footage of *David* with stock dreck so that I wouldn't offend idiots? How could I make a good Hollywood movie when I saw everything as just a steppingstone to another deal? How could I be honest when I was a different person to different groups?

Most of the time, I was biting my tongue. If I wanted to be invited back, I couldn't go on the *700 Club* and tell people that the host was a lunatic. I couldn't go on Dobson's *Focus on the Family* and tell the truth: The host was a power-crazed political manipulator cynically abusing his followers. And I couldn't tell my Hollywood producers that they were full of shit when they cast their girlfriends to star in their movie. I wanted the next job!

By playing along and keeping my mouth shut, I was selling out to be able to find integrity later, something like going to whores to find a faithful wife. But whores just led to more whores.

Once I freed myself from a political and religious agenda, I was able to find inspiration in some very unexpected places. After John joined the Marines in 1999, he and I wrote *Keeping Faith—A Father-Son Story About Love and the United States Marine Corps*. It generated a huge correspondence. Our new readers were barely aware of me as a novelist, let alone as a former evangelical activist. I had stumbled into yet another subculture. Judging by several thousands of e-mails, my new military readers thought of me as one of their spokespeople, telling their story at a time when most Americans didn't even know someone in the military.

Being part of the military family changed me. I found myself connected to a community that believes in service and sacrifice and that lives by what they believe. They contrasted sharply with the leaders of the big-time evangelical world. We evangelical "leaders" had talked about saving America but never made any sacrifices for our country. We left the sacrificing to our "ordinary" followers.

After 9/11, I wrote several more books about being the father of a Marine who was at war. My credibility on the subject of the military family didn't come from my writer's credentials, but from the fact that my son was serving. The reason military parents read what I wrote, and responded to it, was because we shared a profound pride and anguish. It wasn't about politics or who we voted for or whether we approved of the wars in Afghanistan and Iraq; it was about solidarity, brotherhood, and being humbled by the fact that our children were willing to be sent into harm's way for our country. After having spent years talking about America, while knowing almost nothing of our country, I was finally talking about something I actually had a stake in: my country, which my son was risking his life for.

Being exposed to people who led by doing, typified by the Marine Corps drill instructors I got to know on Parris Island (while researching *Baby Jack*), was a turning point for me. It is one of the reasons I wrote this memoir.

After John joined the Marines, I found that I gradually began to understand my life in a new way. I wanted to try to come clean. I wanted to admit my mistakes. I wanted to try to be the same person to everyone I met. I wanted to try to write with the same level of honesty that the Marine Corps drill instructors demand of their recruits and live by themselves.

64

One night Genie and I came back from our walk on Sandy Point, the beach at the southern tip of Plum Island. At low tide, extreme low tide during a full summer moon, Sandy Point opens up to a vast half-mile-wide tidal flat. We walked on the hard-packed rippled ocean's floor late in the afternoon. There was no one there besides us.

We came home at about six-thirty PM, after midnight in Switzerland where John, Francis, and Jessica had all just met up the day before, along with Becky, John's girlfriend. Jessica had flown down from Finland (where she lives with her husband Dani and her children Ben and Amanda), and they were all staying in a L'Abri guest apartment at Chalet Les Sapins, up the back road from Chalet Les Mélèzes. Francis flew over to visit at the same time and was staying with John and Priscilla Sandri.

My son John had traveled to Paris meet Becky. She was there as a chaperone with the Waring School French trip, when the juniors go to France for six weeks to soak up a little European culture. All three of my children, as well as Becky, had made this Waring trip as high school students.

Before John flew over, he had been staying with us, having just returned from his first year at the University of Chicago. It was a triumphant turn of events for the former Marine, who had made it home from war, alive, uninjured, home to be held, loved, spoiled, home to leave dirty socks and scattered running shoes, evidence that he was alive.

John had asked Vincent Hawley, the son of my friend and neorealist painter Steve Hawley, to design the ring. Vincent only had three days. Only at the last moment did John remember that Vincent, who had just completed his training as a jeweler, might be the person to ask. Anyway, there was the ring, produced as if by magic, a band of white gold with eight little diamonds sprinkled through it like a slice of the Milky Way, lovely and small to fit Becky's delicate hand.

She plays the flute beautifully. She will move to Chicago in the fall. Becky is in love. So is John. He asked her in Paris; three days later, she said yes in Switzerland, standing on the back road, *my* back road, looking at the Dents Du Midi, next to Priscilla and John Sandri's chalet.

As we walked in the door from our walk, the phone rang. It was John telling us that he was engaged. They are with *my* family, with Priscilla and John and Debby and Udo. They are in *my* mountains, in fields full of *my* wildflowers where I first kissed *my* Genie. They are in love where I found *my* love. They are in *my* life. And I am in theirs.

65

At the Metropolitam Museum of Art (while strolling as if in a dream through an ethereal exhibition of eighteenth-century Japanese screens), I read a poem that seemed to sum up so much about my restless mother and her relationship with the world:

To love
Unloved
Is more futile
Than to write
On a flowing stream

Mom is ninety-two. Sometimes she talks wistfully about the time when a "real Broadway producer" saw her dance while she was at college. This producer asked her to come to New York. "I had talent. I could have made it," Mom says. "But my parents forbade it. In fact, when I asked them if I could go, they were so shocked that I had been dancing in a school production that they threatened to take me out of college."

In my mother's second childhood, as a very old lady with memory loss, her greatest pleasure, one that literally seems to raise her up, is not Bible study but dancing. When I take her out during my visits back to Switzerland, I have to guide her as we walk. Macular degeneration has robbed Mom of sight, except for a little peripheral vision. And she is unsteady on her feet. But her favorite destination is to go to the Hôtel Trois Couronnes in Vevey.

We head for the piano bar, where Mom orders tea or sometimes buys us both a glass of champagne. But the main attraction is the Italian man who plays the piano. When he sees Mom, he starts playing her favorites, tunes by Cole Porter, some Gershwin, and plenty of Duke Ellington. Then Mom dances.

All of a sudden she doesn't seem old, or blind, or helpless. She stands by the baby grand and sways to the music in an old-lady version of Isadora Duncan free-form dancing, combined with the Charleston. Everyone in the bar watches, and she always sits down to a round of applause.

I have never loved or admired Mom more than when she dances as the oldest of old ladies. And I wish she had been dancing when I was a child. And although this may sound like a cliché, when Mom dances, she literally looks young again. Her face lights up and she smiles at the world she can't see any more. And all the frail uncertainty leaves her body for a few minutes and she is steady on her feet again.

Mom is old, radiant, at peace, and unafraid when she dances. And the paradox is that the woman who I remember no longer exists. The woman who rejoiced that Lynnette was giving up dancing to serve the Lord is gone.

Sometimes I think that maybe the reason that all Mom's heartfelt prayers for her family seem to have been answered is because the old woman, whose life has become so simple, is the woman God saw when he looked at Edith Schaeffer during all those crazy years.

Perhaps God answered the prayers of Edith as she might have been and deep down wanted to be but did not know how to be, because she was working so hard to conform herself to an idea that was false. The sense I have that Mom's prayers for her family have been answered does not seem far-fetched when I meet my mother now, meet her as perhaps God made her before her idea of herself—or her parents' long reach—obscured her.

I am curious about the fact that all those tunes are so familiar to Mom. She has forgotten so much, say where she had breakfast or who she just met, but she sings the old show tunes as if she had spent a lifetime on Broadway. That "jazzy music" was banned from our home when I was young; if we were changing radio stations and hit upon any of the tunes she sings so gleefully in old age, Mom would turn off the radio with a snap and reproachful glare. In the early unreconstructed fundamentalist years, Mom always said "Real Christians don't dance. It isn't pleasing to the Lord."

I never knew how sad that belief must have been making her. And she must have been so torn up inside as she expressed such fierce joy over Lynnette giving up dancing, when buried deep there was the memory of the day she also gave up, or was forced to give up, her talent for God.

EPILOGUE

My son John wrote:

> Although I didn't understand it when I was growing up I've realized since, that my father lives and works on almost everything he does with a kind of frenetic desperation.

In the prologue, I said that the only answer to "Who are you?" is "When?" What was true for prologue is doubly true of epilogue. We never arrive. There are no final answers, only a series of snapshots taken along the path of "frenetic desperation."

Movies

In the mid-1990s, I almost made it through the front door of the movie business again. I co-wrote a screenplay adaptation of *Portofino* with Frank Gruber. We signed on with a producer friend of Frank's. He claimed he had the money lined up. He hired Malcolm Mowbray, a BBC TV and film director who had directed a movie I liked (*A Private Function* starring Maggie Smith and Michael Palin). Malcolm cast John Lithgow to play the father and Dianne Wiest to play the mother and we had a lead on Haley Joel Osment to play my alter-ego "Calvin."

I had breakfast with Lithgow in Beverly Hills, got nice notes from Wiest via her agent, including one saying that *Portofino* was the best script she had read since *Bullets Over Broadway.* I was flown to Italy to scout locations. I got paid top dollar for the option on my novel. There was a double full-page ad in *Variety* announcing the start of principal photography.

Then the German financiers backed out. Lithgow had to shoot the next season of *Third Rock from the Sun*. The window of opportunity closed, just as a new paperback edition of *Portofino* was published with "now a major motion picture" printed on the cover.

I still get e-mail from readers asking me where the movie is. I ran into Lithgow at the Whitney Museum in New York (he was in town starring in the stage production of *Dirty Rotten Scoundrels*). He said that he was sad the *Portofino* deal fell through, and that Malcolm called from time to time trying to get it going again.

The producer gave me a coffee mug with the cover of the original hardback of my novel printed on it, which I use as a paperweight. I never heard from him again until several years later, when he e-mailed me after he saw me on Oprah, talking about *Keeping Faith.*

After the United Artists–Steve Bach debacle, I was stunned. I had thought Steve was one of those gods who had "made it" and that with him behind me I was "in." After *Portofino*-the-movie fell apart, I wasn't surprised, merely resigned. Ten years of knocking around making movies meant that I never allowed myself to get excited about a project. I knew that nothing ever turns out the way you hope, if at all. No one is ever "in." So when a producer at DreamWorks called me in mid-2006 about wanting to option the movie rights on my novel *Baby Jack,* and then after we talked almost every day for several weeks and I didn't hear back from him, I didn't bother to even try to find out why. To give it a second thought would have interrupted that day's writing.

Any time I find myself fantasizing about trying to get one of my novels made into a movie and *almost* pick up my phone to try to revive old contacts and "get something going," I think about the good advice the movie director Sergei Bodrov gave me. We were at a dinner party, and it was right after Sergei's movie *Prisoner of the Mountain* was nominated for an Oscar. I said I sometimes considered trying to direct again, to get my novels made into movies. Sergei, who had recently read *Saving Grandma,* looked at me as if I were crazy.

"*Why* would you want to sit in all those hundreds of stupid meetings that never result in anything?" he asked. "You have the luxury of being at home, writing books that are actually published and read! If I could write novels successfully, I would *never* waste another moment on trying to put movie deals together. Don't let *anything* distract you!"

I didn't need much convincing.

Art

In 1980, when we were about to move to America, I had to pack up everything in my studio in Chalet Regina. It was as if I was packing the belongings of a beloved relative who had died six years before. I hadn't touched a brush since 1974. Everything was lying just as I'd left it when I followed Billy Zeoli into a life that changed everything for me and made me almost forget who I had hoped to be.

There was an unfinished painting still on the easel. As I packed up dozens of tubes of paint, jars full of brushes, my woodcut blocks, sketchpads, charcoal, and pencils, I tried not to look at anything too closely. After we got to our new home in America, I left everything in the boxes.

It was over thirty years before I unpacked my paints. Before that, I hadn't had the courage to face the evidence of my treason. Abandoning painting made everything else I was doing seem half-assed until I had worked hard enough at my "secular" writing to feel that I had rehabilitated myself.

Genie once asked me if I was ever going to paint again. My answer: "I made one false start. I want to be good at something. I'm sticking with the writing for now." But once I had four novels published, and four nonfiction "secular" books, too, it was as if I'd built a wall to keep out the memories of those evangelical pieces of propaganda I'd written so badly and hastily, and the crappy movies I'd made in Hollywood.

That was when I decided I *could* unpack my art supplies. When I did, I felt as if the brushes, unused canvases, paints, and the old crusted palette were shouting "Where the *fuck* have you been?"

Most of the thirty-year-old tubes were still okay. I dragged my old easel out of the barn and set it up in the renovated woodshed attached to our house. I write at one end of the room and paint at the other. I write every day, seven days a week. And sometimes I paint. Not every day, but fairly regularly.

Faith

What represents faith to me these days? It is my father fighting for truth as he saw it, struggling on and saying he was sorry for his sins. . . . My mother battling her demons, wanting to be someone else, failing but still loving her children, reading to me and doing her best, even though she felt cheated by life.

. . . John Sandri forgiving the people at L'Abri who forbade him to teach, and working to keep the mission open when, if he had walked away, he could have shut it down. . . . Gordon Parke striving for long days at Great Walstead and still finding the energy to come out onto the lawn and play a rollicking game of kick-the-can with a hundred eager boys and never letting us down. . . . Genie forgiving me, and her clear-eyed spirituality that is not maudlin or judgmental or pietistic but matter-of-fact and sweet as a long kiss. . . . My children *knowing* that *I know* I failed them in so many ways, and yet reaching out to me to reassure me that they are happy. . . . Christmas dinner with my daughter-in-law Becky's generous family, with her Jewish atheist mother Lauren, and David her lapsed Roman Catholic father, and her brother Alex and our families often agreeing on nothing—except that we love our children and each other, and that is more than enough. . . . Father Chris, kicking my ass and forcing me to treat Genie better, *or else*. . . . Every drill instructor at the Parris Island and San Diego Marine recruit training depots who will get up tomorrow morning and lead his or her recruits from the front, sacrificing everything for them. . . .

Faith is certainly *not* theology to me. Church is just one of the places I look for answers to the only real question I have: Why do we long for meaning?

For me, faith is best experienced in the twilight in the medieval hall of the Metropolitan Museum of Art at Christmastime. Every November, a group of volunteers—mostly middle-aged and elderly ladies working under the direction of the museum's conservancy department—put up the "Angel Tree" and decorate it with Neapolitan eighteenth- and nineteenth-century terra-cotta and wood silk-clad figures: beautifully painted faces gentle and innocent; swirling robes of silk, rich as thick smoke curling heavenward—a nativity scene to break even my cynical heart.

Off to one side is the entrance to the halls holding the Byzantine collection, a glittering reminder of how Greek and Roman art merged seamlessly into the Byzantine world, carrying forward a message of beauty and civilization. People are coming up from the cafeteria downstairs buttoning their coats, getting ready to leave and intending to hurry past the tree. But they linger. I linger.

There are Christmas hymns playing quietly. An art purist might call the seasonal tableau sentimental. But the Met and museums everywhere fight to preserve the human meaning found in our most precious artifacts, and many of those artifacts—from Syrian gods to Italian Virgin-and-Childs—reflect the fact that we humans take hope in the irrational.

Life

The moments that changed me, perhaps for the better, have not been those I chose, let alone was in charge of or planned. America's best movie maker, the late Robert Altman, said "You can pick the best six things in anything I made, and none of them were planned. It's the mistakes I'm interested in. That's where you hit the truth button."

It is no accident that in *Baby Jack* I have God quoting Altman. For me, there have been some pivotal "Altman truth buttons": Marrying Genie because I broke my sullen teenage rule and went to dinner one night instead of huddling in my studio in splendid isolation. . . . Having Jessica, our "mistake," because I was too lazy, horny, and/or stupid to use a condom. . . .John volunteering to serve our country and connecting me to my country in a different way. . . . My finding what I want to do for a living by stumbling into writing novels because of Genie's nudge. . . .

I find little snippets of the answer or, at least, *an* answer, in unexpected places. For instance, I spent a day with Francis at his school recently. I had asked him if I could visit. Francis was teaching a humanities class to seniors. My son answered questions and paced the room. His gestures reminded me so much of my father, the way he put his thumb under the chin, index finger placed alongside his nose, when listening to a question. I felt close to Francis, and through him so unexpectedly close to Dad, as if the three of us were gathered in the room.

I had only planned to see my son in action. (I wanted to take pictures for our family scrapbook.) The "mistake" intruded, and I "saw" my dad as a young energetic gifted speaker, as he must have been back when he was a pastor of his first church.

Meaning

Sometimes the "irrational"—and the intuitive—is the only thing that I count on. Long before John went to war, and long before the afternoon I watched Francis teach, Jessica flew home from Finland with her husband Dani and Amanda. Amanda was only three months old. (Genie had been with Jessica when Amanda was born and came home a week before Jessica came home.) I was counting the days until I could see the baby.

I opened the front door. I didn't know what to expect. Jessica wordlessly held Amanda out to me. Amanda was awake and silent, calm, looking right up at me.

Jessica placed my granddaughter in my arms, a light little bundle, a sweet-smelling package, so light. I turned and went to sit in the kitchen at my usual place. Jessica was there watching her dad, that man who had given her so much grief, who took her all over the world, that man who read her stories, and taught her to box, who had her when he was a child, who slapped her and pulled her hair, that man she hated, that man she forgave who "gave her away" at her wedding, filled the old rowboat with ice, champagne, and strawberries at her reception in his garden, that man who cheered her lacrosse team, that man she watched make deals, make speeches, paint, make films, scream at his wife, convert to a new religion, fail as a movie director, crash, resurrect as a writer, she handed him her baby.

I looked into Amanda's face and she looked back at me with clear brown eyes, and they were the same almond shape, *exactly* the same shape as Genie's, when she was eighteen, the evening I first saw her. And this new love was the strongest I'd ever felt, ever, like nothing else I have experienced. The peace that "passes understanding" seeped from Amanda to me. Jessica watched us both and let us be.

Perhaps Mom and Dad were right. In an infinite universe, everything must have happened at least once, someplace, sometime. So maybe there is a God who forgives, who loves, who knows. I hope so. Anything is possible in a world where a daughter forgives her father, for ignorance, for anger, for failure, and places her daughter in his arms.

Acknowledgments

My wife Genie read this book several times at several stages. I rewrote and added material because of Genie's very good suggestion. My daughter-in-law Becky read it three times and made precise, detailed, and immensely helpful editorial notes. My daughter Jessica, my brother-in-law John Sandri, Frank Gruber, and Holly Meade read the manuscript at various stages. Their comments were so helpful. Thank you all.

My daughter Jessica, my sons Francis and John, my sisters Debby and Priscilla, and my old friends Jim Buchfuehrer, Ray Cioni, and Frank Gruber generously contributed pieces I used. Thank you.

My sister Susan visited me while I was writing. Susan listened as I read her passages from the manuscript. She encouraged me. I'm grateful. On several occasions, my son Francis also listened while I read long sections out loud. His encouragement was wonderful. His suggestions were good. I read several chapters out loud to my granddaughter Amanda over the phone, and she was so very encouraging.

My editor, Will Balliett challenged me to explain, trim, refine, polish, expand, and, as he always does, cut to the heart of the matter. I rewrote the book, twice, for Will and added over a hundred new pages based on his notes asking for more information. I'm so glad that he was the editor for this very personal project. (He even called from his vacation and we did several long sessions on the phone.) It was good to work with a true friend.

My agent Jennifer Lyons, as always, was a good friend. Without her, there would be no book and I would have no career as a writer either. Phil Gaskill did a lovely job on the copy edit. Jamie McNeely Quirk was kind in her capacity as managing editor. She patiently explained the mysteries of checking the final copy edit on a computer file, rather than on paper, as I was used to. I survived and even learned to like the process! I would also like to thank Shaun Dillon, who works with Will Balliett. Shaun was always so very helpful in every aspect of this project and made everything run smoothly in my day-to-day work with everyone at Carroll and Graf/Avalon. Vanessa Crooks very kindly helped sort and scan the photographs herein. She also gave me useful feedback on the text. I thank her for her cheerful kindness. Ryan Jensen is a great friend to Genie and myself. Without his help with our computers, work in our home would grind to a halt.

In the midst of writing, Guy and Marnie de Vanssay were kind enough to invite Genie and me to stay with them for a desperately needed holiday. We rested in their magnificent Château de la Barre. It is one of the most beautiful family-owned chateau/hotels in an "undiscovered" and unspoiled part of France in the Loire Valley region. We drank wine, ate cheese, visited medieval churches, and slept! (www.chateaudelabarre.com)

Later, on that same vacation, Debby and Udo very kindly put us up at the Francis Schaeffer Foundation in Gryon, Switzerland. John and Priscilla entertained us at their home in Huémoz. And my mother and I had breakfast together on several mornings and wonderful conversations in the evenings. Without that timely holiday, I don't think I would have completed this project.

The poem I quoted in the final chapter is taken from "Tales of Ise" (Edo period, eighteenth century, used by permission from the Metropolitan Museum of Art).

I am grateful to Peter J. Boyer, who wrote "The Big Tent," an article reviewing the fundamentalist-versus-modernism conflicts of the early 1900s to 1930s. (*The New Yorker,* August 22, 2005). I borrowed several sections and used them almost verbatim in chapter 18.

Index